DORIS DAY
HER OWN STORY

46 CANADA

MR. GEORGE E.H. FRAIR
296 Woodfield Drive
Nepean Ontario K2G 3W9

Christmas · Noël

Noël

CANADA

—Year 2001—

DORIS DAY
HER OWN STORY

by A. E. Hotchner

WILLIAM MORROW AND COMPANY, INC.
NEW YORK   1976

Filmography compiled by Sheila Smith
Picture Editor, Ursula Hotchner

Library of Congress Cataloging in Publication Data

Day, Doris (date)
  Doris Day: her own story

  Filmography: p.
  Includes index.
  1. Day, Doris, 1924-   I. Hotchner, A. E.
PN2287.D324A34 1976   791.43′028′0924 [B] 75-22354
ISBN 0-688-02968-X

Book design by Helen Roberts

    7 8 9 10   80 79 78 77 76

When I was just a little girl,
I asked my mother, "What will I be?
Will I be pretty?
Will I be rich?"
Here's what she said to me:

"*Que sera, sera,*
Whatever will be, will be;
The future's not ours to see.
Que sera, sera,
What will be, will be."

When I was just a child in school,
I asked my teacher, "What should I try?
Should I paint pictures?
Should I sing songs?"
This was her wise reply:

"*Que sera, sera,*
Whatever will be, will be;
The future's not ours to see.
Que sera, sera,
What will be, will be."

When I grew up and fell in love,
I asked my lover, "What lies ahead?
Will we have rainbows
Day after day?"
Here's what my lover said:

"*Que sera, sera,*
Whatever will be, will be;
The future's not ours to see.
Que sera, sera,
What will be, will be."

DORIS DAY
HER OWN STORY

Prologue

DORIS DAY and I first met in the luncheon garden of the Beverly Hills Hotel in the summer of 1973. Doris's son, Terry Melcher, had picked me up at my hotel and we sat at a shaded table drinking Heineken beer while we waited for her.

"You'll like my mother," Terry said.

"I'm sure I will."

"She has a lot going for her."

I had met Terry the evening before. He is a low-key, thoughtful, attractive young man, drooped hair, drooped moustache, by trade a producer of records and albums. He knew that I had come to Beverly Hills at the instigation of the William Morrow & Company publishers, who were urging me to do a book with and about Doris. I had told Terry (and the publisher) that I had my doubts that a woman who was so apple-pie buoyantly happy and *healthy* (an appraisal exclusively based on observing her on the silver screen) would be a compelling subject for the kind of book that would interest me; but after some Morrow prodding I consented to fly out from New York and have this lunch before definitely making up my mind. I also felt that Doris Day, who, I had learned, had always been rather circumspect about writers, should have a good look at me.

"I'm surprised your mother wants me to do this book with her."

"She admired your book on Papa Hemingway."

"But that was a very frank book that pretty much told everything there was to tell."

"Maybe that's what Doris wants."

"But is there much to tell? I mean, does she have things in her life that are unexpected and that she's never told?"

Terry looked at me soberly, smoothing down his moustache with thumb and forefinger. "Yes . . . yes . . . quite a lot."

9

Doris arrived fifteen minutes late on a chariot of sunshine. Kitsch metaphor or not, that exactly describes her entrance as she came striding into the garden, yellow sweater, beige slacks, yellow straw hat perched on the back of her blond hair, glowing skin, an aura of buoyant euphoria playing off her. The luncheon guests looked up from their tables, as they do at every entrance in the Beverly Hills garden, and you could feel a sort of mass positive response to her smiling, striding presence. (It would be a response I would invariably observe over the ensuing year whenever Doris appeared in public.) I had rather expected this radiation of joyful well-being but what I had not expected, from the Doris Day of *Pillow Talk* and *Calamity Jane* and *Please Don't Eat the Daisies,* was the incredibly youthful, curvaceous, sexy body that was striding toward our table. In a few months she would be fifty years old, but the woman now shaking hands with me, smiling the smile of someone who had enjoyment of life written all over her, infectiously radiating that joy of life—this woman was far short, about twenty years short, of fifty.

"I am late and I am wearing this hat because I've had a fiasco," she said, in the rather musical, slightly throaty voice easily identified as hers alone. She gave the hat a little tug and compressed her lips.

"What kind of fiasco?" Terry asked.

"My hair," she said dramatically, and then she laughed.

"That's about what I thought," Terry said, smiling indulgently.

"Jackie Susann is having a birthday party tonight which I really didn't want to go to—if you *knew* how I don't like parties, even for my best friends! Well, my hair was a mess and I couldn't get hold of the woman who usually does it so I decided just to put in a few streaks myself. Well—what can I tell you?—I'm overstreaked!" She laughed, first lightly, then wholeheartedly. "Boy, am I overstreaked! I look like a psychedelic lemon."

"Now you've got a good reason not to go," Terry suggested.

"No, I said I will go, and I am going. But I'll be the only woman there in a hat, and it's a sit-down dinner here in the Lanai Room of the hotel."

A waiter approached and Doris started to look at the menu, but what he wanted was an autograph for a tourist couple a few tables away.

"They have a marvelous salad here," Doris said, picking up the menu. "The Neil McCarthy." When the waiter returned we all ordered the salad.

"Do you enjoy eating?" I asked. "Or do you have to watch yourself?"

"Oh, do I enjoy eating! But simple things. I'm not a fan of sauces. I've always eaten as much as I pleased but I weigh the same now, to the pound, as I weighed the first day I came to Hollywood—a hundred and twenty-one. I'm five-seven and that's just right for me. I can't cook but I love to eat. My favorite place is a delicatessen on Beverly called Nate 'n Al's—you can't imagine what they bring you from that kitchen!"

The waiter brought the Neil McCarthys, heaping plates of finely chopped salad ingredients. I tasted mine. It was innocuous.

"Uh-uh!" Doris exclaimed. "This won't do!" She motioned to the waiter. "Look at this dressing. It's watery, no taste. Please take it back."

"I think we should return all three," Terry said.

"What *can* we eat?" Doris asked.

"They make a good turkey sandwich on black bread with Russian dressing," Terry said.

Doris and I agreed to that as a substitute.

"I believe in sending things back," Doris said. "There's no sense in sitting and picking at something you don't like."

The couple to whom Doris had given the autograph came over to thank her and tell her how much pleasure she had given them. Doris was gracious to them.

"Now, let's talk about the book," Doris said.

"I came out here to have lunch with you to convince myself not to write it," I said.

"Because you think it will be all sweetness and light, that it?"

"Precisely."

"You know what my mother said when she heard I might do this book? 'Doris,' she said, 'your life just hasn't been that happy that you can do a book. You know the image people have of you, but the truth is—all the terrible things that have happened to you, and all the times you've suffered, well, my goodness, when you think of all the unhappiness you've had—what's there to write about?'"

"Why *do* you want the book?" I asked.

"Because I'm tired of being thought of as Miss Goody Two-shoes, that's why—the girl next door, Miss Happy-Go-Lucky. You doubtless know the remark dear Oscar Levant once made about me—'I knew her before she was a virgin.' Well, I'm not the All-American

11

Virgin Queen and I'd like to deal with the true, honest story of who I really am. This image I've got—oh, how I *dis*like that word 'image'—but it's not me, not at all who I am. It has nothing to do with the life I've had."

"Are you saying that you would candidly deal with the details of your life without censoring out whatever you felt was unfavorable or put you in a light in which you did not want to see yourself?"

"I'm not interested in any of that subterfuge. I have suffered and I have had good times, I am proud of some things I've done, not so proud of others, and I have finally come to a time in my life when I have evolved a personal philosophy which I think others may want to know about."

When Doris walked into Nate 'n Al's the following morning, it was a proletariat Queen Victoria appearing among her loyal subjects. The waitresses and countermen exchanged cheery good-mornings with her, as did many of the breakfast regulars. The atmosphere was that of a club, with a prevalence of booth hopping. Milton Berle slipped in beside her, bestowing a kiss on her forehead, to report to her on the condition of his wife, Ruth, who had been under the weather. When Doris introduced us and said that she and I might do a book together, Berle said, "Don't let her forget the Little Club."

"How could I forget the Little Club?" Doris asked.

"Well, who introduced you on opening night?" Berle asked.

"God, I don't know—do you know how long ago that was?"

"*I* did. That's who. Your Uncle Miltie."

"*You!* Oh, no! Really, Milton?"

"I warmed up your audience and set them up for you and this is the thanks I get." Berle heaved himself from the booth and left in a comic huff.

A writer visited the booth who had an idea for a new television series that he wanted to do for Doris, and an agent named Duke came by to tell an involved, rather vulgar story in a loud voice that seemed to upset an elderly couple in the adjoining booth. Duke smiled at them and tipped his houndstooth hat and apologized.

After a long discussion with the waitress about a dog which the waitress had recently obtained through Actors and Others for Animals, an organization to which Doris is fiercely devoted, Doris ordered breakfast: large orange juice, two eggs, hashed brown potatoes, a plate of sliced lox, a heaping plate of cream cheese, a plate of sliced raw onions, sliced tomatoes, toasted bagels and rye bread, and coffee. To whet her appetite, Joe, who presides over the sandwich counter, had sent over a plate on which there were two rolls of turkey stuffed with pickles and cream cheese and garnished with slices of stuffed olives.

When the ebb and flow of visitors to her booth had subsided, and we were well into the lox and cream cheese, I asked Doris to elaborate on her statement of the day before about how she had suffered.

"You came to Hollywood when you were barely twenty," I said, "you became a star with your first picture, *Romance on the High Seas,* and you've been a superstar ever since—so it's hard to equate that with suffering."

Doris put down her knife and a piece of lox-bearing bagel she was about to attack. "I've had three marriages," she said, "and each was a bitter disappointment in different ways. When I was thirteen, on my way to being a dancer, I had my left leg destroyed in an accident and I was told I might never walk properly again. Before that, I had had to endure the bad marriage of my parents and their divorce and the bizarre behavior of my father. At sixteen I was earning a living on the road singing with bands, one-night stands, living in a bus. Married when I was seventeen and immediately pregnant with a husband who was . . . oh . . ."

Her eyes filled with tears and she looked away. "So many things I've never told anyone," she said, the tears on her cheeks.

"And you would put those things in the book, straight, as they really happened, as they shaped and affected your life?"

"Yes. Everything. Things my mother, my son don't . . . everything."

"That first husband . . ."

"Oh, God, how sick he was! Beating me when I was pregnant . . ." Her tears overcame her again. She used her napkin.

"I've read that after the death of your third husband, Marty Melcher, who was your manager, you discovered that he had cleaned you out—not only cleaned you out but left you heavily in debt."

"Yes, Marty and a lawyer named Jerry Rosenthal, but it was mostly Rosenthal."

"How long were you married to Marty?"

"About seventeen years."

"And you didn't suspect?"

13

"That can't be answered yes or no. You'd have to hear all the details."

"What about the Manson murders?" I was touching on those matters I had heard about to see if anything was off limits. "I've heard that Terry was involved with Manson . . . that actually Sharon Tate was living in Terry's house and that Manson's group was actually looking for Terry that night."

"There was a time that Terry and I both had bodyguards around the clock."

"What about all the rumors about you and certain men—like Maury Wills when he was with the Dodgers?"

"Do you mean will I discuss Maury in the book?"

"Yes—and now there's a sonic rumor going around about you and Sly."

"Who? Sly? Sly and the Family Stone?"

"Yes."

"Oh, no," she laughed. "I hadn't heard that one!"

"But you know Sly, don't you?"

"I've met him. At Terry's house."

"Well, in a book you'll have to deal with all that—and the newspaper accounts that linked you at one time with Elgin Baylor when he was playing with the Lakers. By the way, I find it interesting that most of these rumors over the years link you with black men."

Doris pondered that for a moment. "It may have to do with the fact that my father, who was a staid German bigot, wound up marrying a black woman."

"And you'll go into that?"

"Hotch, I will go into everything that is within my memory. I can't think of anything that I will hold back unless it involves something that will needlessly hurt another person."

"Well, let me tell you the kind of book I'd like to do. I would like to see you every day, so that we develop work rhythm, in a sealed place away from phones and distraction. Four hours every day, taping our sessions, starting with your earliest Cincinnati memories and going right up to this moment."

"Suits me."

"Then, I'd like to talk to many of the people who have been part of your life—your mother, your son, actors you've worked with, like Jimmy Cagney, Rock Hudson, Jack Lemmon, James Stewart— and I'd like to find out about the early days from Bob Hope and Les

Brown and people like that. I'll talk to your producers and publicists and lawyers and whoever else I think can add dimension to this book."

"I'd like that."

"But I may run their interviews as independent sections—the way I see the book there will be sections in which you will tell about your life, then there will be a section, let's say, in which Cagney will tell how he recalls the making of *Love Me Or Leave Me*—"

"I still see Jimmy. We had dinner a few nights ago."

"There may be a section where you'll tell about your son, Terry, followed by a section in which he talks about you. Now, there may be disagreement in all this. You may say one thing about Terry, let's say, and he may say just the opposite—are you prepared to go along with this?"

"Of course."

"Even if it's not favorable about you?"

"I don't even know what you mean by that word. Favorable to what? Some preconceived notion I have of myself? Or what the public may have? That's the reason I want to do this book. These judgments as to what is favorable or not favorable are silly. There are the details of how I've lived and I'd like them to be told as simply and fully as possible."

"Then I see three parts to the book—Doris Day telling about Doris Day, others telling about Doris Day, and then possibly a part in which I may describe whatever may occur while I'm doing the book. If you go on a trip, for instance, I may go along and describe that. But primarily, I'd say, eighty percent of the book will be your story told in your own words."

"I'd love for you to talk to those people you mentioned—Cagney and Jimmy Stewart and Rock and Bob Hope—oh, those early radio days when I was part of Bob's troupe and we played one-night stands by airplane all over the country. We traveled through everything—lightning storms, sleet, zero ceiling—we almost crashed in a landing in Pittsburgh."

I raised what was left of my glass of orange juice. "Well," I said, "here's to our literary adventure."

"Here's to," she said.

A. E. Hotchner

Beverly Hills, California

One

〰〰〰〰〰〰〰〰〰〰〰〰〰〰〰〰〰〰〰〰〰〰〰〰〰〰〰〰〰〰〰〰〰

AFTER twenty-seven years of band singing, radio, nightclub appearances, recording, movie and television acting, my public image is unshakably that of America's wholesome virgin, the girl next door, carefree and brimming with happiness. An image, I can assure you, more make-believe than any film part I ever played. But I am Miss Chastity Belt and that's all there is to it.

And what are some of the sweet, virginal roles I have played on the silver screen? I was slugged and raped by Jimmy Cagney, battled the Ku Klux Klan with Ginger Rogers and Ronald Reagan, was terrorized by Hitchcock kidnappers, stalked by a murderous Rex Harrison, was the long-suffering wife of alcoholic baseball pitcher Ronald Reagan, and became so hysterical with fear of Louis Jourdan that the movie had to be shut down while I recovered.

Well, then, it's my carefree personal life that has given me this image. Sure. At ten years of age I discovered that my father was having an affair with the mother of my best friend. Divorce followed. At thirteen, I was in an auto that was hit by a train, and that abruptly ended my promising career as a dancer—and threatened to make me a cripple for life. I was married at seventeen to a psychopathic sadist. When my third husband died, a man I had been married to for seventeen years, I discovered that not only had he secretly contrived to wipe out the millions I had earned, but he left me with a debt of a half-million dollars. My reward for a lifetime of hard work. Yes, sir, America's la-di-da happy virgin!

And to complete those virgin credentials: I've had one child of my own and a couple dozen movie and television children—in fact, on one occasion Rock Hudson married me on my way to the delivery room!

17

But nothing seems to daunt the persistent image of me as the unsullied sunshine girl of hearth and drive-in. So there must be something about me, about whatever it is that I give off, that accounts for this disparity between who I am and who I appear to be. I cannot account for what I appear to be; that is for others to say, like the English critic who said: "There's something about Doris Day that seems to bring out the boyishness in most of the middle-aged men I know. The moment her short hair and freckled face appear on the screen the sap begins to rise in them and they suddenly realize it's spring again. Let's be off to the woods and gambol with Doris, I can almost hear them say. I can't say I blame them for these daydreams. She's the freshest, cleanest and wholesomest thing on screen today, and never for a moment is she prim or prissy."

If those men knew *me* instead of the "wholesomest thing" they apparently see on the screen, they'd know that they weren't about to go off on a gambol in the woods. It is this other Doris Day, the real-life Doris Kappelhoff from Cincinnati, whom I do know very well, and who is going to be the subject of this book. No holds barred, no pandering to the public image. This is the life I lived, distorted only by the vicissitudes of memory.

My roots in Cincinnati go very deep. I didn't leave there wanting to escape to someplace better. I only left because the tide of events washed me away. And often an ebb tide of misfortune brought me back. I could have happily lived my entire life in Cincinnati, married to a proper Cincinnatian, living in a big old Victorian house, raising a brood of offspring, but preordination, which I sincerely believe in, had other plans for me.

As far as I am concerned, whatever we will be, where we go, what we do with our lives, is locked into us from birth. My predestination was to wander around for a while on bumpy band buses, singing at one-night stands, before coming to roost in Hollywood. But to this day, curiously, I am less emotionally attached to Los Angeles, where I have lived for twenty-seven years, than I am to Cincinnati.

I was born Doris Kappelhoff, named by my mother in honor of her favorite movie actress, Doris Kenyon, a silent-screen star of that year, 1924. (I now live on Crescent Drive in Beverly Hills, and, as bizarre fate would have it, a few houses away from me, on the very same street, lives Doris Kenyon, my namesake, a beautiful,

18

vibrant, chic lady whom I occasionally see.) My parents lived at Greenlawn and Jonathan streets in a red-brick, two-family house in Evanston, a moderate-income Cincinnati suburb. I was born in that house, attended by a good German midwife as my two brothers had been before me.

My father, William, was a music teacher—primarily piano—and choral master, while my mother, Alma Sophia, was a true hausfrau. She moved the furniture around a lot and my father would constantly fall over it. She has told me, "I was so stupid when I was young and first married, and didn't know any better. Instead of waiting until your father came home from work at night to help move the furniture, I did it myself, and believe me, I have suffered! My bladder dropped." That line always breaks me up but my mother is dead serious about it. To this day, if she catches me moving furniture (I am an inveterate furniture mover myself), she will scold me, "Now, Doris, stop moving that furniture—your bladder's going to drop!" She's a darling woman.

Both my parents were born in downtown Cincinnati but their parents were German immigrants. My mother's father came from Berlin. His family was quite wealthy but he ran into trouble when he refused to join the German army on the grounds that he didn't believe in military activity. There was no war then, but he refused to become a part of any military buildup that might lead to war, so he left Germany, forsaking the lucrative family business. He came to Cincinnati, where there was a large German community, and he opened a pretzel factory—the heavy, thick pretzels that are soft and covered with salt. My grandmother and all their many children, including my mother, worked in the pretzel factory, and my mother's brothers sold the pretzels on street corners all over Cincinnati. A big bag of pretzels slung over their shoulders, five for a nickel—five times heavier than doughnuts, but absolutely delicious. With the profits from his pretzel factory, my grandfather bought a building, the downstairs of which he converted into a big bakery and dining room. The family lived in the apartments above the bakery.

Word came to my grandfather that his mother, in Berlin, was dying, so he made a hurried trip to try to reach her before she died. But his sister, on finding out that he was coming, notified the military authorities—after all those years, she still wanted to turn him in for having dodged the draft. My grandfather got wind of it, however, and as the police came barging in the front door of the Berlin house, my

19

grandfather escaped through a rear window. But he never got to see his mother. Nor did he get his inheritance—it went to the German government.

That was my maternal grandfather—a very strict, hardworking, humorless man who died of pneumonia when he was forty. That was before I was born, of course. When I asked my mother to describe him to me, she said, "Well, he was the kind of man, not too many tears were shed when he passed away."

Now my grandmother was something else! She was adorable. After her husband's death, she ran the bakery, raised all those kids, and managed to enjoy her life. Mama Welz. She retired from the bakery when she was in her late fifties—turned it over to her sons —and she came to live with us in the house in Evanston. She died when I was ten.

I don't know much about my father's parents, but as for my own parents, from my earliest memory of the relationship that existed between them, I knew that they were not, in the scheme of things, intended for each other. It was an ill-matched, ill-fated marriage from the word *go*. No two people were ever more opposite. My mother is very barrelhouse, loves to yak it up and enjoy herself, loves parties, and the more people around, the better. Loves Country and Western hillbilly music. She could listen to Country and Western all day long. All through my career, she's asked me, "When are you going to make a Country and Western movie?" She's in her seventies now, lives with me, and I swear she seems to have as much pep and go as she did when I was a girl.

My father was the other side of that coin. He was an introverted, quiet man who loved classics and adored listening to opera. What battles they had over music! My father would get a concert on the radio and settle back to enjoy it. My mother's ears were actually offended by classical music, especially opera, so after enduring the music as long as she could, she would march over and flip the dial to some good old hillbilly music. A few minutes later my father was at the radio, getting back to the symphony or opera. This musical tug-of-war never ceased; but their musical altercations were just symptomatic of their entire relationship.

My father was a handsome man, tall, slender, thick auburn hair, large brown eyes topped by heavy auburn eyebrows. He dressed elegantly, and as a girl I was very proud of his looks. Everyone called him "Professor," although of course he wasn't, and I recall how

20

pleased I was to walk to church with him in his fine clothes and elegant ways and to hear him greeted as "Professor Kappelhoff" as we made our way up the church steps.

My father's whole life was music. As a boy he shunned sports and other boyhood distractions, using all his spare time to practice. At sixteen he was an organist for a Catholic church. By the time he married my mother he was a well-established teacher of piano and violin, and a respected choral master. He gave lessons in our house and also in the houses of his pupils. Evenings were invariably devoted to various German *Gesangverein* choral societies, with which Cincinnati abounded. Cincinnati then was predominantly German (and still is, I suppose), and since Germans love to sing, these big choral groups, with as many as four or five hundred voices, flourished. Once a year they would have their big recital, and my father was the city's most sought-after conductor. I remember once going to watch him conduct a choral group that was singing with the Cincinnati Symphony. He got incredible performances out of these amateur groups.

But with the schedule he had, there was very little time for family life. I had two brothers, Richard, who died when he was two —long before I was born—and Paul, who was a few years older than I. My father spent a little more time with Paul than with me, but that's not saying much. I can't remember a time we ever did anything together as a family—like go out to dinner, or take a trip, or have a picnic in the park. When I came home from school I always checked to see if my father's car was there, then if the door of the music room in the front of the house was closed; and, if it was, I listened for the music of some pupil. On such days I had to use the back door and slip in and out of the house quietly. But on days that his car wasn't there, I could enter in my usual raucous way, with friends in tow.

My father's base of operations was the St. Mark's Catholic Church, which was our church. My father was organist there but it was his choral group that people raved about. I was raised as a Catholic, and I went to Catholic schools, but I'd have to say that the Catholic side of me never took. I found the Latin, which of course I didn't understand, very boring, and so was all the ritual. I went to church on Sundays with my mother, but I was a child who liked to ask questions and I found that the church preferred dogma to giving answers.

21

My father tried to get both my brother and me interested in playing the piano, and he gave us some lessons, but he finally gave up on me because I wouldn't practice. First of all, I was interested in popular music, not the Chopin and Mozart that he taught, and secondly, my overriding love was dancing. When my father had a little free time to give me a lesson, I was invariably at dancing school. My brother Paul did fairly well, and put in long practice hours at the piano, but when my mother and father separated, that was the end of his lessons.

My father was never home for dinner, for he was busy with a different choral society every evening, but considering the atmosphere in the house when he was there, it was perhaps for the best that he was away so much. I suppose I was around eight years old when I really became aware of how things were between my mother and father. I so wanted loving things to happen between them, for them to show some affection toward each other, touching, smiling at each other, I so desperately wanted to see it, to feel it, but there was nothing but quarrels, constant quarrels. They argued about any- and everything. I said that I was eight or so when I became aware of this friction, but the heavy atmosphere around the house when they were together was something that surely affected me for years before that. I remember wondering, when I was in second grade, whether all people who got married acted this way. From then on, when schoolmates invited me over, I watched their parents to see if they behaved any differently.

When my father separated from my mother, and then when they got divorced, it became a scandal that made it very difficult for me. Our family had always enjoyed a certain standing in the community because of my father's position at the church, but when he divorced he had to resign his post. That changed the way people thought of us. Especially when it was revealed that my father had been running around with my mother's best friend. You can imagine how the tongues wagged—this respected "Professor" of the church having an affair with a married woman who was his wife's closest friend.

This woman was tall and slender, a truly lovely woman who lived in a beautiful apartment building right across the street from St. Mark's. She had two daughters, one of whom was in my class, the other in the class behind me. The daughters used to be at our house all the time. My mother would look after all of us. How often she told me to be sure to bring Jane and Virginia home with me because their mother had to go to the doctor, or whatever. What we didn't know was that it was my father she was seeing, not the doctor. The terrible part of it is that I knew about the affair before my mother did.

I have never told anyone this, not even my mother, because the way I found out about my father was so awful that I could never bring myself to mention it. It happened at a party. My parents rarely entertained but this was a big party to which they had invited most of their friends and relatives. It was a rare occasion for me, and exciting, so I was up much later than usual, spying from upstairs on what the grown-ups were doing. Finally, though, I began to get sleepy and I went to my room, which was toward the back of the house. I was in bed, not yet asleep, when I heard whispered voices outside my room, and then the door opened just a crack and I could see my father peeking in. I pretended to be asleep.

Just beyond my room was a little spare bedroom that could only be entered by going through my room. My father was apparently satisfied that I was asleep, and through slitted eyes I could see the door swing open—with the light in back of them I could easily distinguish my father and the woman I have mentioned. My father motioned for her to follow him. They came into my room, closed the door, tiptoed past me and into the bedroom beyond. There I was with the head of my bed against the wall of that room, and I heard everything, God help me, everything. I pulled the pillow over my head and burrowed my crying face into the sheet, but there was no way to shut out the awful things I was hearing.

When it was over, I again pretended to sleep as they came through my room. I held my breath so that my sobs wouldn't escape me. When the door was shut and they had gone, I felt compelled to get out of bed and look at the room where they had been. Then I got under my covers, in the warm tent of my bed, and cried myself to sleep.

You'd think that I would hate my father after that, and turn against him, but I went along as I had been, desperately faking how I felt. Thinking about it, I suppose my drive to preserve our home was stronger than the revulsion of what had happened. I wanted to have my father in that house, part of my life, no matter what he had done. I did not condemn him. That has never been a part of my nature; it is my nature to forgive, to try to accentuate what is good, and not to pass judgment.

Hate is simply not in me. I am often made sorrowful by the disappointments and disillusionments I have suffered in people, but hate or condemnation is not a part of it. Thus, I grieved over what my father had done, but I didn't hate him for it, or reject him.

But, despite my pretense, the marriage didn't last much longer. One evening after I had been to dancing class, my mother and my dancing partner, Jerry, and his mother and I all went to get a bite to eat, as we often did; but afterward, instead of going home, my mother drove toward Avondale, which is another Cincinnati suburb. I was sitting in the back seat gabbing with Jerry and it wasn't until we pulled up in front of an apartment building that I realized where we were.

"What are we doing here?" I asked my mother.

"Just never mind," she said. "We'll only be here a little while."

Quite a bit of time passed, and Jerry and I were talking and playing word games when, to my astonishment, I saw my father parking across the street. He didn't see us. He got out of his car and went into the apartment building across from where we were parked. That's when I realized why my mother had gone there. I knew that the woman he was having the affair with had been divorced and had moved to Avondale. That's when my mother started discussing things with me. My father was still living at home when this happened and this was, in effect, how my mother let me know what my father was up to. I don't know if some lawyer had advised her to spy on my father with the mother of my dancing partner as witness, or if she thought this was a good way to rouse my sympathy for her, but at any rate, looking back on it, I think it was a dreadful thing to have done, for it put me in the middle. But I suppose marital bust-ups are prone to these emotional incidents, especially where children are involved; but I remember my feelings, sitting there in the back seat of the automobile, watching my father through the window as he went into that apartment house to visit another woman, wishing desperately that I was not there, not seeing him do this, with my mother right there too. I felt it belonged to the grown-up world and that I shouldn't have been dragged into it. I kept my face turned away from Jerry so he could not see I was crying. That moment hurt me very deeply.

It was not too long after that that my father moved out. I was eleven at the time. My mother and father had lived together all those years and produced three children but they had nothing in common. Not a thing. The afternoon my father actually left the house, my

24

brother helped him pack. My mother was deliberately not home. Paul was in and out of my father's room, carrying things to his suitcases. While they were packing they were having a long talk. I was down at the end of the hallway, watching all this, hearing the drone of their voices, but not invited by my father to be a part of it. I was crying hysterically, trying to keep it inside me the best I could. My brother was calm and matter-of-fact, as if my father were going off on a little business trip.

When my father was all packed, I went in to the living room and hid behind the draperies, where I could watch the driveway without being observed. It was a lovely, soft drapery and I can still feel it wrapped around me as I pressed my crying face against the window and watched Paul help my father carry his bags into the car. There were no good-byes—my father didn't ask for me and all I wanted to do was hide there in the draperies and watch him. My father got in the car and I watched it move away down the long driveway that ran along the side of our house. Then the car turned into the street and disappeared, and I felt that my life was disappearing with it.

My brother came into the living room and saw me hiding in the draperies. "What are you crying about?" he asked.

I couldn't believe that he wasn't crying.

My father was such a rigid man, so remote, so ungiving toward me, and yet his leaving was an enormous loss to me. I loved him and he had a profound influence on me. But I could no longer fantasize that the happy marriage I wanted for my parents was going to happen. That was my big dream as a girl—that my parents would have a happy marriage and that I would someday have a happy marriage too. It was the only real ambition I ever had—not to be a dancer or Hollywood movie star, but to be a housewife in a good marriage. Unfortunately, it was a dream that would elude me just as surely as it had eluded my mother.

The evening of that day my father moved out, I asked my mother if I could sleep in her room. My father and she had slept in twin beds and that night I slept in his bed beside my mother. It picked up my spirits somewhat. After that, Paul and I took turns sleeping in my father's bed. It made us feel better, not having to see his bed empty with its coverlet smoothly in place.

But in addition to these sorrowful events, I have many good memories of my girlhood in Cincinnati: The traction rides to Trenton to visit Aunt Em and Uncle Ben and Grandpa Bartmann (the traction was a red, one-car vehicle that was somewhere between a train and a trolley); my boyfriend, Alvin Hock, who carved "AH loves DK" on all the telephone poles in the neighborhood; going to the beer garden with Aunt Hilda and Uncle Frank, my mother, and brother, to have roast beef, chili, and orange pop, the lanterns swinging overhead while we sang along with the piano player; going to church on Easter, when everyone looked so beautiful in new dresses and suits; my days at the Welz Bakery when I was seven years old and my uncles let me wait on customers and make change and gave me my own dough and rolling pin and put my bread in the big oven; learning tricks on the trapeze which my cousin Carl had set up in the yard in back of the bakery; swimming in the creek in Trenton, and afterward eating Smitty's homemade ice cream; and in the evening, lingering over a nectar soda in the drugstore and then going back to the front porch and sitting in the swing, reading the funnies while listening to the radio. There were some happy times, all right.

After the divorce I saw my father once a week, on Wednesday afternoon. When I came home from school he would be sitting in his car in front of the house, waiting for Paul and me. My father was staying with his sister and he would invariably take us there for dinner and bring us right back. That's all we ever did. My father said very little to me; I don't think he ever mentioned the divorce, or asked about my problems, but I never expected him to. He had always been so closed, so inhibited, I did not expect him suddenly to be different. I cannot remember one thing I ever did with my father, not the most insignificant thing, like going to the ice-cream parlor. Those Wednesday visits with him and his relatives were terribly boring and I looked upon them as a chore, not as an anticipated opportunity to see my father.

The situation with my father became more complicated when the woman for whom he had left my mother moved into my aunt's house, where my father was living. When my mother found out that this woman, who had been her best friend, was now also living at my aunt's, it upset my mother terribly. But it didn't affect my visits since my father's lady friend rarely showed herself on the Wednesdays when Paul and I were there. I always felt nervous going there, though, because I dreaded running into her. I did see her a few times. She was very thin, elegant, with long auburn hair; a classical singer, soft-spoken, reserved, a personality that perfectly complemented my

Doris, age three, astride a Cincinnati pony with her brother Paul, whom she adored; his life was destined to be cut short as a result of a baseball beaning.

After strewing the flowers at the wedding of her Uncle Frank and Aunt Hilda, Doris Kappelhoff became petulant when she was not allowed to wear a veil for this official photo.

Doris's father played a romantic and tragic role in her life. At left, with her mother and father—it was Doris's dream to have a harmonious family life, but her musician father was an introvert who paid more attention to his piano, and other women, than to Doris.

Talent will out—even in the Kappelhoff backyard.

father's. They lived at my aunt's for quite a while until they got married. But by then I was singing with a band and not visiting on Wednesday anymore. My father, in his fashion, did not tell me about the marriage, which, I heard, worked out very well for him for a time. But, tragically, she died of cancer. For a time my father was alone, but then his life changed, changed more drastically than the life of any man I have ever known. He was a rigid man who had been so set in his ways and views, so unyielding, so bigoted—Italians were wops and dagos, blacks were niggers or coons; Jews were always kikes. Since there was not one member of any of these ethnic groups in our neighborhood, I had no reason to question any of these abstract prejudices. But something happened later on that turned my father around, to an amazing degree. It was years later, though, after I had become a movie actress, and the telling is best left for later in the book.

My mother never went with anyone after my father left. She certainly could have. She was relatively young, a very attractive woman, and there were men who were interested in her, but she was not interested in them. As I got older, I made many an effort to get her to go out, and there were a few times that she actually went out on a date, but after an hour she'd be back home, complaining about a headache. My mother's lack of interest in developing a new life for herself had an enormous advantage for me, of course, since she could devote all her time to me, not only in my growing years, but afterward, too, when my own marriages collapsed.

My first public performance was in the olio of a minstrel show when I was in kindergarten. The olio consisted of a string of performances that preceded the minstrel show itself, a little floor show designed to warm up the audience. My contribution to the olio was a recitation and dance; my mother, who made all my clothes, had costumed me elegantly in a red-satin top, red panties, and a tarlatan skirt. Unfortunately, I can still remember the opening lines of that recitation:

> "I'se goin' down to the Cushville hop,
> And there ain't no niggie goin' to make me stop!"

There was an interminable wait backstage while the long line of performers ahead of me went out to do their stuff. When it was finally my turn, disaster had already struck my act. I came out, did

27

a bow, saw my mother sitting in the first row, right in front of me, started my recitation:

"I'se goin' down to the Cushville hop . . ."

I could hear the audience starting to giggle.

"And there ain't no niggie goin' to make me stop . . ."

The giggling was getting louder. "I'm sorry, Mommy," I blurted out, "I couldn't help it!" And with that I started to cry. During that long wait backstage, I had wanted to go to the bathroom but my mother had pinned me into the costume and no one could get me out of it. Besides, I didn't know when they would call my name to go on and I wanted to be ready. But the woeful consequence was that I had wet my pants and the red satin had turned black where I was wet. I did a little curtsy and ran off the stage. That was my debut in show business. Wet-pants Kappelhoff. Maybe that's why I have such an aversion to performing before live audiences.

I was still in kindergarten when, having been nagged to death, my poor mother finally agreed to take me to Pep Golden's for my first dancing lessons. I was crazy about dancing. Pep Golden's was for tap-dancing and for what was called "personality dancing." I was in a few recitals there but my mother didn't like Pep or his studio very much. She had heard about a ballet school, Schuster Martin's, and I went there for a while. But the third school I went to, Hessler's, is the one I fell in love with. Hessler's was in the suburb of Mt. Adams, and we had to take four streetcars to get there. They taught everything, including elocution. Every week I had to sing a song, one chorus, and make up a dance to go with it. I could pick any song I wanted, and my mother and I would go to downtown Cincinnati, to the dime store, where there was a lady in the sheet-music department, who played on the piano any music you selected. You handed her the music and she'd play it and sing it for you. My favorite of all the songs I bought at the dime store was "Life Is Just a Bowl of Cherries." I fell in love with it the minute the dime-store lady played it. I made up a tap dance to go with the song, but there was nobody at home to play for me. I sometimes tried to get my father to play but he wouldn't touch the music I brought home. "You call that music?" he'd bellow at me. He hated it.

But I worked out a way to devise tap routines without musical accompaniment and it all came very easily to me. I was also in the plays at school. I vividly recall one play we did, *The Poor Little Rich Girl,* in which I played a girl from a rich family in which there was no love in the house. I met a little girl from a poor family in which there was love, and with this as an example I was able to bring my parents to love each other again. For a long time I cherished the notion that I could do this with my own parents.

Hessler's also taught acrobatic dancing, which came to me as easily and naturally as my first steps. They had a contest, with twenty-five free lessons as the prize, to determine who could stand on their hands the longest. For weeks I was never on my feet. People would have to talk to me by bending over and tilting their heads downward. I went up and down stairs on my hands. I got up in the morning on my hands and went to bed that way. I was always on my hands around the house. I won the prize easily.

Even though my father had not been home very much, I missed him terribly after he separated from my mother. He was the head of the house, a presence whether actually there or not, and the house was less a house and we were less a family after his departure. I found that I missed hearing the piano of his students, the loud arias emanating from the Victrola, and the frequent aroma of my father's homemade beer. Hops have a peculiarly satisfying smell, and on "beer days" I loved to have their pungent odor greet me when I came home from school.

But now when I came home from school, it was quiet and empty. My mother had taken a job in the Evanston Bakery, selling baked goods. But despite her job she made time for me. And the large Welz clan, my mother's family, were always coming to the house or inviting us. There was one aunt, Tanta Re (Aunt Maria), of whom I was particularly fond. Very funny woman. I remember telling her one time that there were only four things in the world I really wanted —a permanent, a brassiere, high heels, and false teeth. Can you imagine? False teeth. My grandmother had false teeth, uppers and lowers, which made a clicking sound when she ate, and I simply adored that sound. I tried copying it when I ate but it didn't work.

Another saving grace for me was my dancing. I now had a regular dance act with a twelve-year-old boy named Jerry Doherty, whom I had met at dancing school. We'd sing a chorus of a song and then go into our tap routine. Our big number was "Clouds":

"Clouds drifting through the sky,
How I wonder why my love never said good-bye . . ."

A ghastly little song that we would render with Jerry standing behind me with his hands on my hips as we walked first to one side of the stage and then the other. Then he would come around beside me and off we'd go into our fast buck-and-wing. My mother made our costumes (she made all of my clothes), which were a symphony in blue—mine was ice-blue satin with a little skirt that had silver worked into it, and Jerry wore a pale-blue coat with tails. Hessler's sent us all over Cincinnati to perform—church affairs, Odd Fellow temples, Elks lodges, Masonic temples, and other boring places. We were paid a few dollars for our performances, just about enough to cover our expenses.

We didn't stay in the Evanston house very long after my father left. My mother moved us to smaller, less expensive quarters in a suburb called College Hill. I had to go to the Our Lady of Angels school, while all of my friends entered Regina High. It was a painful transition for me, losing all my friends like that. And I was not happy at the school. I resented the parochial system, the attitude toward the students; the arbitrariness of what was and was not taught. They seemed to avoid teaching anything about life as it was lived. My one and only ambition was to get married and have children, but nothing they taught me was concerned with that. After my parents divorced, my ambition for a happy marriage became stronger than ever. But the Catholic schools, it seemed to me, wanted uniform thoughts on safe subjects, and I resented that.

The dance team of Doris & Jerry scored a resounding success by winning the grand prize of five hundred dollars in a big city-wide amateur contest run by one of the department stores. The contest was held every weekend in a local radio studio and it went on for months. Hundreds of amateur performers were competing for the prize. Our act was a comedy song-dance routine called "The Bird on Nellie's Hat." It was really quite funny. My mother dressed me in an assortment of old-fashioned clothes that she had found in an antique store—high-button shoes and pantaloons, with the crowning glory a wide-brimmed hat with a big bird squatting atop it. During all those weeks of competition, it never occurred to me that we wouldn't win the grand prize. It wasn't that I had any particular interest in the money. It was just my basic confidence asserting itself, that I could achieve anything I set out to do.

My mother and Jerry's mother discussed what they should do with our five-hundred-dollar windfall. They asked us if we'd like to spend it on a trip to Hollywood, where the nationally famous dance school Fanchon & Marco was located. Of course, I found that very

30

exciting but I had no thoughts about the movies, only about my dancing. My interest in films was simply that of a moviegoer. Every Friday after school my mother and I would go downtown and have a spaghetti dinner at Caruso's and then see a show at one of the big downtown houses, the Shubert or the Albee. And every Sunday afternoon I would go to the neighborhood theater, the Evanston, for the horror films. I can still feel my fright on those afternoons, hiding behind my hands from the terrible monsters that roamed the screen.

The most exciting thing about going to the Shubert or the Albee was that after the film they had a stage show, and a Hollywood star would often put in a personal appearance. That's how I fell in love with Betty Grable. She was married to Jackie Coogan then, I think; I had seen her movies, of course, but she was nowhere near as exciting in films as she was dancing live and in person on the stage of the Albee. At that time I thought her dancing was spectacular, and she was part of the reason I too wanted to be a dancer; but as I look back on it now, she really didn't do anything much, just an ordinary, routine tap dance.

But much as I adored Betty Grable, when we played movie stars I was always Ginger Rogers. My cousin Jean always chose to be Jeanne Eagels but that infuriated me because I didn't know who she was.

"How can she be a movie star if I've never heard of her?" I demanded. "There's nobody named Jeanne Eagels. You're making it up, and you can't play the game with us if you're going to be some dumb old Jeanne Eagels which everybody knows is a name you just made up."

"She's a big star in *Rain*," my cousin would say, "and I'd rather be one Jeanne Eagels than one hundred dizzy old Ginger Rogerses."

When we played movie stars, I had only one movie boyfriend —Lew Ayres. I think that was because at that time he was married to Ginger Rogers. I'm not sure. At any rate, when I was doing my television series a few years back, he came on as a guest star. He's super, a beautiful person, and we had a lovely time working together. Also, we discovered a mutual passion for chunky peanut butter.

But my journey to Hollywood that summer when I was twelve had nothing to do with the movies. Our mothers felt that Jerry and I had learned just about all we could in Cincinnati, and that Fanchon & Marco would teach us more advanced routines. We saved our money all that winter.

We set out in July with my mother driving, stopping at inexpensive motels along the way. At the conservative pace my mother drove, it took us almost a week to get there. Along the way my attitude toward the restaurants and diners we ate in became a standing joke. I suppose it was the result of the scrubbed and sweet-smelling kitchens of all my German relatives—whatever the reason, I was terribly finicky about the kitchens of the places we ate in. Wherever they chose to eat, I would sneak a look into the kitchen to be sure it measured up to my Cincinnati standards. If it didn't look clean enough to me, no matter how hungry I was I'd only order a container of milk.

The hottest place at which we stopped on the trip was Needles, California. Blistering. It was exciting to be in the far west, but eggs could literally have been quickly fried on the sidewalks of Needles. My mother scouted around and found a small, clean place to eat— by now she knew that if it wasn't sparkling clean, I wouldn't eat. At any rate, this lunchroom in Needles was freshly painted and well scrubbed, and we all sat down at the counter and ordered. Between the counter and the kitchen there was a sliding panel which opened when an order was ready to be passed through to the counterman. Well, the first time that panel opened, I made a beeline out of that lunchroom. The cook was a Chinaman.

There was one Chinaman in Evanston. He had a laundry but I'd never been in the place because of all the strange things I had heard about Chinamen. Sometimes when I passed his shop I would peek in the window where he and his wife were hard at work. I would see this little man with his long pigtail come shuffling out from the back of the store with a big package that he'd give to a customer, and then shuffle away. I can't say why, but I was terribly frightened of him. I'm sure my fear was all bound up with my father's prejudices. At any rate, that day in Needles, I was not about to eat anything cooked by a sinister Chinaman. So I just upped from the counter and went back to the car and sat there in all that heat, waiting for them. I was starving but there was no way I could touch that food.

When they came back to the car, my mother said, "Now, Doris, that place is absolutely clean as a whistle. What in the world is wrong now?"

"I'm just not hungry," I said. "I don't feel like eating."

Later that day, I rather reluctantly told them why I had left the lunchroom, and they all roared with laughter. But they didn't realize how many times at night, coming home from the movies or from the place we went for sandwiches and chili, shivering with fear, I'd pass the Chinese laundry, where a single light bulb hanging from the ceiling menacingly illuminated the interior. And they were always working in there, no matter what time of night. I was afraid to pass too close to the laundry, for fear something sinister might happen to me. Those poor people, working so hard, washing and ironing, and I had no idea of the reality of their lives. But that's how it was in Evanston with all minorities. There was not one black. Not a Jew. It wasn't until I began singing with the bands that I learned about the real people who lived inside the skins of those prejudices.

My mother had rented a little apartment for four weeks, and we all four stayed there, taking turns on who slept in the bedroom and who slept on the Murphy-in-a-Door that folded out of the wall in the living room. All of our meals were cooked in the apartment's closet-sized kitchen.

Compared to Hessler's, Fanchon & Marco was really big-time. Our teacher was Louis De Pron, who had danced in films and whose name I had seen in credits on musicals. He liked our dancing and right away Jerry and I were sent to perform at events in and around Hollywood. My dancing received a lot of attention, and I began to dream that someday I might come back to this Hollywood as the Betty Grable who had danced on the stage of the Albee. There was something indefinable about Hollywood that made thirteen-year-old spirits soar.

We bought a movie-star map and drove all over Hollywood, gawking at their houses—but all the time I was there, I never actually saw a movie star. My big hope, of course, was to catch a glimpse of Ginger Rogers, but the closest I got to her was driving slowly past her house—at least the house that the movie-star map said was hers. My mother wanted to stop and ring her gate bell, but I wouldn't let her. Even then I felt about their private lives the way I feel about mine today—but if it were up to my mother, every tourist who rings my gate bell would be invited in for a grand tour of the house and high tea.

By the time our four weeks were up we had received such encouragement from Fanchon & Marco, and we had all become so enamored of Hollywood, that my mother and Jerry's mother decided to move to Hollywood for good. The plan was to go back to Cincinnati, rent our apartments, say our good-byes, and move our belongings to the Coast. The people who had seen us dance were so enthusiastic about our ability that I had no doubt that we would do very well. But, then, running the risk of sounding immodest, I must emphasize what I mentioned before—that I have never had any doubts about my ability in anything I have ever undertaken. I hope that doesn't sound arrogant; what I mean to convey is a natural sense of security about what I do. Dancing, singing, acting—the demand seems to create a rise in me that satisfies it. It is not a conscious effort. It is not anything I have control over. It is automatic and natural and as reliable as my breathing.

When we went back to Cincinnati, my mother did not enroll me in school since the plan was to leave at the end of October. We rented our apartment and packed all our belongings and said good-bye to our friends. On Friday, October 13, 1937, a good-bye party was given for us by our friends the Holdens, who lived in Hamilton, a little town about twenty-five miles out of Cincinnati. While I was there, I received a phone call from my boyfriend, Larry Doherty, the brother of my dancing partner. He was with two of our friends, Albert Schroeder and Marion Bonekamp, and they wanted to pick me up and go nearby for a hamburger and shake.

We drove to a hamburger joint on the other side of Hamilton but only stayed a short time for I had to get back to the party. Albert was driving, Marion in the front seat beside him; I was in the back seat behind Albert, with Larry on my right. It was a cold, rainy night. The steamy car windows were all closed, the radio going full blast. We were driving rather slowly, talking, Marion with her head turned toward us in the back. There was a flash of the locomotive's light, a moment when I became aware of its black, looming hulk, but no sound, no warning, a crossing with no lights or signs, just the giant presence hurtling at us, a split moment of our screams, then crashing into us, not once but twice as we were struck again by a freight car in back of the locomotive. Albert and Marion were both driven through the windshield, embedded in the shattered glass. Albert's seat had first pitched forward, driving him into the windshield, but the second impact knocked him free of it and his seat came crashing back. Marion's head was trapped in the windshield, and she was severely cut and bleeding profusely.

The initial crash knocked me down in the seat with my legs forward, but as the train screeched to a halt and I was able to react to what had happened, I felt all right, that I hadn't been hurt. Larry was all right too.

People were running to our assistance. Albert, bleeding heavily, was helped from the front seat. I pushed his seat forward and started to get out to see if I could help Marion, who was still pinioned in the shattered windshield. I collapsed. My right leg wouldn't support me. I pulled myself along the ground over to the curb. I felt no pain. I probed along my leg and discovered I was bleeding. Then my fingers came to the sharp ends of the shattered bones protruding from my leg. I began talking to myself about my leg. "How will I dance? How can I dance?" I kept repeating it. Then I fainted in the gutter.

The sound of the ambulance's siren brought me to. Some bystanders were looking after me. Through foggy eyes I watched the ambulance crew working to free Marion from the windshield. They were having a terrible time with her. A wave of nauseating pain washed over me. I passed out again and I did not recover consciousness until I was in the hospital.

The police had gone to the Holdens' to get my mother; she was in my room at Mercy Hospital when I regained consciousness. When I looked up and saw her, I started to cry. "What about my dancing?" I asked her. "What do the doctors say?"

"You're going to be all right," she said. This was no time to tell me that my right leg was shattered and that the doctors were not concerned about my dancing—at that point they were worried that I might never be able to walk again.

Two

~~~~~~

THE X-rays showed that I had a double compound fracture, and there were shattered bone fragments that had to be fitted back into place. A steel pin was inserted in the bone and an extra-heavy cast encased my leg from my thigh to my toes. But despite the long and complex surgery, the doctors were optimistic about my being able to regain normal use of my leg; they were not optimistic, however, about my ability ever to dance again.

My mother was able to induce the people to whom we had rented our apartment to return it to us, so it was there that I went when I was finally released from the hospital. Jerry Doherty and his mother had visited me the day after the accident, but when he came into the hospital room Jerry didn't know the nature or extent of my injury. When he found out that I would be on crutches and in a wheelchair for at least four months, he realized that his Hollywood dream was fractured as badly as my leg. I felt terrible that day Jerry came, not for myself, but for him. I guess I hadn't realized how much our dancing career had meant to him. He sat there looking at me, not believing his bad luck, and I couldn't help but feel a little guilty, as if, somehow, I had let him down. As it turned out, he never did have a career. He finished high school and became a milkman.

I tried going back to school on crutches but it was just too difficult. My mother couldn't take me, since she was working, and I had to take three streetcars to get there. You can imagine what it was like, transferring from one streetcar to another in the winter on crutches. Also, I couldn't manage getting around in school. In the classrooms, the crutches were always in the way, and I was in constant peril of being upended in the crowded corridors. I just couldn't get around and, besides, I felt that I, who had been so active and rather dynamic around school, was now being pitied—and pity is an emotion which I despise.

My mother finally agreed that until my leg got completely well, I should stay out of school. Little did we know how long that would be. As it turned out, that second year of high school was the last formal education I was to receive.

It was not long after I began my convalescence that we moved to Price Hill. My uncle Charley had retired from the bakery business, sold the family bakery, and built a beautiful home in Sailor Park. But after all those busy years in the bakery, retirement was driving him crazy, so he bought a tavern in Price Hill and went back into business. My mother agreed to take over the kitchen for him to provide such tavern staples as roast beef and chili, and Uncle Charley provided an apartment for us that was upstairs from the tavern. Charley and my mother were very close and they had a good time running Charley's new tavern.

As for me, I couldn't have asked for a better place to convalesce. The jukebox was going all the time, and whenever I got hungry I just scooted down the stairs on my fanny, holding my crutches above my head, and helped myself in the kitchen. Looking back on that period, I ask myself whether I was depressed and whether I brooded about my fate—after all, dancing had been the biggest thing in my life. But I think I'm being honest when I say that I did not moan over what had happened. It is my nature to accept events as they happen and adjust to them. By sheer coincidence, a song was written for a picture I made twenty years later, "Que Sera, Sera," which precisely stated my philosophy, a philosophy which has not been dented over the years by the arrows of what occasionally has been rather outrageous misfortune. Whatever will be, will be, and I have made the best of it.

The predicted four-month recovery did not materialize. The bones were not knitting although my orthopedist was giving me calcium and all kinds of things to promote the healing. During this long, boring period, I used to while away a lot of time listening to the radio, sometimes singing along with the likes of Benny Goodman, Duke Ellington, Tommy Dorsey, and Glenn Miller, who was just then starting to make a name for himself. But the one radio voice I listened to above others belonged to Ella Fitzgerald. There was a quality to her voice that fascinated me, and I'd sing along with her, trying to catch the subtle ways she shaded her voice, the casual yet clean way she sang the words. When I was dancing, singing was just incidental to the dance; but now, with all that enforced time on my hands, I began to get interested in singing for its own sake. Not with any thought of following it up, but just for my own amusement.

My leg had finally started to mend, and the doctor was beginning to talk about removing the heavy cast, when, in one impetuous moment, I undid everything. My mother had put a recording of "Tea for Two" on the Victrola, a song that is the tap dancer's national anthem. Its stop rhythm is perfect for the clickety-clack of tap shoes and I responded to its call by standing on my crutches and moving my good foot in a kind of tap-shuffle to the music.

"Now, be careful what you're doing," my mother warned.

But too late—one of my crutches slipped on the edge of the throw rug and I did a complete flip and landed on my busted leg. This time the prognosis was really bad. All the partially knitted bones had been broken, with some further damage, and I was medically condemned to stay in my cast and on crutches for at least another year. My mother was concerned about how I would react to this latest misfortune, and she discussed it with our doctor. A year's forced inactivity for someone who had always been as lively and as full of get-up-and-go as I had been might put me in a deep depression. The doctor advised her to keep me as busy as she possibly could; he warned that although I was an avid reader, reading was not enough, and that enforced idleness like this often led to severe depressions.

My mother had a friend, a musician, who had heard me singing around the house and who had said quite often that she thought my voice had potential for classical music. So to distract me from my idleness my mother decided to give me singing lessons. I was excited about that, but disappointed to find that the first song assigned to me by my new teacher, who thought my voice had "possibilities," was "Indian Love Call." Never having been a fan of the Jeanette Mac-Donald-Nelson Eddy genre of operatic kitsch, I lasted only three lessons before telling my mother that I loved the idea of singing lessons, but there were no Indians to whom I wanted to warble this love call.

Through an acquaintance of hers who was a song plugger, my mother came up with a new voice teacher by the name of Grace Raine. If I had to name one person who had the greatest effect on the career that was in store for me, that person would be Grace Raine. She lived in a second-floor apartment which I reached by going up backward sitting on my fanny. (I never did learn how to master stairs on crutches.) A gentle, smiling woman, she led me over to the piano, which was covered with sheet music. I picked out something. Grace sat down at the piano and played it, and I sang for her.

After three lessons, she told my mother, "Doris has tremendous potential. I'd like her to come three times a week."

"I'm sorry," my mother said, "but I can only afford once a week." The lessons were only five dollars but that's all my mother could afford on her earnings.

"All right," Grace said. "The other two lessons are on me."

Those first weeks with Grace Raine were tremendously exciting. My mother didn't own a piano but I've never needed musical accompaniment to practice. Or to do my exercises. Of course, it's nice if you have a piano to sing to, but in a way you have to be more alert when you sing without accompaniment. I cannot read music but, after glancing at a piece of sheet music, I can usually sing it correctly first time through.

Grace Raine really taught me virtually everything I ever learned about singing. Of course, no one can teach you to sing—either you are naturally endowed or you are not—but you can be taught how to make the most of whatever your natural talent is. Grace taught me the importance of singing the lyrics correctly. "When you sing the words to this song," she'd say, in that sweet, gentle way of hers, "imagine that you're singing to one person, just one, a very special person, and that you're singing it in that someone's ear. Don't just belt out a song, because that's impersonal, just putting it up for grabs. Remember that when you're singing a lyric it's really like playing a scene, and you can make it mean something to you. How many times have you heard marvelous singers with beautiful tone quality whose song means nothing to you because it doesn't mean anything to them?"

I worked very hard on projecting lyrics, *feeling* them, putting them within the framework of some imagined scene that fitted the song. It was this early work on lyrics, I'm convinced, that later helped me make the transition from band singing to movie acting.

My mother helped and encouraged me in every way she could. I've often been asked whether, in light of her involvement with my dancing and singing, she was one of that ogre species of stage mothers. I really can't say. When you're a child you're not aware of your mother in those terms. So many times I have worked in pictures with children who had horrendous stage mothers, suffocating them with their ambitions, and yet the children seemed perfectly happy with their mothers and blissfully unaware that they were being exploited. Of course, later on they often do come to realize how their mothers truly were and they begin to resent them. "My mother was an absolute brute," I've had them confide in me. "She wanted to be in show business herself but she didn't get anywhere, so I became her alter ego and she pushed me and had me working when I was barely out of diapers to compensate for her own failure."

I don't think my mother was that kind of stage mother. I made up my own mind about everything from the time I was a little girl and my mother respected how I felt. She did exert herself in aiding and abetting me in whatever I decided on, but I don't think she tried to impose her will on mine.

Grace Raine had been, for many years, the voice coach at radio station WLW, and she was very well-connected with the music people at all the stations; one of her contacts was with Andre Carlin, who ran a local radio show called "Carlin's Carnival." Carlin was a small-time Major Bowes, who had a two-hour Saturday-morning program that featured students from the Cincinnati schools who wanted to perform. There was a piano player in the studio who would play any sheet music you gave him, and Mr. Carlin would tell a little about each performer—where he lived, went to school, his teacher's name—before he did his stuff. Grace arranged for me to sing on this show so that she could hear how my voice sounded on radio.

The song I chose to sing was "Day After Day," a song that was destined to play an important part in my life. The studio audience was mostly composed of relatives of the performers. My recollection is that I was more curious than nervous—curious about how it would feel singing into a microphone. Grace stayed at home and listened to me. She later told me that she thought I had an attractive radio voice but that I needed to work on my delivery. She warned me not to pop my *p*'s, that I should lean away a little on a *p* sound to soften it. She had me work on my *s*'s to make them cleaner, and not hiss. Painstakingly, she taught me all the tricks of radio singing, which were to prove of such great value over the ensuing years. For instance, when I sang a word like "people," she showed me how to turn my head slightly to the side so that the double *p*'s would not pop.

Grace's husband was a song plugger who told Grace about a

40

Chinese restaurant in downtown Cincinnati that was looking for a girl singer on Saturday nights. Grace thought that this would be good practical experience for me to have while I was studying, and she arranged for me to have a tryout evening at the restaurant, which was called Charlie Yee's Shanghai Inn. The restaurant was on the second floor and I had to reach it by scooting up backward on my bottom. I still nurtured my fear of Chinamen, and I approached the restaurant full of trepidations, but Charlie Yee and his lovely wife and their large clutch of kiddies quickly dispelled my fear of the yellow menace. I think Charlie was a bit taken aback by a girl vocalist on crutches, but he good-naturedly agreed to a tryout anyway. There was a three-piece combo to back me up, and the pay was five dollars for an evening's singing.

The sensation of standing in front of a roomful of people who are eating, waiters moving around, much talking, is hard to describe. Unsettling, to say the least. You are singing more to a plate of *moo goo gai pan* than to people. I was so unsure of myself, so nervous, at this, my first professional engagement, that I had trouble getting enough breath for my debut number, "Ain't Misbehavin'." But once I got over that, I began to relax and have a good time. The crutches were no handicap. I stayed with bouncy, strong-rhythm songs like "Murder, He Says," and I was happy to see that as the evening progressed I was keeping up with the chop suey. Charlie Yee (who, by the way, was the mayor of Chinatown) and his family were eating in a big rear booth, and after each number they gave me a standing ovation. Looking back on it, I can't think of a nicer way to have made my debut. I was only fifteen, but I said I was eighteen and no one seemed to question it.

Over the ensuing months, my singing lessons, weekend appearances at the Shanghai Inn, and rather regular unpaid stints on "Carlin's Carnival" helped keep me distracted from my slow-mending leg. And so did Tiny, the little black and tan who was my constant companion during these long tedious months of convalescence. I had had dogs and other pets before Tiny, but I had never developed the kind of relationship I had with this gentle, understanding creature. He seemed to understand my moods, adopting them as his moods, and he never left my side. Those long days of companionship gave me a beginning insight into what it is that sets a dog apart from all other animals. It was the start of what was to be for me a lifelong love affair with the dog. I care about them deeply, but no matter how much I have given them in the way of love and concern for their well-being, they have given me much more. Tiny taught me how much love, and affection, and undemanding companionship a dog can give—and what an antidote for loneliness he was! As a matter of fact, all my life I have never felt lonely with a dog I loved at my side, no matter how many times I've been alone.

As for Tiny, who was indeed the sunshine of my life, he was destined to hurt me in a way that I would feel for the rest of my life. Not through any fault of his own, God knows—but through my own fault, really. Twice a day I would take Tiny for a walk. He invariably walked alongside me as my crutches carried me along the sidewalk. I never used a leash with him because he was so well trained in staying close beside me, and also because a leash might have become entangled with my crutches. But there came this day when we were walking along as on all other days when, for absolutely no reason that I know, Tiny dashed away from me and out into the street. Perhaps there was another dog—I don't know. I screamed at him but of course I couldn't dash after him. There was a screech of brakes, and a sickening thud that I can hear to this day. I hobbled out to him where he lay inert on the street. I dropped my crutches and picked him up. What had been so vital and animated a moment before was now a still form in my arms. He seemed so small. I leaned my face against his lifeless cheek and cried my heart out. By letting him run free, I had betrayed him.

It was a searing, indelible experience. I cried for days. My loneliness was intolerable. And so was my guilt. I could not stop running what had occurred through my mind. From then on, and to this very day, I would berate anyone I saw with a dog who was not on a leash. If I now find a dog running free, I will corral it; and if it has a tag, I will deliver it to its owner along with a blistering lecture about unleashed dogs that he will not soon forget. But as for Tiny, all I could do was bury him and grieve for him. It certainly made the rest of my convalescence much harder to take.

Finally, eighteen months after the accident, I was given permission to trade in my crutches for a cane. And just about that time, Grace Raine received a phone call from a band leader friend of hers named Barney Rapp, who had heard me sing on "Carlin's Carnival."

Barney Rapp and his New Englanders were a good, small-time band that traveled around the country playing smaller hotels. Barney explained to Grace that he had decided to settle down in Cincinnati and start a club, The Sign of the Drum. He was looking for a girl vocalist to replace his wife, who had always been his singer but who was pregnant now and permanently retiring. Barney Rapp told Grace that he liked what he had heard of my voice on the radio and he wondered if I would like to try out with his band. He was then playing at the Hotel Sinton in downtown Cincinnati.

I had heard Barney Rapp's music on radio remotes from places around the country where he had been performing, and I knew he had a big band, with a big sound. My mother drove me downtown to the hotel—and to demonstrate how nervous I was, even now, just thinking about that evening, I feel as nervous as I did then. My nervousness was not that I might not be good enough. In all my life I never thought or felt that way. It was the nervousness of having to put myself on display for professionals in a public place. Barney Rapp wasn't an amiable restaurant owner who was just looking for someone to sing along with the won-ton soup—no, Mr. Rapp was a hard-bitten professional who would be judging me according to the tough standards of the big bands.

The band was already playing in the downstairs dining room when I got there. Barney Rapp was a relaxed, affable man who very obviously enjoyed leading his band. He came over to us at the end of the set.

"Let's do 'Jeepers Creepers,' " he suggested. "Do you know it?"

I knew it, all right, and I hated it. It was possibly the last song I would have chosen to sing. The lyrics were "Jeepers creepers, where'd you get those peepers? Jeepers creepers, where'd you get those eyes?" A really awful song.

"We'll open with a chorus, vamp into your key," Barney said, "then you do a chorus and we'll wind up. Okay, here we go."

That's all the preparation I had. I sat on a chair at the side of the stage while Barney wound up the band with a one-two-three and they belted out the number. At the start of the vamp, I walked over to the mike. I was still limping and unsure of my bad leg, which during the long time in the cast had shrunk to half the size of my good leg. Barney fixed the mike for me while he said, "Ladies and gentlemen, Doris Kappelhoff," gave me a nod, and I was into the song.

The first few bars, I felt unnatural, but as I sang my voice began to thaw, and by the time I got to the bridge I was doing all right.

I later found out that over the course of his engagement at the Sinton, Barney had auditioned two hundred vocalists; but he later told Grace that I had been first on his list right along. The band manager fixed my salary at twenty-five dollars a week, which, as it turned out, was not quite enough to cover my expenses. It wasn't until I had been working for Barney for a long time that I discovered that my salary was fifty a week and that the manager had been ripping off half of it for himself. That incident should have forewarned me of the many rip-offs during my big-band, movie, and television careers that were to follow, especially the movie rip-off that lasted twelve years and just recently resulted in a court judgment in my favor for $22,835,646. I suppose from the very beginning I was just too naïve and trusting in a business that attracts predators. But it is my nature to be trusting—I wouldn't have it any other way. How can one exist being suspicious of everyone around him? No, I trust in people, and mostly my trust has been rewarded with solid, long-lasting friendships. Those who have abused it—well, I pity them, for I am none the worse, really, for their abuses, but they are.

Barney Rapp's new club, The Sign of the Drum, was on the outskirts of Cincinnati, on Reading Road near Bond Hill, in a huge place that looked as if it had once been a warehouse. I had just turned sixteen, but on the records I was listed as eighteen so that I could work in the club. My mother drove me there on opening night. She had made me a lovely new gown for the occasion, and I sat in the back seat, holding it carefully in my lap lest it get wrinkled. My hands were damp with nervousness and I had serious doubts that any sounds would come out of my dry throat. My nervousness was compounded by the fact that many of my relatives and friends were going to be there.

When we got to the club it was already very crowded and noisy with that special air of excitement that an opening engenders. I asked Mr. Rapp, who was wearing a tuxedo, where I would find the dressing room. He looked stunned. "Dressing room?" he said. "Why, we don't have a . . . you see, we all dress before we get here."

I was ready to cry, but my mother took me firmly by the arm and pushed me into the ladies' room. It was still in the process of being decorated and there were paint buckets and loose plaster all over the floor. "Now I'll hold the door so no one can get in," my mother said, "and you dress as fast as you can."

My mother did her best but a couple of insistent women forced their way in—and there I was, trying to dress among the paint cans and plaster while ladies drifted in and out, staring at me. I nearly fainted with embarrassment. When it was time to go up to the bandstand for the opening number, my legs were so rubbery going up the steps I had doubts I was going to make it. Barney smiled at me and winked, trying to give me confidence, but I don't know if I was holding up the mike or the mike was holding up me. My opening number was "A Foggy Night in London Town," but I have no memory of singing it. I saw familiar faces floating around in front of me on the dance floor, a relative smiling, a friend waving; I was just grateful that I wound up the vocal without getting too far ahead of the band. Later on, I found out that my voice had been so constricted that no one had heard one note of that first number, but Barney, sweet man that he was, never said a thing, just let me find my way, and by the end of the evening I was really lighting into the lyrics of such songs as "Old Black Magic," "St. Louis Blues," "Beale Street Mama," and "Day After Day," which the people particularly liked. Also, and this was the most important thing, I was enjoying myself. There is no way that a performer who does not like what he is doing can communicate a sense of enjoyment to his audience. I really like to sing; it gives me a sense of release, another dimension; it makes me happy; and I think the people who listen to me instinctively know that and feel it.

I worked for Barney Rapp six nights a week, from early evening to two in the morning. After the first few days, Barney had a talk with me about my name.

"Doris, I want to put your name on our marquee and in the ads we're running, but Kappelhoff is just too much of a name. We'll be having radio remotes and the announcer will fall all over your name. Now my name was Rappaport, why don't we change yours to Kapps?"

"No," I said, "Doris Kapps. No, that's pretty awful."

"Well, what about your mother's maiden name?"

"Welz."

"Doris Welz—not bad."

"No, but not good."

"Doris Kappel?"

"No!"

"Well, there must be *some* name you'd like."

"I was named after Doris Kenyon—that's pretty."

"No, people would come expecting the movie queen herself. What about naming you after the song you sing that everybody likes so much—'Day After Day'? Doris Day."

"I'm not crazy about it."

"Why? Doris Day—it has a nice lilt to it."

"It sounds like a headliner at the Gaiety Burlesque House. It sounds phony."

"Well, think about it. I think it's just right. Has a nice fresh sound to it—like the dawn of a new day."

I tried Doris Day out on my relatives and they all liked it, and since I couldn't come up with anything else, Barney put it out on the marquee. But I never did like it. Still don't. I think it's a phony name. As a matter of fact, over the years many of my friends didn't feel that Doris Day suited me, and gave me names of their own invention. Billy De Wolfe christened me Clara Bixby—with the result that many of my friends now call me Clara instead of Doris. Rock Hudson calls me Eunice (I call him Ernie because he's certainly no Rock), Gordon MacRae and others call me Do-Do, and lately one of my friends has taken to calling me Suzie Creamcheese. I like them all better than Doris Day.

It was a long drive from where we lived in Price Hill to The Sign of the Drum. My mother had to drive me there and then come back at two in the morning to pick me up. It was, of course, very hard on her and after a week or so she asked me if there wasn't someone in the band who lived near us with whom I could hitch a ride. I found out that one of the trombonists, Al Jorden, lived in Price Hill. He was a tall, slender, attractive man who had not spoken two words to me. He was an extraordinary trombone player, one of the best musicians in the band. I asked him if he would mind giving me a lift.

"You have to go right by my door to get here," I told him, "and I'll gladly help pay for the gasoline if you'd let me drive with you."

I could see he was not too thrilled. "I'll tell you, Doris," he said, "I have to be here a quarter to seven for the theme, and the one thing that will make a guy late every time is a girl vocalist." Every evening we started off with a fifteen-minute remote on a local radio station, and the band's theme song featured Al Jorden on the trombone. "I know how girls are," he went on, "always keeping you waiting—I've never had any luck with band vocalists. I'd like to help you out but I can't afford to be late."

"Al," I said, "I promise, listen, you don't know me, I'm an *on-the-mark* girl. . . ."

"Well, I don't know . . ."

"It's just that my poor mother—"

"Sure, I understand. I'd like to help your old lady, but I got myself to think of."

"Listen, the first time I'm late, I mean, you give the horn one honk and if I'm not right out of the door and into the car, you take off and that'll be the end of it."

With great reluctance, Al agreed to my experiment. I was never late, not once, but the arrangement had other complications. To begin with, Al had one of the glummest personalities I ever ran into. In the beginning, I would get in the car and we would drive all the way there with him not saying a word and looking straight ahead. That eventually improved somewhat, thanks to my efforts, but what didn't improve was his irascibility on the return trip. When a band finishes playing, they usually like to sit around for a while, having a few drinks, unwinding from the long night's work, perhaps having a little something to eat. The men in Barney's band were lively and funny and I adored sitting at the big table with them at the end of work. Also, I was always ravenously hungry and I looked forward to the big onion-bearing hamburger and thick milk shake that I invariably ordered from the kitchen. But I never knew in advance if Al was going to sit with the boys or if he had a date (he was going with a singer in another band) and wanted to get away in a hurry. There were times when I was just about to bite into my hamburger when I'd hear his impatient *beep-beep-beep* on the horn in the parking lot.

"Oh-oh, it's Mr. Jorden—he's really angry again!" I'd gather up my hamburger and malt and hurry out to the car while all the guys at the table screamed with laughter.

I would get in the car and continue with my sandwich. "What in God's name are you eating?" he'd ask.

"A cheeseburger."

"Why does it smell like that?"

"Well, it has a lot of raw onions, catsup, pickles, and mustard on it."

"Christ! I'm picking up a date after I let you out, and this whole car smells like a delicatessen. Besides, the last time I picked her up she got catsup all over the bottom of her dress from where it dripped out of your sandwich onto the floor." The more he talked, the angrier he got, and the angrier he got the faster he drove.

"Listen," I said, "do you have to drive like a nut?"

"I *am* a nut," he exploded, "for ever having agreed to cart you around! Look, here I am driving all the way back to Price Hill when I've got to go in the opposite direction to get my date!"

He would take the corners on two wheels, spilling my malted all over my dress. As I got out of the car, he'd shout, "How the hell did I ever get myself into this? Why can't you eat your damn sandwich during an intermission?"

"They're too short—and besides, I would have to sing on a stomachful of food. It's so nice to sit around after work with the guys—"

"You, Doris, you are a pain in the ass!" he'd say, as he slammed the door and screeched off into the night.

I would clump up the stairs and unload the whole thing on my mother. "Why do I have to ride to work with the one guy in the band who is a grump, always out of sorts, never a good word for anything or anybody, always picking on me? Why couldn't it be Don?" Don played clarinet and although he was totally unaware of it, I had a fierce crush on him.

But no matter how annoyed Al had been the night before, he always showed up the following evening at the appointed hour. We continued like this all through the winter until Barney announced that we would all have to take a two-week vacation without pay while he brought in an out-of-town band. The first day of that enforced vacation, I was out when the phone rang and my mother answered. It was Al Jorden. "Tell Doris I'll call her later," he said. "I wanted to know if she'd like to have dinner and see a movie tonight."

When I got home and my mother told me about Al's invitation, I broke up laughing. "Come on, stop teasing me," I said. "What did he want?"

My mother insisted that that's what he had said. "Why, he's got a steady girl," I said, "and besides, the way he treats me, why in the world would he want to be with me on the first evening he's got free? Anyway, he's a creep and I wouldn't go out with him if they were giving away gold nuggets at the movie."

"Well, I don't think he's so bad. Nice-looking. Just the right age. You don't have to get involved with him, just go out and see a movie—you work all the time and you deserve an evening out on the town."

"I don't deserve him with his bad disposition. I should say not!"

By the time Al called, my mother had talked me into going out with him. That's the way mothers are sometimes. If I had said, "Oh, how nice, a date with Al Jorden," she probably would have said, "Why do you want to go out with that creep?"

The surprise was that Al Jorden as a date bore no resemblance to the surly Al Jorden who was my chauffeur. He was amusing and relaxed and I had a really good time. I was baffled by the fact that a man who had been so consistently dreadful to me could have changed so completely. This Jekyll-Hyde switch from grump to charmer should have forewarned me about Al Jorden, but when he asked me to go boating with him the following day, I innocently said yes.

Al invited the band's drummer, Wilbur Shook, and his wife, Virginia, to come along with us. Al owned a sixteen-foot speedboat that was one of the fastest boats on the Ohio River. Also plying the Ohio that Sunday was the *Island Queen,* a huge steamboat that made excursions up the river to Coney Island. I had taken that trip many times, and going up the beautiful, winding Ohio on the *Island Queen* is one of the dreamy memories of my youth. It was an hour's ride and there was a band aboard to dance to and great fun in the Coney Island amusement park when you got there. The *Queen* carried fifteen hundred people or more, and was powered by a big paddle wheel on her stern. This wheel churned up a mountainous wake, with high waves rolling out from the wheel. Al Jorden decided to give us a big thrill by zooming along in back of the *Queen* and riding that wake, crisscrossing into the churning waves.

There was something manic about the way he gunned his boat across and through those waves, the boat shuddering and pitching from the impacts. We were screaming at him, drenched with spray, but he kept getting closer to the *Queen*'s paddle wheel, and as he got closer the wake waves got higher and higher until we struck a wave as high as a house, and the next thing I knew I had been pitched in the muddy water and Al's speedboat was burbling its way to the bottom. The boat's cushions were life preservers and all four of us were hanging onto cushions in that filthy water screaming and

49

waving at passing boats to pick us up—but boat after boat went by, and all the occupants did was wave back at us, thinking, I guess, that we were enjoying a nice swim in that filthy water!

Finally, we were rescued by a boat manned by Jerry Hurter, who was a reporter for the Cincinnati *Times Star*. The next day our mishap was front-page in the newspaper. Looking back on it, it's hard to explain why, in the face of his erratic and rather spooky behavior, I continued to date Al. I suppose that to a sixteen-year-old, there was something glamorous about this twenty-three-year-old's behavior. He called me constantly and we went out every night. He was mostly on good behavior, but he did become angrily jealous whenever I so much as spoke to another man. At the time I thought his jealousy was flattering. Too late I was to discover that it was a pathologic jealousy that almost destroyed me.

Another signpost about Al that I should not have ignored, but did, involved an incident that occurred at his house. Al had been hurt in a motorcycle accident, and my mother and I went to pay him a visit. This was the first time I had met his mother. After we had been in the house for ten minutes or so, Al's mother managed to get me off by myself. "I think I should make something very clear to you," she said, looking right at me with eyes that burned, "and that is that Albert is never going to get married. He has promised never to leave me and his father, and I think it's only fair that you know that."

"But, Mrs. Jorden," I said, "Al and I have no plans—"

"Marriage is just something that does not figure in Albert's life, you understand? It's all right that he has a good time with girls—"

"We're just dating, Mrs. Jorden—that's all."

"Yes, well, I know how girls get once they get their hands on an attractive man like Albert, and I thought it was only fair to let you know that Albert will never be serious about you or anyone else."

As I later told my mother, I didn't feel that she had anything against *me*—she probably had made the same speech many times before to girls Al had gone with. I asked myself, What kind of mother talks like that about her son? I should have asked, What kind of son allows it?

Al received a telegram from the drummer Gene Krupa, who was leaving Benny Goodman to organize his own band in New

York; he wanted Al for the trombone section. It was a great opportunity to break into the big time, but I was heartbroken. He sent me his itinerary as he traveled the country playing one-night stands, and I would write to him every day. He wrote to me and telephoned quite often. I was back singing with Barney Rapp and meeting new people, but I only cared about Al. He wrote marvelous letters which underscored that old saw about absence making the heart grow fonder. I think that if Al had not gone off our relationship would have lost its steam, but as it was, I only had eyes for my absentee boyfriend.

The Sign of the Drum limped along for a while, but Barney finally folded it and decided he'd be better off going back to playing band dates. We played about four one-nighters a week, often traveling fifty or a hundred miles for a night's work. The pay was a little better but the work was a darn sight harder. A hundred miles in a broken-down band bus, singing for six or seven hours, then a hundred bumpy miles back to Cincinnati, was not an easy night's work. So when Grace Raine, dear Grace Raine, came to me with a new opportunity, I responded enthusiastically. Grace's husband, Ferde, was a song plugger who often went to Chicago to try to get the big bands to play the songs he handled. During his last trip he had discovered that Bob Crosby was looking for a vocalist, and Grace suggested that I go up to Chicago to audition for the job. Bob Crosby and his Bobcats! I had never really thought about ever singing beyond the Cincinnati city limits. I really had no ambition about my singing, and never tried to create opportunities, but neither was I ever loath to embrace one if it came my way.

The Raines drove me to Chicago, and we went directly to the Blackhawk, where Bob Crosby was playing. Crosby's Sunday afternoon jam session was already in progress. It was jam-packed with teen-agers; and up on the stage was the famous Crosby band, with well-known musicians like Jess Stacy and Irving Fazzola and Bobby Haggart, the bass player, and Ray Baduc on drums, Matty Matlock, Billy Butterfield—I knew them all from my records and from reading about them in magazines. And there was I, little Miss Cincinnati, sitting there at a table beside the bandstand, waiting to sing with the likes of *these* men.

I had never laid eyes on Bob Crosby before, and there was no rehearsal or preparation of any kind. "Grace," I whispered desperately, "I don't want to go up there! I'm not good enough for this

51

band—they're all going to laugh at me. Why should I disgrace myself? Let's go!" Grace was trying to mollify me and I was tugging on her when Crosby suddenly put an end to my fright flight with a drum roll and an announcement.

"Now, cats," he announced into the microphone, "we have a little lady who's come all the way up from Cincinnati to audition and let's all be very nice to her, okay?"

Polite applause while I wanted to crawl under the table and die. Why did he have to say it was an audition and to be *nice?* Now, even if I stank they were duty bound to give me a big hand out of sympathy. But Grace was already giving me a friendly push toward the stage. She had arranged in advance what I was to sing but my only memory of that afternoon was the way the band improvised as I sang. I sang three songs, I think, and I was no sooner back at our table than Crosby's business manager, Gil Rodin, joined us and offered me the job at seventy-five dollars a week. My eyes popped out of my head. But to be honest about it, despite my nervousness and reluctance to sing for these mighty professionals, it never occurred to me that I wouldn't get the job. I never have tried out for anything that I failed to get. And all of my tryouts were tinged with reluctance —I'm very secure about what I know I can do even though I have very little ambition for doing it.

But that's not to say that I wasn't very excited and pleased that I was to be a singing Bobcat. I joined the band right then and there. My mother brought my clothes and belongings to Chicago and stayed with me. Later she traveled with me when she could, but when we went on a one-nighter tour on the Crosby bus, I had to travel alone. My mother was uneasy about her sixteen-year-old being thrown to the wolves, but actually I never had a hard time with any of the men in the band. I was their kid sister. They knew that I was completely devoted to a boyfriend who was traveling with another band —Al had left Krupa for Jimmy Dorsey—and they used to tease me unmercifully about my postal love affair.

In the beginning, traveling with the band was exciting. It seems to me I learned a little something every time I sang, those little things that only come with experience and which are summed up in the word "style." Bob Crosby himself contributed little or nothing to my singing education because he was really only a front man for the band. He didn't play a musical instrument nor did he have any-

Thirteen-year-old Doris and her dancing partner, Jerry Doherty, knocked 'em
cold in Cincinnati and were on their way to the big time in Hollywood . . .

A few days before she was to leave for Hollywood, Doris posed for this happy picture with her brother Paul. On the eve of her departure a car-train wreck smashed her leg and with it her dream of a career as a dancer.

But during her convalescence, Doris developed a talent she didn't know she had.

With Barney Rapp, Cincinnati bandleader who gave Doris her start as a singer, and Joseph Cheriavsky, musical director of station WLW, who started her on radio.

In Rapp's band was a trombonist named Al Jorden whom Doris married with disastrous results.

Big time on the road started with Bob Crosby and his Bobcats, then on to Les Brown and his Band of Renown, pictured here on a New Year's Eve.

thing to do with the arrangements, but, for me, experience itself was the teacher.

As for the travel, there was a peculiar quality to big-band travel, playing one-nighters, that's difficult to describe. I did get a pretty good view of the country from the bus window, but the strenuous physical demands of touring, of performing every night until very late, of having to squeeze in rehearsals in order to work new numbers into the repertoire, of trying to get laundry done, buy new clothes, get to the hairdresser, of living out of a suitcase but having to look glamorous every night—all this made band travel a kind of challenge to survive. The sensation I most vividly recall, working for the Crosby band and later, for Les Brown and for Bob Hope, was that of awakening in a hotel room and not being able to remember what city I was in. It was a constant struggle to meet a string of little deadlines, and I slept more hours in my bus seat than I did in a bed.

The only time I felt sad, singing with the bands, was when we played the big proms at the colleges in the South. Sitting up on the bandstand, looking at all those college kids who were my age and who looked so attractive in their prom formals and tuxes, I had sharp pangs of regret that I wasn't one of them. I often had long reveries that I was one of the coeds, and I'd choose some boy on the dance floor as my boyfriend and imagine my exciting life as a student at that school. More than once, these reveries almost caused me to miss my cues.

Sometimes, sitting in the bumpy bus, the day after we played a college dance, I'd confide my sadness at missing college to Jess Stacy or Bobby Haggart or whoever was sitting beside me. They'd try to cheer me up. "Do you know how many of those girls are dying to be a band singer like you?" Jess would say. "Why, you've got the glamour job they all envy. Hell, anybody can go to college, but how many girls are there who are lead singers with the big bands?" I suppose that was true, but the next time we played a big prom, I'd get sad all over again.

But it was lucky that I did have this job and was able to send most of my paycheck home, because my mother needed expensive medical attention for my brother. Paul was a truly marvelous baseball player who had played first base for his school team at St. Joseph's College, in Collegeville, Indiana. A scout for the Cincinnati Reds had spotted him at one of the games, and signed my brother to a contract. The Reds' office was very high on Paul and assigned him to one of their top farm teams. He was more than fulfilling their faith in him when misfortune put an end to his baseball career. This was in the days before batters were required to wear hard helmets, and during one of the games a pitch hit my brother squarely in the head. Not only was his skull fractured, but he suffered brain damage which resulted in a kind of epilepsy. Later on, when I was established in Hollywood, he came to live there with his family and worked for my company, but the epilepsy got increasingly worse and he eventually died. Still a young man. And what a lovely man he was. I loved him dearly and always felt very close to him. His death shook me very hard.

The Bob Crosby itinerary eventually took us to the big apple, New York City. We were booked to play at The Strand, a big Broadway showplace, but the excitement of my first New York performance was muted by a visit I had from the band manager, Gil Rodin, a few nights after we opened. It concerned Crosby's other girl singer, Bonnie, who handled the vocals on his weekly commercial radio program. I knew that Bonnie was the girl friend of the man who handled the radio account and that that was why she had this radio plum instead of me. But Rodin had now come to tell me that there was too much expense involved in flying Bonnie to wherever we were for each radio broadcast, and it had been decided to let her do the one-nighters as well.

"Then you mean I'm out of a job?"

"No," he answered, "I don't think so. I hope you're just going to change jobs. I brought Les Brown to hear you and he wants you to join his band. There are other bands that would also like to have you, but I'll tell you, Doris, Les Brown has a new band with a new sound that is really catching on. He is getting a lot of big play dates. Just between us, Bob's band is well established, but Les has the band people are talking about."

It was true that bands like Crosby's were beginning to fade, and I had heard that Les Brown and his Blue Devils from Duke University were one of the exciting newcomers. In fact, I had heard them a few times on radio, a band with a big, driving sound that was quite distinct.

Les Brown was a marvelous man who, despite his youth, was a strong father figure. He was also a first class musician. He played the clarinet and did most of his own arrangements, with the help of one of the members of the band, Frank Comstock, who had previously been the arranger for one of the black bands of the period. These arrangements were the heart of the band. The big bands all played virtually the same songs and it was only the style of playing them that distinguished one band from another. There was a certain precision in the style of Glenn Miller's band; a sweet, swing style in Tommy Dorsey's band which featured the trombone, which is a soft, ballad instrument; Benny Goodman's style was jump—escalating arrangements that fired the blood. Les Brown's sound was staccato, exemplified by his theme song, "Leap Frog," and he had wonderful arrangements full of twists and surprises.

The Les Brown band was markedly different from the Dixieland Sound of Bob Crosby's. There were eight men in the brass section, six saxophones, and four men in rhythm. We played some set dates, but the big money was on the road, and when our New York engagement ended, Les handed me our itinerary—three months of nothing but one-nighters! Living on a band bus was by now part of my being. When you're with the same people all the time, there's nothing much to talk about, so life aboard the bus was reading and sleeping—mostly the latter. I did spend a little time memorizing my new songs but I was always a quick study and that didn't occupy much of my time. It was too bumpy to write but I'd daydream about Al, who always had a letter waiting for me at the next stop. Al wrote wonderful love letters—how was I to know that this was a side of him that was split from his "other" personality? If only this hadn't been a paper romance, if only we had had a normal courting period, I am sure that Al and I would have parted company. But as it was, every letter made me miss him more. There was no doubt, from his letters, that he loved me intensely—but what I couldn't tell was what an overly possessive, destructive love it was.

As for life with the band, it couldn't have been more pleasant. The men all fitted into Les's image of a "clean-cut" band, and nobody fooled around with drugs or drank while working. Many of the men were such consummate artists that it was thrilling, night after night, to sit on the bandstand and listen to them perform. Si Zentner on the trombone, Ted Nash on tenor sax—the great Wolfie Tannenbaum was tenor sax when I first joined the band but he decided to leave the band and stay in New York. I never before or since heard a tenor sax sound the way it did when Wolfie blew it. There's no doubt that when you sing backed up by great musicians like that, you are inspired to sing at the top of your form.

Les helped me in many little ways. At our first recording session, he picked up something I was unaware of—a little southern drawl in my pronunciation. Cincinnati is just across the river from Kentucky and some southern accent has crept into Cincinnatian speech. Les had the recording played back for me and carefully pointed out where the southern influence had affected my pronunciation. For instance, the way I sang "ah" for "I." Les also helped me with phrasing, but for the most part he let me sing the way I wanted; apparently he liked whatever it was that was developing naturally.

LES BROWN

In 1940 I went to the Edison Hotel in New York to hear Doris sing with the Bob Crosby band. I had heard that she was dissatisfied and ready to leave. I listened to her for five minutes, immediately went backstage, and signed her for my band. She was every band leader's dream, a vocalist who had natural talent, a keen regard for the lyrics, and an attractive appearance. Actually, she didn't look too much different then than she does today.

Our first engagement with Doris was at Mike Todd's Theatre Café in Chicago in 1940. Gypsy Rose Lee was the headliner and we did two twenty-minute dance sets, with Doris singing four or five songs. Her pay then was seventy-five dollars a week; by the time she left me in 1946, it had risen to five hundred.

As a singer, Doris belongs in the company of Bing Crosby and Frank Sinatra. None of them can read a note of music, they depend on memory and ear, they are very fast reads; and I'd say that next to Sinatra, Doris is the best in the business on selling a lyric. The reason her salary rose so precipitously was that virtually every band in the business tried to hire her away from me. Hollywood people were constantly making her offers to do screen tests, but Doris was very loyal to me, primarily, I think, because she liked the nature of my band. I ran a tight ship, no dope, no booze, no hard language. One reporter wrote that the X band played on booze, and the Y band band played on dope, but Les Brown and His Band of Renown played on milk shakes. The label stuck, and we became known as the Milk Shake Band. And if ever there was a milk-shake girl, it was Doris!

The next time we played New York, Jimmy Dorsey's band happened to be there at the same time, and Al and I got to see each other. All we had was the fragmented time between shows, and late at night when the last shows were over. But we did get to stay together every night, and on the fourth or fifth night, Al presented me with an engagement ring. As rings go, it wasn't much, but to my young eyes it was the Hope Diamond. We only had a week together in New York, but by the time our bands took off for the road again, we had agreed to get married as soon as we could.

As it turned out, "soon" was not very soon. Les took us on a long tour, months of one-nighters, which culminated in a month-long engagement at Michael Todd's Theatre Café in Chicago. It was there that Al telephoned me. Jimmy Dorsey had a long engagement in New York and Al wanted me to quit Les Brown and come to New York to get married. I couldn't say yes fast enough.

Les was shocked when I told him what I was going to do. "You're young, Doris," he said, "just beginning what is going to be a glorious career, and now you want to ruin your life. You know what it is to be a band wife—look at the married men in my band. What kind of a life do you think their wives have? Alone at home when we're traveling, and hanging around some hotel when we're booked for a stand. Now, as for you, it'd be a crying shame for a girl with your potential, with all the talent you have, to throw it all away on a guy like Jorden. He's a good musician but, if you'll pardon my saying it, he's not any prize as a husband. I like you very much, Doris. You're like my sister, someone special, and I'm not telling you all this just to keep a good singer from leaving my band—no, I'm telling you this because I like you and care about you."

Nothing Les said could dissuade me. From the time I was a little girl, my only true ambition in life was to get married and tend house and have a family. Singing was just something to do until that time came, and now it was here—home and marriage was the only career I wanted. And the only career I have ever really wanted.

So I quit the band and went back to Cincinnati to pack my things before joining Al in New York. My mother was beside herself. She was after me for days to change my mind. "Nobody likes Al Jorden, not Les or anybody else. But that's not the point. Here you are just starting out and getting somewhere after all that struggle, and now you're not giving yourself a chance. What's the hurry?"

I could not explain it to my mother and I don't think I can explain it now. Perhaps it was that I wanted to belong to somebody, to share a life rather than be on my own anymore. Although I was a member of a group, the fact was that I was alone and lonely. The engagement ring on my finger bound me to someone who wanted me

57

and loved me. I suppose that was the overriding drive toward getting married. I'm just a hausfrau at heart.

When she finally realized that it was hopeless to try to dissuade me, my mother helped me prepare a wedding costume, and then she drove me to New York. Al and I got married between shows in City Hall. One of the guys in the band and his wife came along as witnesses. There was a hotel directly across from the stage entrance to The Strand, where the band was playing, and Al had a little reception there in a small room, where a couple of waiters passed around a tray of hors d'oeuvres and poured some domestic champagne. Our wedding guests were the boys in the band and some of their wives. Since everyone had to get back to The Strand for the next show, it was one of the shortest wedding receptions on record. A slurp of champagne, a couple of quickly wolfed hors d'oeuvres, and whisk, everyone was gone—including my new husband.

Al had rented a two-room apartment for us at the Whitby, a Times Square place across from the Martin Beck Theatre, off Eighth Avenue, that featured seedy, furnished accommodations. Most of the band men who had wives visiting used to stay there because the apartments had little kitchens and they were inexpensive. Of course, the only band wives who could follow their husbands like this were those who didn't have children. My mother returned to Cincinnati the afternoon of the wedding.

The walls, furniture, rugs, and kitchenware at the Whitby showed the sad, soiled effects of a thousand abusive occupancies— there was just no way to make it look cleaner and less dingy than it was. I tried, all that first afternoon, with scouring pads and scrub brush, but the results were negligible. Also negligible were the results of my first effort to cook a dinner. If I had had a more reasonable marriage, there would have been time for me to have learned how to make a few basic dishes, but as it was, I had had no time to prepare for anything. The first time I made spaghetti, I literally made enough to fill the kitchen sink. If I had had a bridal shower, I would have had a few decent pots and pans of my own (all of the other wives brought their own kitchen things), but I only had the beat-up Whitby pots with their permanently blackened bottoms.

As for my life as a band wife, Les Brown had not exaggerated how difficult it would be. The dreariest, loneliest life you can imagine. Band wives didn't hang around the band. We went on opening night, or when there was something special, but most nights I just waited at the apartment, knitting or writing letters or visiting with the other wives until Al got home, which was usually around two in the morning. Since that's when we would eat, I had to stay up to do the cooking. It would be three or four when we got to bed, and by the time we got up the following day, there wasn't much time until Al had to go back to work. It would have been a better life, of course, if I could have worked alongside Al as vocalist with the Dorsey band, but Jimmy had Helen O'Connell and Bob Eberly, just about the best band vocalists at the time.

But the real difficulty for me was not band-wife boredom but the shocking revelation of the kind of man I had married. What had been represented to me as love emerged as jealousy—a pathologic jealousy that was destined to make a nightmare out of the next few years of my life. I do not mean that Al didn't love me—I think he did, and in the beginning I certainly loved him; but Al's love was destructive, a fire of uncontrollable jealousy that eventually burned out my feelings for him.

This dark side of Al's makeup showed itself immediately. On the second day of our marriage, I was to meet him at The Strand at the dinner break. Just inside the stage door there was a little waiting room with benches. On one side of this waiting room were the steps that led down to the orchestra pit; on the other side of the room were steps that led upstairs to the dressing rooms. These were open stairs that you could look through and see the landings above. On the first landing, just above the waiting room, was a combination office and dressing room that was shared by the band's manager, Billy Burton, and Jimmy Dorsey. On this day I was sitting in the waiting room as the show was ending. I could hear the theme song. At this point the door to the dressing room on the first landing opened and Billy Burton looked down through the open steps and saw me waiting there.

"Doris—hi!" he called out. "Listen, can you come up for a minute? I have something for you—a wedding present."

I jumped up. "Oh, how lovely!" I started running up the steps to the dressing room just as the musicians began coming up the lower steps from the pit. I went into the dressing room and Billy, an adorable man, handed me a big package, beautifully wrapped. "Congratulations from Jimmy and all the band," he said. "I just hope you're really going to be happy. In a way, I hate to see you stop singing, because it's a shame to lose a voice like yours, but I can understand that maybe it's more important to be with someone you love."

"Yes, it is, Billy," I said. "I don't actually feel I've given up anything because singing never meant that much to me. Marriage means a lot to me and I honestly feel I've gained something."

I opened the package. Inside was a beautiful leather makeup case, completely fitted. I was just about to tell Billy how thrilled I was with it when the door slammed open and there stood my husband of two days. "Oh, Al," I said, "come and see . . ." The look on his face stopped me. He was absolutely white. His eyes seemed to extrude from their sockets. His whole face was drawn and tense. He was obviously making an effort to hold himself back from attacking me. I turned frantic when I saw the look on him. I had never before seen anyone's face look like that.

Billy saw all this too, and he didn't know what to say. He finally said, "We . . . we thought . . . as a wedding gift . . . you know, traveling and all, Doris might like a case like—"

"I'm sure she will," Al snapped, then he grabbed my arm, just below my armpit "We'll be going," he said, tightening his grip on my arm. I gathered up my present with my free arm and managed to mumble a "Thank you" as Al steered me out of the room and down the steps and out on the sidewalk. He propelled me along the sidewalk so fast I had to run to keep up with him. I was frantic to find out what was wrong. I kept asking him but he wouldn't say a word. Just that terrible look on his face and his fingers digging ever deeper into my arm. People stopped and stared at us as we hurried past them. I felt fear. For the first time in my life, I really felt afraid of someone.

The minute we walked into our apartment, he spun me around and hit me in the face. I put up my hands to protect myself but he hit me again and again, knocking me into the furniture and against the wall. All the while he was yelling at me, in uncontrollable rage, shrieking at me. "You tramp, you no-good little whore, you call that a wife, running up those stairs so all the men could take a good look up your skirt! You thought I wouldn't notice it—do you think I'm blind? You timed it just right, didn't you, you little two-bit bitch! Well, you ever do it again, I'll kill you! You're my wife now, and you better behave like one!" And on and on as he slammed me around.

I was hysterical. Even if I had been able to talk, what do you say to an insanity like that? At seventeen, how could I handle such an attack? I finally collapsed on the floor, sobbing into my arms, with him standing over me with his fists clenched. A minute or so later, I heard sounds coming from Al. I turned my head and looked up. His body was slumped, his head against his chest, and he was sobbing. He lowered himself to the floor beside me and held me against his crying face. "Oh, please forgive me, please," he sobbed. "I love you too much. I shouldn't have hit you. I'm sorry. Please forgive me. I just can't stand the thought of anyone else looking at you. Can you forgive me?"

I tried to believe that this was a singular outburst that would never be repeated. For the most part, Al was loving and humorous and enjoyable to be with. Sexually, we got along fine. I admired him as a musician. And I loved him. I really and truly loved him, but it didn't take long before his psychotic jealousy again broke out, not just in one incident, but in endless incidents. For instance, I used to shop in the little Italian markets on Eighth Avenue just around the corner from the Whitby. One day he went with me. As we shopped, I became aware of the same psychotic change in him, his body going tense, his face becoming grim and pinched. By the time we got back to the apartment with our packages he was in a white fury. He slammed the door and then started to knock me around the room, sending the bags and their contents all over the floor, raging that he was "on to me," the way I knew all those Italian shop-keepers and they knew my name. I wasn't fooling him, I was playing around with these guys while he was working, pretty convenient with all of them just around the corner, hitting me in the face, grabbing my wrists when I tried to protect myself, and flinging me onto the floor.

Then the scene of contrition would repeat itself. The fit would boil out of him and he would beg my forgiveness. There were times when we would lie in bed at night warm and loving, when I could rationally discuss these jealous outbursts with him. He freely admitted that they were all groundless and destructive but he said he couldn't help himself. That he could feel a jealousy attack begin to boil up in him but that he was helpless to stop it. No more than he could stop an epileptic fit. It was the price of loving me too much. But he would try to be better about it. He was sure he'd be better and not to worry about it.

But he wasn't better. In fact, it got worse. The tension of not knowing what I might say or do that would set off one of his attacks

61

became an unbearable burden. In fact, I most certainly would have left him soon after the marriage if I hadn't become pregnant. It happened in the second month. I didn't know how Al would take the news. To my surprise he wept. I hoped in joy and not in sorrow. He didn't say anything, he just wept. As for me, after the initial shock of finding out I was so soon pregnant, I was suffused with joy. My dream of marriage and children was being fulfilled, and even though the husband had brutalized the dream, I suppose I hoped, optimist that I am, that my pregnancy would make him less jealous. But that was a rational hope, and Al was an irrational man. Actually, the period of my pregnancy was horrendous.

It would not have been so bad if Al had been away on one-nighters, but when a band had as big a name as Dorsey's, it could pick and choose its dates and Jimmy preferred playing long hotel engagements in big cities, especially New York, where he lived. Shortly after I had told Al about being pregnant, he came home with the name of an abortionist recommended by someone in the band. Band men always had good contacts with abortionists. I was appalled. Now I knew Al's tears had been anything but tears of joy.

"I'm not going to give my baby to some grimy abortionist in the Bronx," I said.

"We're too young to have kids," Al said. "You won't be able to travel, you'll have to spend all your time with the kid. Listen, let's just get rid of this one and then we can have one we really want later on."

"No way! You hear me, Al? No dirty abortionist is going to get his hands on me! Now that's the end of it!"

Al knew I meant it and that was the end of his attempt to get me to an abortionist, but it had succeeded in draining off any good feelings I might have had about having my baby.

A short time after the abortion proposal, Al came home to the Whitby one night with a new plan for getting rid of the baby. He went over to the stove and put on a big pot of boiling water. I asked him what he was doing.

"You were right about the abortionist," he said, "but I'm right about not having that baby. I'm a traveling musician and we just can't be saddled with a baby. I would resent it—you wouldn't want that, would you? I want you with me at all times. I want us to have complete freedom to do what we want and go where we want. We really can't have this baby. Now it's right at the beginning—

there's really nothing in your belly yet and all we have to do is bring on your period and everything will be all right."

He got the water from the stove and made me put my feet in it. I was so heartsick at his attitude toward the baby that I offered no resistance. He took a small box from his pocket from which he extracted several large pills that he gave to me to swallow. They made me deathly ill. God, was I sick, but Al kept me sitting there with my feet in the scalding water and said over and over that everything was going to be all right. He kept me there like that for most of the night but nothing happened.

I had become ambivalent about the baby. On the one hand, I wanted it very much; it had an importance to me that was difficult to describe but nonetheless very real. But I also realized that I should not be having this baby under the conditions into which it would be born. I was indeed terribly young and Al certainly would be a rotten father. But after that night with the pills, there formed in me a desire to somehow get through my pregnancy with Al and then leave him as soon as the baby was born. I did not have a dime to my name. Another of Al's hang-ups was about money; he didn't trust me with any. Not that I was profligate—I never had a chance to be. But he made me account for every penny. Most purchases I made, he came along to handle the money himself. So my plan was to stick it out until I had the baby, and then go back to Cincinnati to live with my mother and get a job. But as it turned out, sticking it out proved to be almost beyond my endurance.

In the third month of my pregnancy, Dorsey booked an engagement in Chicago and Al decided that we should stop and visit in Cincinnati on the way. We stayed at his parents' house, which was not too far from my mother's apartment over the Welz tavern. This was only the second time I had laid eyes on Al's mother, who was just as withdrawn and unfriendly as she had been the time before. But I had a joyful visit with my mother, who spotted that I was pregnant the minute I walked in. I was surprised because I was not aware that I had physically changed in any way except that my breasts were a little larger.

"How do you know?"

"You just *look* pregnant, that's all. There's a look about you."

I was glad that she had been so intuitive about me, because Al had forbidden me to tell anyone, including my mother. I was relieved to be able to talk about it.

63

That evening Al and I went to my uncle's tavern, where all my relatives and friends showed up to see me. It was a typical Cincinnati tavern with beef barbecue and hot potato salad, homemade chili and fabulous beer. We all had a good time, Al included, I thought. Good music from the jukebox, lots of laughs.

The gathering broke up around midnight, but Al and I were no sooner in the car than I knew he was bugged. This time he was furious because my mother knew I was pregnant and my aunt and uncle and others had happily drunk to the impending event.

"I didn't tell her, she just took one look at me and knew."

"You're lying! Don't lie to me! You told her. After I told you that no one was—"

"Oh, Al, what difference does it make?"

"The way they all looked at you. Those men looking at your belly—at your tits. I saw them. I warned you."

By the time the car arrived at the house I was upset and frightened because he was on the verge of violence. I knew where this black mood might lead him and at all costs I wanted to avoid an outburst in this house where his parents were. But he hustled me up the steps to the front door, grabbed my arm in that terrible grip of his, and started to push me into the house.

"Let go of me!"

"Don't you raise your voice and awaken my mother!"

"Then let go of me!"

I wrenched away from him and ran up the steps and into our bedroom, which was on the second floor. A second later he burst into the room, locked the door in back of him, and then started knocking me around the room. I'm certainly no weakling but he was terribly strong and there was no way I could defend myself. He threw me around the room, hitting me, pushing me, knocking me over the furniture. The racket awakened his parents. His father pounded on the door and shouted at us to open up. Finally, mercifully, Al went over and opened the door.

"Albert, what in the hell is going on in here?" his father demanded.

Al went out in the hall where his mother and father were and I closed the door and locked it. I sat down on the bed, crying hysterically, feeling the hurts and pains of where he had struck me. Outside, I heard the men go down the steps. Then there was a knock on the door and his mother asked if she could come in. I went over and opened the door.

She came in and looked at me; I couldn't stop crying. She looked at me with a cold, hostile expression on her face. "What on earth was going on here?" she asked. "All that racket—what will the neighbors think?"

"Your son was hitting me, that's what happened," I said. "It's not the first time and I think you should know it."

She looked at me more intently. Then she said, "Well, from the looks of you he didn't hit you very hard."

I jumped up from the bed. "Get out of this room," I said, starting to push her. "Get out of this room and out of my sight. I never want to see you again. You hear? Never, never again!"

I pushed her into the hall and locked the door behind her. I sat down, trembling, a captive in this strange house with these weird people and this sick man who was my husband. All I could think of was somehow getting to the corner to catch a streetcar that would take me to my mother's. But there wouldn't be a streetcar now until morning and somehow I'd have to last through the night here. Al came to the door but I wouldn't let him in. His father, a really decent man, wanted to talk to me but I said no, I didn't want to talk to anybody. Finally, I heard doors closing down the hall and then it was quiet. I sat there for the rest of the night, alert, fearing some other evil in that house.

At daybreak I tiptoed out of my room and down the stairs and let myself quietly out of the house. I was petrified that they might hear me and stop me. The few coins I had in my purse would get me on the streetcar, but the wait for the streetcar seemed interminable and I was stiff with apprehension that they might find me.

I didn't tell my mother the whole story, just what had happened the night before. She was appalled and urged me to leave Al then and there. But I explained that I did not want to burden anyone, that I had never borrowed a dime, and I told her about my plan to come back to Cincinnati as soon as the baby was born. We didn't have much time to discuss it because Al showed up. He was contrite and apologetic and gave his usual speech about loving me too much. At times like this he could be very appealing, and I think my mother felt rather sorry for him. But before we left, I made secret arrangements with my mother. I would have the baby in New York, where my doctor had offices right in the Whitby; I would go to the Medical Arts Center hospital; and my mother would stay with me after I had the baby. Then, the first time Al went on the road with the band, we would hightail it back to Cincinnati and I would start divorce proceedings.

I really don't know how I got through those nine months. One time we were driving to Buffalo for a two-week engagement at a hotel there. Al had worked up a head of steam over some innocuous incident, and as his fury increased, so did the speed of his Mercury convertible. We were driving on a winding mountain road and the speedometer was at 110 miles per hour and he was yelling and screaming at me.

I said, "Al, please, slow down, you're going to kill us."

And he said, "I want to kill us, I'm going to kill us both. What's there to live for? So you can make a fool out of me, you and that baby of yours? I'm going to kill us, we're going right down to the bottom of this mountain!"

That mountain road descent, the car slipping and sliding perilously close to the guardrails, for all time ruined the automobile for me as a pleasurable way to travel.

Another time we were again driving in the car when Al had one of his rages. We were in New England somewhere, perhaps on our way to Boston. In the midst of ranting at me, Al reached over and opened the glove compartment and took out the pistol he always carried there. He flipped off the safety and thrust the barrel of the gun against my stomach. Even now I can feel the cold nozzle of that gun as it dug into my stomach. "You and your baby, I'm going to shoot both of you!" he shouted. We rode like that for miles. I was literally frozen with fear in the truest sense of the word. Every bump and tremor in the road, I expected the gun to discharge. My voice was frozen—I couldn't speak, I couldn't move. Finally, in disgust, Al pulled the gun away and tossed it back in the glove compartment. He stopped talking. By the time we got to our destination, he was pleasant and attentive and it was as though nothing had happened. (Years later I learned that while driving in his car one day, Al pulled that gun out of the glove compartment, put the barrel against his head, and committed suicide.)

The worst of all his rages occurred when I was eight months' pregnant. For many weeks we had had a reasonably tranquil relationship, and I was hopeful that the calm would last for the remainder of my pregnancy. Instead, it was ruptured by the most brutal attack of all. The band was playing an engagement at Michael Todd's Theatre Café in Chicago. We were staying in a place on the north shore that had small furnished apartments—many of the musicians stayed there. A little place with a Murphy-in-a-Door bed and a tiny kitchen. (I had stayed there when I played the Michael Todd with Les Brown. Al and I had just gotten engaged then—it seemed a long, long time ago.)

On this particular night I hadn't been feeling very well so I had fixed a little dinner and gotten into bed. The baby was kicking and turning and raising all kinds of hell. Al was late coming home, but that was not too unusual because musicians often have a few drinks after working to unwind. So it was late, around two-thirty, when the door of the apartment banged open and Al came charging in. He was in a blind rage, yelling every kind of foul word at me. He flung off my covers, grabbed my feet, and pulled me out of the bed. I fell heavily on my back. He pulled me all around the room like that, then he jerked me to my feet, and began slamming his hand against me, knocking me against the wall. I kept my arms around my belly, trying to protect the baby.

"You lousy, dirty bitch! You two-bit whore! You and that wop bartender! I want you out of here when I get back! Out of here or I'll kill both of you!"

He stormed out of the room. My fear of being deserted at this moment was so intense that I threw on a raincoat over my nightgown and went running after him. It was cold as only Chicago gets cold in the winter. As I ran out of the apartment building, some of the musicians were coming home. They offered to help me but I went running off, looking for Al. I went up and down all the dark streets in the neighborhood, a bad district, calling his name, going into the rough, dimly lighted bars looking for him. But he was nowhere to be found.

I returned to the apartment, hoping he might be there, but he wasn't. My body was badly bruised. One of my eyes was cut. I felt sick, really sick, a sick feeling I had never before in those months experienced; I was sure I was going to have a miscarriage. I had become chilled from my night's excursion and I was shaking, from the cold and from the fright I was experiencing. I buried my head in the pillows and cried as I had never cried before. No matter how

67

many lows I would have in my life, none would ever be lower than that night in Chicago.

Al returned at dawn, calm and contrite. He explained that after work he had had a few drinks with some of the boys at the bar at Michael Todd's. On finding out who he was, the barman there, a lovely, fatherly man, had said, "Oh, I know your wife from when she sang here with Les Brown. That's some gal you've got—she used to sit here talking about you all the time, I just love her, showed me the ring you gave her," and so on, and Al had interpreted all this to mean that the barman had had an affair with me when I was singing there. Al wept and begged me to forgive him. He got into bed with me, wanting to be comforted. As I held him, listening to his poor, sick sobs, I thought, Oh, if only I can last till my baby is born. If I had had any money at all I would have left him there and then. But I didn't have a dime. Also I was mortally afraid of him, afraid of what, in his blackest fury, he might do to me and my unborn child when he found out I had left him. After I had the baby, if I were able to escape to the sanctuary of my mother's home, surrounded by my relatives and friends, I felt I had a much better chance of defending myself against him. But now, here he was beside me in the Murphy bed, seeking forgiveness and consolation, and it was all I could do to force myself to hold him while he wept. My body ached where he had hit me, and my heart ached for my baby, who would come into the world with this man as a father.

My mother was staying with me at the Whitby on February 7, 1942, when, at midnight, my water broke. Al was playing in Buffalo. The doctor had said I was due but Al went to Buffalo anyway. Before he left, I told him that I thought I would go back to Cincinnati with my mother after I had the baby since I could no longer travel with him and didn't want to stay at the Whitby with the baby alone.

My mother tried to reach Al in Buffalo to tell him what had happened, but couldn't get him on the phone—she left word. Then we took a taxi and went to the hospital, barely avoiding a head-on collision on the way. The admitting nurse thought that my mother, who was a rather heavy woman then, was the one to be admitted. She couldn't believe I was about to have a baby. I'm five-seven and I weighed 134, which was just twelve pounds over my normal weight of 122. The doctor came right away and warned me not to drink anything, despite the fact that I was unbearably thirsty.

I was in labor for twelve hours, agonizing, painful, knots-in-the-sheet, old-fashioned labor. The following morning a nurse's aide brought me a big glass of grape juice by mistake; in my pain-ridden thirstiness I wolfed it down. Two minutes later everything in that hospital room was purple! Toward the end the pain got so bad I became rather delirious, but my doctor, I discovered, was one of those horse-and-buggy types who didn't believe in medication or any other measures to help the mother. Of course, I had had no preparation for natural childbirth or anything like that. I had foolishly expected that Al might hurry down from Buffalo, but he didn't get to the hospital until two days later.

At high noon, February 8, the ordeal ended. I produced an eight-pound, one-ounce boy whom I promptly named Terry, since Terry had been a favorite name of mine ever since I started to read "Terry and the Pirates" as a little girl. I had previously discussed it with Al, who didn't care about the name one way or the other.

~~~~~~

ALMA (KAPPELHOFF) DAY

Al Jorden had come to me and urged me to help him persuade Doris to have an abortion. I was always afraid of Al, because of his uncontrollable temper and his fierce ways, but I stood right up to him about the abortion.

"Now, you leave her alone about that, Al," I told him. "She wants to have that baby and she's going to have that baby." My knees were shaking but I knew that if any real trouble developed I could depend on my brother, who loved Doris with a passion and would have gladly killed Al Jorden on the spot if need be. Of course, you never knew what crazy thing Al was going to do next. Like deliberately driving on the wrong side of the street, trying to cause an accident, while Doris screamed in terror.

When the baby was due, Al was in Buffalo and I tried to locate him. All the time Doris was in the hospital in labor I tried to get Al on the phone; by the time my message finally reached him it was too late, the baby had been born. He came in the apartment two nights later and I told him he had a son.

The following morning, as he left he asked me to give his suit to the valet for cleaning since he needed it for work that night. The valet took the suit but came back shortly afterward with an envelope that was in one of the pockets. I opened it up. It had been written by a girl who said how wonderful the three days were that they'd spent together, but what if she got pregnant, how would she get in touch with him to tell him since she didn't know his address? "Maybe," she wrote, "I'll never see you again. I hope not. Please don't do that to me. I love you."

No wonder I hadn't been able to locate Al Jorden to tell him his wife was having their baby. I never told Doris about the letter—what was the point? We both knew what kind of man Al was and there was no sense upsetting her even more. One of the cruelest things he did was to forbid Doris to have the baby in the bedroom with them. The baby had to stay with me in my room all the time. There were times, I can tell you, when I was fearful that he might harm the poor little thing. I kept my eye on him all the time.

~~~~~~

When I returned to the Whitby with the baby, I impatiently bided my time until Al was to leave with the band for a string of one-nighters. Then back to Cincinnati I would go, finally escaping from Al Jorden. My mother had already alerted my cousin, who was a lawyer, to be prepared to start divorce proceedings immediately. But Al was not to be handled so easily. In the midst of our preparation to depart, Al walked into the apartment and announced that he had quit the band and was going back to Cincinnati with us. I was stunned.

"I'm sending your mother back on the train with the baby," he said, "and you and I are going in the car."

"No, I think I should stay with the baby—"

"I'm not driving by myself," he said, his voice beginning to rise. "Now you do as I say. Your place is with me—your mother knows how to handle a baby."

"All right," I said. I was afraid of him, just plain afraid, and now with the baby there, there was just no telling what he might do if enraged. All right, I thought, I'll just keep peace until we get back to Cincinnati, where I'll have the protection of my uncles and brother. I was not able to breast-feed the baby so there was no reason why we couldn't make the trip as Al suggested.

My mother had found a little home for us (at the time she thought it would be for me and the baby and herself)—a cute little house, not far from my uncle's tavern, that was directly across from a pretty neighborhood park. When Al found out about the house, he gave my mother the down payment she had made and took over the mortgage for himself. All my well-laid plans were suddenly defeated and here I was again, trapped with him. He immediately got jobs playing with local bands and with a band on radio—with his kind of musicianship, he found work easily.

The most sadistic thing he did after we moved into the new house was to buy a little dog. Now that may sound strange coming from me, an abject dog lover, but what Al did was to bestow on that dog all the love and attention that normally a father would give to his newborn son. He knew, of course, how much I loved dogs— but he had never showed much feeling for them one way or another. Now, however, he made that little dog the center of his attention. He would walk in the house and walk right by the baby, who was purring and being adorable, and go straight to his dog and lavish all his attention on him. This was his bizarre, convoluted way of getting at me. And it worked. It bothered me terribly.

But I was no longer as isolated and insecure as I had been in New York. My aunt Marie lived right next door to our house. Aunt Marie's nickname was Rocky, a solid, hearty, adorable, funny woman who was indeed a rock. With her alongside me, I had resolved not to absorb any more of Al's abuse. For the first few weeks he was on good behavior, but after a few minor outbursts, he came in late one night and threw one of his black, yelling tantrums. He didn't hit me, but he pushed me and abused me, the racket awakening the baby, whose crying intensified the abuse.

The next day when Al came home from work he couldn't get in. I had had the locks changed and all his things were in his bags on the porch. I was next door at my aunt's. Al banged on the door and shouted my name, but after a few minutes, to my surprise, he picked up his bags and left. I had expected him to crash the door down or smash a window. But he was gone—*gone!* To be heard from again, I knew, but for the moment I was alone with my baby and no longer living in fear. I didn't have ten cents to my name, so for the first and only time in my life, I was forced to borrow money— ten dollars from Aunt Rocky to buy groceries.

"How will you get along?" my aunt asked.

"Why, I'll get a job," I said. All my life I have known that I could work at whatever I wanted whenever I wanted. This is really not conceit—I do not have feelings of superiority. Nor do I have a large ego. I just feel secure in what I know I can do. I just never have thoughts about it—the "My God, what if I don't get a job" syndrome—I simply know that I'll get along all right.

The very next day after Al left, I made an appointment with a Mr. Weiner, who ran radio station WLW. "Mr. Weiner," I said, "I need a job desperately—to start right now."

"Well, Doris," he said, "after Les Brown and Bob Crosby you could go with any band you wanted to."

"No, I don't want to go with a band. I have a baby now and

71

I want to stay here with him. I know I can go on the road—that's easy. What I'd like is a radio job. I know that radio singing is different from band singing but I'd like to audition for you, if I may, and then see if you think there's a job for me here at WLW."

"All right," he said. "I'll find a pianist and we'll have an audition."

I went into a studio with the pianist, and without practice or run-through, I sang for Mr. Weiner, who was sitting in the adjoining control booth. I tried to make my voice a little smaller, more intimate and subtle than the way I had sung in front of the band. Singing for radio and for records is quite different from singing in front of a band. The radio mike is much more critical, the background music less imposing. After I sang just one number for Mr. Weiner, he opened the control booth mike and said, "Okay, Doris, you've got the job."

He came into the studio. I thanked him. "Of course," he said, "you must realize that you'll only be making scale unless you get a sponsored program."

"How do I go about that? I *have* to make some money."

"Well, whenever we have a sponsored show coming up, we'll let you audition for the sponsors—they're the ones who have the say-so on the performers."

Within no time I had several sponsored shows. My first show was for MGM, "The Lion's Roar," advertising MGM movies. It was a fifteen-minute show, five times a week, a little variety show. I'd chat with the announcer about whatever MGM movie was in release, and sing a couple of songs with the studio band. I also did a beer show on weekends, and then I became the vocalist on "Moon River," which was the biggest radio show out of WLW. Every night at midnight. A great organist, love poems read by a sexy-voiced announcer, and I was the vocalist four nights every week. It was a silky, seductive show that was highly successful.

Two days after Al had left, the little dog disappeared from his run in the back yard; I knew Al had taken him. My cousin had immediately started divorce proceedings. The first few nights after Al's departure, my mother and I were very apprehensive that he might come barging in—but, no, Al had a much more sinister way to make contact with me. On those nights when I did "Moon River" I usually stayed in the downtown area rather than go all the way up to Price Hill and back again. I often had dinner in restaurants with friends. Wherever I went, Al Jorden was invariably there, sitting at a table across the room, staring at me, making me apprehensive and uncomfortable. He had me under constant surveillance. It was terribly spooky (years later I made a picture called *Love Me Or Leave Me,* in which my estranged movie husband, played by Jimmy Cagney, shadowed me in much the same way). Al would never come up to my table or talk to me, just sit there in the restaurant staring at me, watching my every move, not taking his eyes off me.

It got so at WLW that the doorman was primed to watch for him, and when it was time for me to leave the studio, the doorman would often get me on the phone and warn me that Al was parked outside. So I would leave through some other door, or I'd go to the rear parking lot with a friend and duck down in the back seat so that he couldn't see me as we drove away. It was awful.

One night Al finally confronted me. I had double-dated with a friend of mine at the station, Vivie, and two announcers. Vivie was going to spend the night with me. We said good-night to our dates on the sidewalk in front of the house and they drove off. Vivie nudged me. She knew Al's car and she saw that it was parked directly behind us. I had told her about Al's furies; she was panic-stricken but she stayed right at my side. Al put his head out of the car.

"Get in," he said. "I want to talk to you."

"Al," I said, my voice quaking with fear, "it's late and I'm very tired—and so is my guest who's staying with me."

"I said get in."

I started to move up the steps to the front door, Vivie and I clinging to each other. "Some other time, Al. I just don't want to talk when it's late like this."

He got out of the car and stood there, glaring at us as we hurried up the steps and escaped into the house. I had heard from mutual friends that he was in a bad way and was still telling everyone how much he loved me and how desperately he wanted me back. But that night the only feeling I got from him was one of menace.

There was a night, a week or so later, that I finally did have a talk with him. Again I was returning home with Vivie, and there he was parked in front of the house. Vivie spotted him the moment we arrived. "I better see him and get it over with," I said.

Vivie was horrified. "Doris, don't you dare! You said he has a gun in there—now, Doris!"

This time Al got out of the car and came over to me. "I want to talk to you," he said. "Are you afraid to *talk,* for God's sake?"

"You go on up, Vivie," I said.

"No, that's all right, I'll wait."

"No," I insisted, "you go on up and tell my mother I'll be in shortly."

Reluctantly, Vivie did as I asked and I got in the car with Al. I could feel myself trembling. Al was quite subdued. He said he had had a long time now to think about things and he really felt that if I took him back we could have a good life together and be a happy family. He said how much he needed me and missed me, and how much he wanted his baby son. It was really quite touching, what he had to say, but I had been through this too many times now for it to have any effect.

"I'm sorry, Al," I said, "but the feelings I once had for you are dead and gone. There's no way to resurrect them. I don't love you anymore, and without love it just wouldn't work. There's nothing to talk about—the good feelings are gone, and it's over. All over."

Before I left, I agreed that he could come to see the baby once in a while, and occasionally take him out for an afternoon at his mother's. I was plenty apprehensive about that, but I knew it would have to be part of the legal arrangement anyway. As I started to get out of the car, he put his hand on my arm. I looked at him. His face was full of pain and he was near tears. I thought to myself, No, I am through comforting you. I felt a curious kind of revulsion. The pain was his and his alone, and I would have nothing to do with it. I looked away from him and got out of the car and quickly went into the house.

Al did come to see the baby a few times, and once or twice he took Terry to his mother's house to visit, but it was not long afterward that he left Cincinnati to go into the service. He was sent to the Great Lakes Naval Station, where he was made a member of the splendid service band they had there.

I had found work and we were managing all right, but in the beginning of my return to Cincinnati I was dispirited and disillusioned. My dream of happy home, husband, and baby had gone bust. My marriage had had no substance, so that when it ended, it was not two people who had once enjoyed a good relationship who were now dissolving it with some dignity and mutual respect. I had had a marriage with no substance and no enjoyment that had come to a shabby end. My girlhood dream had been destroyed and there was nothing to take its place.

My mother became increasingly concerned about the uncharacteristic depression I had fallen into, and suggested that it might be helpful if I had a talk with the parish priest. Of course, we were in a new neighborhood and this priest was a stranger to us, but my mother suggested that perhaps in talking out things with him I might be able to help myself.

Although I had been raised a Catholic and had attended parochial schools, I had my reservations about Catholicism. When as a little girl I was told that I would have to go to confession before I went to communion, I asked the nun, "What do I tell him?"

"All your sins," she said.

"My sins?"

"I suppose you're going to stand there and tell me that you haven't sinned?"

"I haven't."

"Get on with you—you know what you've done wrong and you just go in and tell him what you did wrong."

I used to make things up because, at the age of seven, what sins do you have? Telling your mother that you washed your hands before dinner when in fact you didn't? From the very beginning I thought the concept of sins and sinning was repugnant. I also missed mass whenever I could because I felt it was an empty ritual without meaning. I had my own built-in church. It allowed me to question a lot of Catholic dogma. As a child I could not understand why the Protestant children whom I used to meet at the Evanston swimming pool were not getting the same good deal that we Catholics were getting. I began to feel sorry for them, being shut out of such desirable places as heaven. And I could never accept that a few minutes in a confessional booth would purge a person of whatever grievous wrongs he had committed against his fellowman.

But despite my reservations about it, Catholicism was the only religion I knew, and I did finally go to see the parish priest at my mother's insistence. I was desperate to find some way to restore the positive view I had always had toward life. I told the priest about my marriage and child and how things had turned out, and he looked at me rather smugly and said, "My dear, you don't have a thing to worry about because you have never been married."

I said, "What did you say?"

"You weren't married in the church. You were never married." He was a middle-aged, rather fat priest, and as he sat there expounding on his theme that I had never been married, I thought about all my friends who had been married by judges and whose children were in the same fix as mine.

"Father," I said, "are you in effect saying that my son is illegitimate?"

"Well, my dear," he said, patronizingly, "I can only repeat that in the eyes of the church you have never been married."

As anger began to rise in me I could feel the Kappelhoff lower jaw jut out from its moorings. "And all the children of my Protestant friends—all illegitimate?"

"The Catholic church offers a binding and consecrated marriage," he pronounced. "Let us hope that you will find solace in marrying properly and enjoying the fruits of such a marriage."

I knew that I should get out of there fast before my temper got any worse. "Thank you, Father," I said, "you've been a great comfort."

Les Brown called and tried to get me to rejoin his band. He had heard me singing on "Moon River" and he was elated to find out that I was divorcing Al Jorden. But I told him that I would not leave Terry even though it was a struggle to make ends meet. He urged me to think it over and said he would keep after me until I said yes.

My mother was all in favor of my going back with Les. I had taken the house back from Al and the mortgage was a heavy monthly burden.

"What future do you have scrambling around at WLW?" my mother asked. "It's a dead-end local station. I can take care of Terry while you travel, and then when you light anywhere I'll bring Terry and we'll stay with you in between the one-nighters. We could give up this expensive house and I'd take a little apartment across the street from the tavern where Terry, Paul, and I could live comfortably and a lot more cheaply."

It was indeed a struggle. The idea of alimony was repugnant to me—as long as I was healthy there was no reason why I should not support myself. As far as I am concerned, the American notion that the husband is "guilty" and must continue to support his ex-wife "in the manner to which she has become accustomed" is preposterous. Two people decide to go their separate ways, each to start a new life. That should be the end of it.

So I asked nothing of Al Jorden, and although my earnings

barely supported us, I nevertheless enjoyed living in Cincinnati. And I really felt no ambition toward a career. I was perfectly content to get by, by singing on my radio shows. There was a group who sang at WLW, the Williams Brothers, a really marvelous group, and one of the brothers, Andy, asked me if I'd like to join them. I said I had never sung with a group before and that I thought I was fundamentally a soloist because of my stylized way of singing and phrasing; I felt it would be very difficult for me to be regimented in the way a group demands.

But Andy, who was a very appealing young man, urged me to give it a try. They were going to rehearse the following Monday night at their house and they invited me to join in. Andy's mother, father, and sisters were all there, as well as his three brothers, and we had a wonderful time. Actually, I blended into their group very well. Although we never sang professionally, every Monday night I would go to the Williamses' and his mother would fix hot chocolate and bake cookies and we'd have a songfest. Those Monday nights were part of what I enjoyed about life in Cincinnati. I was really heartbroken when Andy told me they were going to leave town to start working in New York. I don't know when Andy split from his brothers to sing on his own, but I knew from those Monday-night sessions he was a young man of immense talent.

Les Brown called me for the third time the day after the Williams Brothers left Cincinnati, and I guess their leaving put me in the mood to leave also. My mother and my aunt had been working on me, and I was at the point where I felt I should give it a try. I met up with Les in Columbus. For my opening, Les staged "Too-ra-loo-ra-loo-ral" for me so that I sang it on a darkened stage with a pin spot on me, backed by four trombones that were grouped right behind me. Just the lovely trombone harmony, nothing else. It was musically very exciting and made me glad to be back with the band. Also, Les and the men were old and dear friends by now and I had the feeling I was back with family.

Les was constantly putting new material into our repertoire. We would rehearse these new songs and arrangements late at night when we finished playing. Although I cannot read a note of music or play any instrument, I can usually sight-read a song in my own funny way. Also, the band always went through a new number a couple of times before I rehearsed the vocal. I usually memorized the lyrics the following day on the bus.

We were playing the Pennsylvania Hotel in Newark, New Jersey, when, at a late-night rehearsal, Les gave me the sheet music for a new song that he had helped compose, "Sentimental Journey." The band went through it and I scanned the lyrics as they played. I felt a distinct rise in my scalp. I *always* feel a rise in my scalp or on the backs of my wrists when something is special, whether it be song or man. I stepped to the microphone, and on the second run-through I sang the lyrics. I loved the song, I loved singing it, and we all thought it was going to be a big hit.

Les introduced "Sentimental Journey" the following night. I started to sing the lyrics and by the end of the first eight bars the couples had stopped dancing and were just standing there, arms around, listening to me. It was an overwhelming success. They just stood there, wildly applauding, until we played it again—and again. There were requests for it all night long. I sang it on a network remote, and mail came pouring into the hotel from all over the country. A short time later, we recorded it on the Okey label and it became my first hit record. Everywhere we went, that's what people wanted to hear. The song had somehow captured how the war was affecting the emotions of the men who had gone off and those who had to wait for their return. In a sense, "Sentimental Journey" became the serviceman's theme song. For the rest of the war, I received a flood of mail from G.I.'s all over the world, telling me over what army juke or radio they had heard me sing the song, and what it meant to them. Some of them wrote me love letters. It was very touching. I got sick and tired of having to sing the song but I never tired of reading the mail from the servicemen.

I had other hit records with Les, like "My Dreams Are Getting Better All the Time," but none rivaled the success of "Sentimental Journey." I was usually pretty good at guessing which new songs would be hits, but I also had some notable misses. When the composers first played "Que Sera, Sera" for me, I thought it was a nice, simple little child's song that would never get out of the nursery.

~~~~~~

LES BROWN

Shortly after Doris joined the band, my arranger, Ben Homer, came to me with an original song that he had been trying to peddle in the Brill Building without success. He had eight good bars but that's all. I added a bridge, smoothed out what he had, and got Bud Green, who had written "Flat Foot Floogie" and other winners, to write a lyric for it. The song was called "Sentimental Journey," and Doris introduced it during our stand at the Pennsylvania Hotel. Most often you don't know what a new song will do, but the minute Doris sang that song I knew that it was going to be a big love affair between her and the public.

In a funny way it was Doris who got me into my long association with Bob Hope. A recording of Doris singing "Sentimental Journey" had been taken to Hope, who was considering a replacement for Frances Langford, who had been the long-time vocalist on his radio show. Hope listened to the recording and decided he wanted the band, not the singer. It wasn't that he didn't like Doris's singing; it was a question of Hope's loyalty to Langford, who had a drinking problem, and Hope, who is one of the few truly compassionate people in our business, didn't want to compound Langford's problems by firing her. I tried to convince Hope that he was making a mistake, that he could get Doris at that time for a reasonable amount, but I warned him that if he waited, her price would be way up. Hope didn't listen to me. He waited a year and at the end of that year, when he did sign Doris up, he had to pay her ten times more.

As for Doris's first husband, Al Jorden, he was a very peculiar, very selfish man, who played a good, solid horn, but was certainly not a man Doris should have married. I tried to tell her that. I told her he was a sick character and she was making a mistake, that he was bad medicine, but she wouldn't listen. I liked Doris, really liked her. She was young and vulnerable and I felt responsible toward her as a father would feel toward a daughter. One time there was a picture in Downbeat magazine of Doris sitting on top of a trunk with her legs crossed, her skirt at her knees— a typical publicity photograph. Al saw that picture and went wild. He grabbed Doris by the arm and yanked her out of the office, down the stairs, and out on the street. I watched them as he dragged her along the sidewalk, shouting at her. The street was crowded with people. Al stopped suddenly, hit Doris across the face, and then continued to drag her along the sidewalk.

Whoever planned Les's tour was a sadist—we played Canada in the dead of winter and Florida in August, but whenever we had a stand of a week or more, I'd bring Terry and my mother there, whatever the weather. Terry was almost two by now and into everything. Once, when I was having an argument with the particularly obnoxious landlord of an apartment we had rented in Miami Beach, Terry picked up a garden hose that was running and turned it on him. When we were in New York we stayed at the Piccadilly Hotel in Times Square. Terry would wander off down the hall and return with clocks, shoes, books, and other booty that he would collect from rooms that had their doors open. We'd have to call the housekeeper to get them returned. Terry would fill up containers with water and toss them out the window, to land on the heads of unsuspecting pedestrians. He was a terror.

When my mother took him for a walk, she used a tiny-tot harness to ensure that he would not suddenly dart away from her into the traffic. But this precaution backfired one afternoon when Terry spotted a policeman sitting on his horse. As Terry made a beeline for the horse, his harness cord caught my mother around the ankles, knocking her over. She landed heavily and broke her leg—in fourteen places. When she came back from the hospital she had a heavy cast on her leg from thigh to toes. And the day after she came back from the hospital, Terry threw her crutches out of the window.

But Terry was as lovable as he was mischievous and the men in the band and their wives were always helping to look after him, taking him to the park or the zoo or wherever. Despite the little troubles he caused, he was a joy.

I had not heard from Al since he left to join the Navy. But when the band bus rolled into Chicago for an engagement at the College Inn and we checked into the Sherman Hotel, somebody handed me a message to the effect that Al Jorden had called and wanted me to phone him at the Great Lakes Naval Station. I crumbled up the paper and threw it away.

I had no sooner checked into my room than the phone rang and there he was on the line. He said he was coming in to see me perform and asked me to have dinner with him afterward. I told him I didn't think that was a good idea and that I'd prefer it if he didn't show up.

"Don't you want to *see* me?" he asked. "I mean, what I look like and all?"

"No, I don't."

"But I'd like to know about things—you know, catch up on things. Why can't we be friends?"

"Considering everything, Al, it's just best that we keep our distances."

"Why, do you have a boyfriend—somebody you don't want me to meet?"

"Al, that has nothing to do with it. I just don't want to see you. I'm getting my life in order, and I'd like to keep you out of it."

Although I went out occasionally, there was no man whom I was interested in. One of the men I dated was a United pilot named Dick Cooley, who would often appear in places where I was singing. He was an engaging man who loved a good time and we'd often go out with other pilots and stewardesses. There was also a song plugger who was my age whom I'd see occasionally, but I had little time for dates and certainly, considering what I had been through, no enthusiasm for getting emotionally entangled with anyone.

I was standing in the wings of the little stage at the College Inn, watching the band, when I became aware that someone was standing behind me. It was Al, looking very attractive in his uniform. Some of the men in the band saw him and they looked grim. By now most of them pretty well knew how awful Al had been.

I decided to go out to dinner with him, and afterward we came back to the hotel and talked. We talked most of the night. Al was making his last desperate pitch to get me back, and I was determined, once and for all, to convince him that my feelings for him were dead and gone, and that we should never see each other again. Some of the things he said were very touching, and I believe he did still love me in his way; he pleaded with me to come back to him, that he had no life without me—if I had had any positive feelings for him I think they would have been rekindled by his plea, but there was nothing, and I told him so and he could tell I was telling the truth.

Finally, when he had talked himself out and the early dawn light was in the windows and he knew that his cause was hopeless, Al put his face in his hands and wept. I felt great pity for him. He was two men, and the good part of him deserved what the bad part had taken away. Out of compassion, I wept too. He slept with me.

When he left he said that he was going to write to me—that maybe there was still a spark of something that would keep us alive. He just wouldn't give up. He wrote to me several times after that, and finally I wrote to him and asked him not to write anymore. I told him in as final terms as I could that there was no hope that I would ever have any feelings for him again. I urged him to make a new life for himself, just as I was trying to make for myself.

That did it. I never heard from him again. Not too long afterward, I heard he had gotten married to a woman from around the Great Lakes area, a woman who had a child. After his discharge he moved back to Cincinnati. One time when I was in Cincinnati on a short visit between band dates to see Terry, I went into a drugstore and there was Al with his new wife. They were on the other side of the store. He pretended not to see me. I guess he didn't want to have to introduce me to his wife.

Three

~~~~~~

Y̶OU would think that after my experience with Al Jorden I would
never have anything to do with a musician again, but I did. This time,
however, I learned once and for all that I could not make beautiful
music with a musician.

I had been with Les Brown for several months before I "noticed" the lead alto sax and he "noticed" me. It is a curious phenomenon, isn't it, the way someone we have been around a lot will suddenly
capture our fancy, a daffodil bursting into bloom? George Weidler
was his name, brother of the actress Virginia Weidler, hired as first
alto sax when the regular lead sax man, Steve Madrick, was drafted.
He was tall, slim, dark, with deep-brown eyes, a moustache, soft-
spoken—a quiet man, and very gentle. Just the opposite of Al.

In no time at all I fell in love with George and we saw each
other every day and slept together every night. The way I felt about
love then was different from the way I feel about love now. I have
come to realize that there is loving someone and there is being in love
and the difference is that one involves physical love and one doesn't.
There are men I love whom I've no desire to go to bed with. On the
other hand, a dynamite sexual relation may not have anything to do
with love. A strong physical reaction can addle your senses, but it can
also wear off as quickly as it sprouted, and suddenly you are saying
to yourself, "Hold on, I can't be in love with him, I don't like him.
Imagine, I don't even *like* him! I don't like the way he thinks and we
don't really have all that much to say to each other. I like him in
bed—my heart flutters when I see him and all those experiences I'm
having in bed with him are super—but how can I be in love with him
if I don't like him?"

But I wasn't wise enough to make this distinction way back then in my late teens and I really thought that George and I had a total love that would last forever. The thing that I particularly liked about him, after the brutality of Al Jorden, was his gentleness. He was a gentle man in the true sense of the word. I would say that, for me, of all the attributes a man must have, gentleness would be at the top of my list. Gentleman. A beautiful word.

My blissful band life with George came to an abrupt end when Steve Madrick returned from the service. Les had promised Steve that he would restore him to his old position as lead sax, but George was not willing to be demoted. Also, George was a native Californian who longed for the warm climate of Los Angeles, and although he was torn by his desire to stay with me, he eventually decided to leave the band. So there I was again, reduced to a postal love affair. I missed George terribly after he left, and my spirits, after their brief restoration, again plummeted.

Almost a year passed, of passionate love letters and equally passionate phone calls, before George decided to come to New York, where I was performing at the Pennsylvania Hotel, to get married. Now the peculiar thing is that I have no recollection of the details of our wedding. I do recall that we went to Mount Vernon (don't ask me why) to get married by a justice of the peace, but I can't for the life of me recall who went with us, who were the witnesses, or anything about the ceremony itself—or even where we went afterward.

But there is one thing that I sharply recollect. On the way to Mount Vernon, I remember looking out the window of the car and thinking, What am I doing here? Why am I getting married? It's a mistake, another mistake—so why am I doing it? Why? No bride ever went to her wedding with more misgivings. I should have worn black.

George stayed in New York for a couple of days before returning to the Coast. I gave Les notice but promised to stay on until he found a replacement. Poor Les, again he tried to talk me out of marriage. He pointed out that I would have a tough time finding adequate work in Los Angeles. He also felt that I should give myself more time to recover from Al Jorden. But I had decided to strike out on my own as a singer without band attachment. An agent named Al Levy, who was associated with the Century Artists agency, had been coming to the Pennsylvania Hotel and he had been urging me to try to make a career for myself. But I was not much interested in that, as I've never been fixed on a career—I was interested only to the extent that

83

I could go to California to be with George. I planned to stop in Cincinnati on the way to get Terry. George had seen little Terry and had not seemed to respond to him one way or the other, but I felt that he would accept him and like him once we all started living together.

But it was not to be as easy as that. The war had just ended and there was a severe housing shortage in Los Angeles. Months passed while George hunted for a place to live, and finally all he could come up with was a trailer in a place called the Midway Trailer Camp. Many musicians were living there, the attraction being that when the trailer was purchased, you were guaranteed a space in which to park it. The space itself was located in an awful industrial area on Sepulveda Boulevard. Of course I wasn't able to bring Terry as planned. I can assure you that the new Mrs. Weidler was less than uplifted when she first laid eyes on her home-to-be, packed in, as it was, among all those hundreds of trailers in that busted-down trailer court.

But once I settled in, I actually didn't mind it all that much. While George went off to work in radio bands, I scrubbed and painted and did the laundry in the trailer court's community washhouse. Our neighbors on one side had a new baby who cried all night, and there were two loud winos on the other side, but I had a peculiar illusion that I was in a frontier town with pioneers, which helped alleviate some of the stress.

I still had the responsibility of supporting my mother and Terry—George didn't have much money and I wouldn't have taken it from him if he had. I made the rounds and wound up as vocalist on "The Sweeny and March Radio Show"—Bob Sweeny and Hal March, who were comics at that time on a local CBS station. I didn't at all like singing on that show. To begin with, I had never been comfortable doing radio—it always made me nervous because there was no way to do it again if you didn't like the way you sang a number. But what I particularly didn't like was singing by myself without a band in back of me. However, I was making enough, even though I was working for scale, to support Terry and my mother.

Al Levy came around quite often, to tell me of things he hoped would open up for me, and to discuss my "potential," which he thought was fantastic. I remember one time he came by the trailer in that big, black, four-door Cadillac of his, and as usual began telling George and me what a big star I was going to be. "Al," I said, "I'm not interested."

"You're not interested? How can you be not interested?"

"Oh, Al, of all the people for you to latch onto as agent I'm the worst. I'm just not ambitious. I'm not interested in being *somebody* because I feel I already am. I'm the somebody I want to be. Just cozy here in this trailer."

"Are you nuts? Do you know how many girls want to be in your shoes right now—on the brink of a big career?"

"Look, Al, whatever radio shows I can get I'm grateful for—I'm really glad you got me the Sweeny and March show—but don't talk to me about being a big star, because I'm just not directed that way. Whatever comes along, fine, as long as I can make enough money to take care of my family. But don't try to build me up—I don't want any more than I've got right now."

Al turned to George. "George, listen, do something—your wife has got to stop talking like that."

Another time, after he'd been to London for two weeks, Al drove up to the trailer in his big Caddy and honked. When George and I came out, Al presented me with a big box he had brought back for me. I opened it on the fender of his car; inside was a beautiful houndstooth sports coat, brown-and-white check. I loved it, but protested his having bought it for me—you know, the usual "I want it but you shouldn't have" response. I tried it on and it was really a super coat. I asked George if he liked it; he said he did but there was a funny look on his face.

Despite Al Levy's enthusiasm, his attempts to get me going in Hollywood were fruitless. Months passed with only local radio work available to me. Al introduced me to his partners at Century Artists, Dick Dorso and Marty Melcher, who agreed that I was on the threshold of something big, but during the passing months I never got over that threshold.

The one definite offer that finally did materialize was to appear for a month in New York at Billy Reed's Little Club, a new spot that was just opening its doors. I didn't want to leave George but I would be getting four times what I'd been earning in Hollywood—and we were badly strapped for money. I talked it over with George, who urged me to go. It was only a month, he reasoned, and it would be good money and good exposure. And on the way I could stop and see Terry. I think that's what decided me. I missed Terry very much and I could spend a few days with him on the way out and perhaps find a place where Mother and Terry could stay with me in New York.

SOL JAFFEE

My introduction to Doris Day involved two men, Monte Proser, who then owned the Copacabana in New York, and Mannie Sachs, who was a vice-president at NBC. I was attorney to both men.

Proser was in Hollywood making his first movie that involved his famous Copa girls, but being inexperienced he was way over budget and behind schedule and running into all kinds of trouble. He had phoned me and frantically asked me to come out to help him. I didn't want to—I knew quite a lot about Broadway but not very much about movies—but finally I agreed to go as a favor to Proser.

In the meantime, I received a call from Sachs about a girl singer named Doris Day. Mannie Sachs was one of the most well-liked men in the music industry, always helpful, never said no to anyone. Sachs had received a call from a song plugger friend of his, telling him about Doris Day, who had once sung with some of the big bands but was now down on her luck in Hollywood, living in a trailer, little baby to support. Sachs knew I was going to Hollywood to work with Proser and what he wanted me to do was to try to get Proser to give Doris Day a job.

I phoned Proser, who said he had no time to see anyone, but I put it right on the line with him—either he did this favor for Mannie Sachs or I wasn't going to come out to help him. Proser agreed reluctantly.

A few days after I got to Hollywood, I set up a meeting between Doris and Proser at the Goldwyn Studios, where Proser was shooting his film. Doris, whom I had never seen before, showed up in an old white sweater, her hair windblown, no makeup—hardly the getup of a girl eager to make her mark at her audition. Proser gave me a look but I pressed right on for the audition. We went in and out of rooms, looking for a piano, but none was to be found. Proser was dying to get back to the movie set. Finally, he just dragged Doris into a bare room and said, "Sing." No music, nothing. To Doris's credit, she just dug in and sang.

Afterward I got Proser out in the hall. "Well, what do you think? Nice voice and she'll be pretty when she's fixed up, you can see that."

"Yeah," Proser said, "she has a nice, small voice but it's not big enough to fill the Copa. I just couldn't use her."

"What about the new club you're going to open that Billy Reed is going to manage? The Little Club. A little voice for a little club."

Proser was so anxious to get back to his troublesome movie that he agreed. The funny thing is neither of the two men who were instrumental in starting Doris on her way at the Little Club—Proser and I— had ever laid eyes on her before this strange New York-Hollywood ploy.

Billy Reed was a lovable old vaudevillian who was a joy to work for. The Club was long, narrow, very elegant, with an intimate atmosphere that lent itself to my style of singing. There were two shows, dinner and late, with a small combo to back me up. Al Levy brought in Marty Melcher to help with selecting the songs I would sing. We selected a program of things I liked to sing, with no attempt at special material for the occasion. "How Are Things in Glocca Morra?," "How About You?," "Too-ra-loo-ra-loo-ral," and, of course, "Sentimental Journey" and "My Dreams Are Getting Better All the Time." I had to overcome a terrible case of jitters—nervous diarrhea and all that—before I could go out and face the opening-night crowd, but once I started to sing everything sorted itself out inside of me. By my third number I was having a good time. As I came off the stage, Billy Reed told me that he was picking up my option for another month.

I enjoyed the dinner show, but every night the late show was a struggle. My nature is to fold early; I should have been a bird or a flower. I had had to struggle through the late hours when I sang with the bands and now I struggled to keep myself from falling asleep before the late show—not only before, but during!

I did not have much time to enjoy my success at the Little Club, because a couple of days after I opened I received a letter from George that devastated me. Married only eight months, and here was this letter telling me that he thought we should put an end to it. There had been nothing between us to prepare me for this. We had never exchanged a cross word. An easygoing relationship, I had thought, rather bland but very compatible. Our sex life, as far as I could tell, was perfectly all right. We had been struggling to make ends meet but we were succeeding and there was something rather romantic, I thought, about living in our neat little trailer.

I suppose what bothered me most about the letter was the letter itself. That George didn't discuss this with me before I left Hollywood, or at least have had the courage to tell me this on the phone. It was obviously something he had thought about and planned. In his letter George said that it was the hardest thing he had ever had to do, writing this letter, but that after much deliberation he felt that we should go our own ways. He said it wasn't right for me to be stuck in the trailer and living that kind of life. "You are going to be a huge success," he told me, "Al says so and I believe it. You are going to be a star and I'm never going to be anything more than just a side man in a band. You're going to outgrow me and sooner or later the imbalance will destroy our relationship—so rather than wait until that happens I think we should break up right now. It's easier. We haven't yet put much into our marriage. We won't have lost very much."

Pride. A commodity I'm very short on and put down when I see it in others. But George felt that I was on my way to becoming a headliner in New York with a glittering new career, and he did not want to become Mr. Doris Day. But in fact I was no such thing. I loved him, or at least I thought I did, and with all the hardship and struggle I was enjoying my trailer wifedom. If I hadn't been a good wife, he should have said something about it, some indication, but as it was there had been no intimation at all that he wanted to end our marriage.

The letter shattered me. I tried to reach him at the trailer but he had moved out. I phoned around but no one knew where he had gone. I took it very hard. My engagement at the Little Club was a battle with tragedy. I was crying all the time. Poor Billy, such a dear man, tried to console me but there was no way to stop my interminable flood of tears. I even cried while I was out on the floor singing! "Little Girl Blue" was one of my numbers, and I cried all the way through it. And every night I had to struggle to finish "Glad to Be Unhappy" before my tears overcame me. I'm sure the audiences had never heard a performer so touched by her songs.

I asked Billy to let me out of the second month. I was in no shape to continue. I wanted to get back to Hollywood to find George to see if there was some way we could be back together again. Finally, toward the end of my month at Billy's, I contacted George through his mother. I told him I was coming back and he agreed to meet the train when it arrived in Pasadena, so that we could sit down face-to-face and talk about what had happened.

All the way to the coast on the train, I was fidgety and depressed and nervous but intermittently buoyed with hope that we might be reconciled. I spent long hours rehearsing just what I'd say to him. As the train neared Pasadena, I changed into the most attractive dress I owned, and prettied myself up as best I could. My heart was on one sleeve and my hope on the other. But George wasn't there. The train pulled out and I waited and waited on the empty platform but George never came. I finally took a taxi and checked into a hotel. I phoned his mother, and mutual friends, with the result that later that day George called me at the hotel.

He came to get me that evening and we went back to the trailer. He was gentle, as always, but quite firm in repeating what he had told me in his letter—that I was going to be hugely successful, a star (how I dislike that word!), and the kind of life he had and the life I would have just wouldn't fit together. I tried to convince him that a good and happy marriage was all that I wanted, but he insisted that stardom was not something that could be avoided—that it reached out and grabbed you and thrust you up there and there was nothing you could do about it.

We talked for hours, but nothing I said changed his mind. Finally, when it was late and we were all talked out, we went to bed and made love and I could not doubt his strong desire for me. But I guess his desire not to be Mr. Doris Day was even stronger, for in the morning we parted, and I knew it would be final.

I walked to the nearest bus stop and sat down on the waiting bench. The optimist in me rummaged among the debris of my ruins but found nothing of comfort. My second marriage, after eight months, was over. I had only a few dollars in my purse. I had no prospects other than going back to New York to pick up the second month's work at the Little Club. And then? Nothing else but to return to Cincinnati to try to get on again at WLW. But our little house was gone and we'd have to find a place to live. Either that or I could go back on the road with Les Brown. Those interminable one-night stands. By the time the bus arrived I was crying so hard I didn't get on. I tried giving myself a pep talk—listen, no matter if you miss the bus, there's always another. Just be patient. There *will* be a man, there *will* be a good life, you *will* have a home where you can bring your little boy. The next bus arrived but I just sat there. The pep talk wasn't working.

I had had misgivings about this marriage even as I drove to the wedding. There was no joy, no eagerness, no keenness in either of us. We were frustrated at being apart, but I had found out that that was not a valid reason for getting married. You don't really know a person until you live with him, not just sleep with him. Sex is not enough to sustain marriage. I have the unfortunate reputation of being Miss Goody Two-shoes, America's Virgin, and all that, so I'm afraid it's going to shock some people for me to say this, but I staunchly believe no two people should get married until they have lived together. The young people have it right. What a tragedy it is for a couple to get married, have a child, and in the process discover they are not suited for one another! If I had lived with Al Jorden for a few weeks, God knows I would never have married him. Nor would I have married George Weidler. But I was too young and too inexperienced to understand any of this. Now my heart was busted and I had lost my way. I hated Hollywood and I hated New York. And I had come to hate

89

the long night bus rides with the band. Cincinnati was all right but the thought of going back to WLW radio was as depressing a prospect as everything else. The bottom. I had landed rock bottom with no sign of a way up. I finally got on a bus and went back to my dreary hotel room.

There were a few things I had to do before I could leave Hollywood, like selling the trailer. George had gone out on the road with Stan Kenton and it was up to me to dispose of our mobile love nest. I needed my share of the proceeds to get back East. Al Levy did what he could to help me and try to cheer me up. He sent roses to my cheap room at the Hollywood Plaza. He took me to dinner and oozed sympathy while I cried in my soup dish. His enthusiasm for my mythical future was undiminished, but as for my unmythical present, he had nothing concrete to offer me. I sat in my room and stared out the window, hours at a time, feeling nothing, seeing nothing, waiting for Al to sell the trailer so I could be on my way.

The evening of the third day Al phoned to say he had sold the trailer at a good price. "Now," he said, "you've got to get out of that room. There's a nice party tonight and I'd like to take you."

"Oh, thanks, Al," I said, "but I'm really not up to going to a party."

"Come on, it will do you good. Meet some people, have a few drinks, you can't just mope around there. . . ."

"I'm ready to go back East."

"I'll pick you up at eight and that's that!"

The party was at Jule Styne's house on Elm Drive in Beverly Hills. It was my first good look at the Beverly Hills houses with their beautifully manicured grounds. The trees and the flowers did indeed make me feel better than sitting in my hotel room. Most of the people at the party were entertainers—musicians and singers. There was good food and lots to drink and an air of jollity and good fellowship. I was glad I had come, until Jule Styne and Sammy Cahn and all of their friends started to get up and perform, one after the other; I began to get uneasy. These people loved singing for each other but I am painfully shy at parties, and particularly shy about performing impromptu as they were. Oh, God, I thought, I hope they don't ask me to stand up there and sing.

They did. When I tried to beg off, Sammy Cahn put his arm around me and guided me firmly over to the piano. Jule Style was at the keyboard. "Just a chorus of 'Embraceable You'—come on, it won't kill you." "Embraceable You." Every girl singer at every audition in Hollywood sang "Embraceable You." Jule started to play; I had no alternative but to sing. Before the evening was over, Jule, Sammy, and Al got me in a corner. They explained that Jule and Sammy had written the score for a musical, *Romance on the High Seas,* that was ready to go before the cameras at Warner Brothers, under the direction of a famous director, Michael Curtiz. They had written the score for Judy Garland, but the deal with her had fallen through. Then Betty Hutton had been set to play the lead, but they had just found out that she was pregnant and there was a frantic search on to find someone to replace her. How would I like to come to Warners in the morning and audition for the part? They were smiling at me in the expectation that I would jump out of my skin with delight.

"Well, I'm leaving in a day or so—"

"You're leaving!"

"Oh, she'll put it off, of course she'll put it off," Al Levy said.

"Who is Michael Curtiz?" I asked.

They told me.

"But you see, I'm a singer—I don't know a thing about acting, or movies."

"Leave her to me," Al promised. "I'll have her there in the morning."

Acting in films had never so much as crossed my mind. I was a singer and whatever talent I had was motivated toward that; even when Jerry and I had gone to Hollywood as a fledgling dance team, I had not given a thought to becoming a movie actress. But there was Al Levy, picking me up at my hotel the following morning and driving me to Warners for a screen test. All the way there, Al enthused about what a great director Curtiz was, how lucky I was to be testing for the *lead* in a major musical, how many girls would die to be in my shoes, but I was sitting there glumly looking out of the window, only half listening to him. Nothing mattered to me except my personal life and my personal life was a melancholy ruin. My mind was on George and Terry and how I would manage in New York. On what should have been a tremendously exciting morning, I was a study in abject despair.

Curtiz had his own bungalow on the Warners lot, a tribute to his eminence at the studio. I could tell from the furnishings that Mr. Curtiz was a man of good taste. Tall, handsome, expensively tailored, steel-gray hair, thick Hungarian accent.

"So what you do?" he asked. "You stand up in front of band and you sing?"

"Yes, when it's my turn to sing, I get up and sing, and then I sit down."

"You do that for whole evening?"

"Yes."

"You ever act?"

"No."

Al Levy was sitting beside me and he gave me a knock on the ankle with his shoe. "Well," Al said, "she went to elocution school."

I was in no mood to play games. My life at the moment was too bleak for that, and I was always one to show my true face. "Oh, I was only this big," I said. "No, I don't know a thing about acting."

"Would you like to be actress?"

"Oh, I suppose. I guess it might be interesting."

"Well, I am about to begin film—"

"Yes, I know."

"Do you think you'd like to be in movie?"

"To tell the truth, Mr. Curtiz, I'm on my way back to New York."

Al Levy's shoe was tattooing my ankle. "Of *course* she'd like to make a film, Mr. Curtiz. She'd *love* to make a film!"

"Well, truthfully, I don't really know if I'd love to or not, because I've never made a film. But I do have this four-week job in New York at the Little Club, and besides I'm pretty depressed because I've just separated from my husband and I've got to do something about my mother and little boy, who are in Cincinnati. They're waiting for me to pick them up."

Mr. Curtiz patiently listened to all this. "I see. Well, would you sing for me?"

"Where? Here?"

"Yes, the piano here. I have a man here will play. What you sing? 'Embraceable You'? He plays 'Embraceable You.' "

The last thing I felt like doing that morning was to sing, but I gave the pianist my key and started the song. I sang maybe six bars and then broke down completely, crying my eyes out, on the verge of hysteria. The lyrics of the song had gotten to me. My mascara was running, my nose was running. "Where is the ladies' room?" I blubbered. Mr. Curtiz showed me. I went in and couldn't stop crying. All the frustration and despondency and sadness—it must have taken me twenty minutes to get myself under control.

While I was gone, Curtiz said to Levy, "What's the matter with her—she sick?"

"No, no—she's fine!"

"Why she crying? Any other girl would be bubble with joy to get chance at movies."

"Well, you see, she's had some marital trouble. . . ."

Curtiz was relieved. "Oh, that—just so she's healthy," he said.

When I came back, Mr. Curtiz was smiling at me, just couldn't have been more understanding. "I'm sorry, Mr. Curtiz, I'm just going through a very bad experience. I don't think I'm the girl to brighten up your musical comedy. But if you'd like me to, I'll try the song again."

I got about halfway through this time, when again I broke down and started to cry. "I'm sorry, I shouldn't be taking up your time." I started to leave.

"I would like to test you for the part," he said. "Here, I give you script, you study, and day after tomorrow we do test."

"You mean, after all this, you're still going to test me?"

"You're very sensitive girl—to be good actress is to be sensitive."

I took the script. "What part?" I asked.

"The lead."

"How can I possibly be the lead? I haven't had any experience—I don't know how to act. That seems pretty crazy to me."

"You let me decide that."

Al Levy was having a heart attack.

"I sometimes like girl who is not actress," Curtiz said. "Is less pretend and more heart."

After we left I found out that Curtiz had already tested a hundred women for the part and planned to test fifty more, many of them established movie actresses with names. So I knew my chances were very slight. It would have been a help to know one end of a camera from the other. However, the test was really not of much importance to me. I was preoccupied with my busted marriage and all that went with it. Work has always been a secondary consideration to me, even later, when my career was so demanding.

Mr. Curtiz had given me three scenes to do, and in those scenes were two songs. I went over the script several times in my hotel room, and found that I memorized the material as quickly and easily as I had memorized lyrics for new Les Brown songs. The night before the screen test, I set the alarm for 5 A.M. and went to bed early. Whether you are a fledgling taking your first test or a big star, movie life begins at 6 A.M. in the makeup department—this was the first film commandment that Warner Brothers taught me.

While I was under the dryer, I fell sound asleep. The hairdresser had to poke me awake. "I never saw this happen before," she said, "and I've been here a long time. Usually they're so nervous we can't keep them under the dryer. Aren't you nervous?"

"No," I said.

"But this screen test may be the only chance you'll ever get."

"Well, however it goes is all right with me—either I get the part or I don't and there's nothing to be nervous about." Down in the dumps where I was, I could only ask myself, How important is this dumb screen test compared to what's happening to my life?

When Makeup finished with me and proudly showed me the results in the mirror, I dropped lower in the dumps. I think they were trying to make me look as much like Betty Hutton as they could. Stereotyped blonde. They had covered my freckles with an inch of guck that made me look as if I were wearing a mask, heavy eye makeup, lacquered hair piled up—just the reverse of what my makeup should have been.

Curtiz shot the test himself. Jack Carson was to be the star of the picture, but I did the test with an actor named Don McGuire, who couldn't have been nicer to me. The first time on a set is a rather overwhelming experience—I was startled by the number of technicians who are busily involved in the shooting of a simple scene. Breakaway walls and the camera traveling on its track and being told to move to precise marks on the floor while trying to remember lines and listen to directions were all rather baffling. But after a few minutes of induction, it all fell easily into place for me. I found I could enter a room and move easily to my floormark without actually looking for it. I felt a nice exhilaration at hearing the word "Action!" and then responding to the pressure of the rolling camera. It was effortless and thoroughly enjoyable. After the first shot, Curtiz did not tell me very much, but when we ran through my first song he suddenly dashed over and began to move me around the set rather frenetically. I was amused, because I immediately sensed what he was doing—trying to get me to sing in Betty Hutton's bouncy, energetic style. But when we shot the scene, I did it in my own way. I guess I instinctively understood something then that was to sustain me through all the years of acting that followed—to thine own self be true. Don't imitate. Don't try to imagine how someone else might feel. Project your honest response to your movie situation, quite the same as you would respond honestly to a life situation. I have never been one for artifice. It is a characteristic I despise. I am always exactly what I am, I always show exactly how I feel. If I am happy, I bloom with it. If I am depressed or grouchy, everyone around me knows it.

I really had a fine time doing my screen test but, being a realist, that afternoon I booked a reservation for Cincinnati and phoned my mother to tell her when I'd be there. Al Levy took me to dinner at the Brown Derby that evening and tried to cheer me up and talk me out of leaving, but my mind was made up. It would probably be weeks before Curtiz made a decision on the part, and if he was looking for a Betty Hutton type for the role, I sure wasn't it.

Late the following afternoon, I was in my room packing when the phone rang.

"Hello, is this Doris Day?"

"Yes."

"This is Jack Carson—"

"Oh, now, who's kidding who?"

"No, really. Don't you recognize my voice?"

"Well . . . I've seen you in a lot of pictures and it *sounds* like your voice. . . . Oh, come on, who is this?" I started to laugh.

"Now, listen, I'm Jack Carson—why wouldn't I be Jack Carson?"

"Honest to God?"

"Yes, and I'm calling you to tell you that your test was sensational. I just saw it and I wanted to call you and tell you myself."

"Oh . . . oh, aren't you nice! Was it *really?*"

"Have you really had no experience?"

"No, this was my first—"

"Well, I don't know if I'm talking out of school but I'm almost certain. . . . You haven't heard from anyone?"

"No, and I'm leaving for Cincinnati tonight."

"Miss Day, you're not going back to Cincinnati."

"Oh, sure, my mother and my little boy are waiting for me. I've given up my room here—"

"You're *not* going back to Cincinnati, Miss Day."

"I'm Doris."

"Doris, listen to me. You're not going back to Cincinnati. You're

95

going to stay here—a long time. I think you have that part in the picture. I want you in the picture and so do they."

"Do you think so? Do you really think so?"

"I'll see you soon. I just wanted you to know I'm happy for you."

A few minutes later, Al called me, doing a Highland fling somewhere in a phone booth. It was official. The part was mine.

Four

$\approx$

IN *Romance on the High Seas* I was Georgia Garrett, a singer in a sleazy nightclub where Oscar Levant is the pianist. During the day, I hang around the neighborhood travel agency because I have never been anywhere and I dream of going to faraway places. Into the travel agency comes rich Janis Paige, who is supposed to go on a fancy cruise but has decided not to because she is worried that her husband has a mistress. So she hits on the bright idea of having me go in her place so that she can stay in New York and spy on her husband. Meanwhile, her husband is just as suspicious of her faithfulness and he has hired a private eye, played by Jack Carson, to go on the cruise to spy on her—only it is me.

It was really quite funny, and above all, it had some marvelous songs: "It's Magic," "It's You or No One for Me," and a song that went, "Put 'em in a box, tie it with a ribbon, and throw it in the deep blue sea." This was 1948, before it was common to make albums of movie music, but I recorded "It's Magic" as a single and it had enormous success—well over a million in sales. It was at the top of "Your Hit Parade" for many weeks.

The first scenes scheduled to be shot took place aboard the cruise ship. When I came to the studio, I walked on the sound stage and asked when we'd be leaving for the boat. This broke everyone up. Of course, all the boat scenes were played right there on Stage 6 and we never saw a drop of water from one end of that cruise to the other; but in all those hundreds of movies I had seen back in Cincinnati, Hollywood's deviousness about such things had never occurred to me. Boats were on water. Airplanes were in the sky. Men in a trapped submarine were on the bottom. I discovered that in this deviousness is the essence of movie making: it's all real—and it's all make-believe.

My contract with Warners, riddled with the usual options, only provided a few hundred dollars a week, but that would have been enough to bring out Terry and my mother to live with me if I had had the time to look for a house and all that. But Curtiz went into immediate production, six days a week, and I had all I could do just keeping up with the demands of this strange new profession I had fallen into. I didn't even have that basic Hollywood necessity, a car— in fact, I didn't yet know how to drive.

In the evenings I usually ate alone in the Brown Derby across from my hotel. I was painfully lonely and my thoughts often went to George, wondering about him, out there on the road with the Stan Kenton band. I wondered if he ever thought about me. I still cried over him, or perhaps it was our failed marriage I was crying over.

At the start of the picture, I began taking lessons from the Warners acting coach, Sophie Rosenstein. But Curtiz soon put a stop to that. "Doris, I tell you about acting," he said. "Some people, the lessons are very good for them. But I tell you about you—you have very strong individual personality. No matter what you do on screen, no matter what kind part you play, it will always be you. What I mean is, the Doris Day will always shine through the part. This will make you big important star. You listen to me. Is very rare thing. You look Gable acting, Gary Cooper, Carole Lombard, they are playing different part but always is the same strong personality coming through. But you take other actors, maybe better actors, who become the character they are playing and lose all of themselves. They can be fantastic but big stars, never. Because there is not that personality, always there, that the audience identify with. Always there is Humphrey Bogart himself coming through every part he play. So with you. You have very, very strong personality. Is you. Is unique. That's why I don't want you to take lessons. You have a natural thing there in you, should no one ever disturb. You listen to me, Doris. Is very rare thing. Do not disturb."

From the first take onward, I never had any trepidation about what I was called on to do. Movie acting came to me with greater ease and naturalness than anything else I had ever done. Often before a take, despite all the pictures he had made, Jack Carson, jittery and on edge, would show me his hands, which were wet with nervous perspiration; I never had a qualm. Water off a duck's back. Curtiz would explain what he wanted in a scene, I would do it, and that would be that.

Traveling with Bob Hope made a nightmare of the airplane, but the radio broadcasts helped prepare Doris, shown here with Hope, Les Brown, and Hy Averback, for her transition into films.

With Terry during her band travels.

Doris on her first day on the set for her first movie role in *Romance on the High Seas*.

With Jack Carson, wearing the heavy Warner Bros. pancake make-up and lacquered hair she abhorred.

It's a Great Feeling had Jack Carson, Bill Goodwin, and Dennis Morgan in the cast but Jeffrey Bushfinkle stole the show.

During the making of the film, Jack Carson began taking me out, and I spent more and more time with him. He was divorced and lived in a beautiful home in Longridge out in the Valley. A couple who once worked with him in vaudeville lived there and took care of the house for him. Jack was a very sweet, considerate man whom I liked very much, but I wasn't in love with him. I spent a lot of time at his place and often stayed there with him, but Jack was a closed man who couldn't communicate. He was amusing and we got along very well, but I was just out of a marriage where there had been no communication and I wasn't about to repeat that mistake.

Perhaps Jack was in love with me. I don't know. He was basically a lonely man who drank too much. When he became too serious about us, I eased away from him and eventually stopped going with him. But I have fond memories of Jack, of how much fun we had at parties where he was comical and entertaining—but then when we got back to his place, he would often sit with a brandy bottle, the party spirit gone, lapsing into a kind of quiet sadness. My second picture, *My Dream Is Yours,* was also made with Jack, but after that we fell out of touch. Some years later, after a long and painful illness, he died of cancer.

Romance on the High Seas turned out very well. Curtiz immediately picked up my option and put me in his next picture. (I eventually made four pictures with Curtiz.) However, when I saw the first print of *Romance on the High Seas,* I was terribly disappointed. I couldn't imagine why the people at Warners were so enthusiastic about me. I hated the way I looked, especially my heavily pancaked face, and the horrendous hair. Curtiz had me wear a long blond wig and it looked just terrible. I'm a casual person and my whole manner is casual. I wear very little makeup and I let the freckles fall where they may. I've always worn my hair in a Dutch bob. But there I was on the screen, a pancaked, lacquered Hollywood purse made out of a Cincinnati sow's ear. As for my acting, I had the feeling then I have had every time I've ever had to sit through one of my own movies—I wanted to redo every shot. I always felt I could do a scene better than the one I was looking at.

But the one thing that really pleased me about my new career was that it made me into a lunch-bucket lady. The bell rings at noon, you go to lunch; the whistle blows at six, you go home. You have the evening to yourself. I love that kind of organized life. Probably my German upbringing. The chaotic, nighttime life of big-band singing just wasn't my dish. How many times I had been up there on the bandstand with a swinging orchestra, having trouble keeping myself awake!

One evening the phone rang and it was George Weidler. I was terribly pleased to hear his voice. Even though we were divorced by then, it had bothered me that we had parted so acrimoniously. I had been angry with him and as deeply hurt as one could be. I could not emotionally understand why he was ending our marriage. We had shouted at each other and argued like children. Later I reminded myself what negative feelings I had had on our way to our marriage, but that really didn't do much to assuage the hurt of rejection. I have never been one to shout or even raise my voice, except in joy, laughter, and ecstasy, but that parting with George had been a high-decibel yelling match.

So I was pleased to hear from him again because I was very fond of George and I didn't want our last exchange to be an ugly one. He asked me whether I'd like to have dinner and I unhesitatingly said yes. I was feeling positive again and I knew I could see George without getting upset. Or getting involved. My picture, although not yet released, was being highly touted at Warners. My second film, *My Dream Is Yours,* was about to get under way. I was looking for a little house where I could bring Terry and my mother. My social life was just fine—besides Jack Carson, and the usual constant attention of Al Levy, I had also been regularly dating Hal March, who was an amusing man and a good friend.

George never looked better. We were really happy to see each other again. We drove to a place on the beach to have dinner, and it seemed to me that George was much more open and communicative than he had been when we lived together. He seemed much more at peace with himself. I told him so. I noticed also that he was not smoking, and when we got to the restaurant he did not have a drink. We had both smoked heavily and drunk moderately, and his abstinence surprised me. I myself smoked about two and a half packages a day, and when I was singing with Les he constantly tried to get me to cut down because by the end of the evening my voice began to sound a little like Jimmy Durante's.

George and I had a lovely evening and spent the night together somewhere on the coast. He invited me to go with him to Balboa on the weekend, where he was playing with Stan Kenton's band.

That weekend we found a pretty little place, overlooking the water, and in the evening I went to the ballroom to hear the band. I

100

knew Stan and many of the musicians and it was fun being around band life again. The following day, George said, "You know, you've been saying I've changed and you've asked me about it. Well, it's really something I've found."

"What's that?"

"A way of life. I know that sounds pompous, but that's what it is—a way of life. It is something beyond your wildest imagination. It is the opposite, the complete opposite of everything you thought was true and real."

"What are you talking about?"

"I'm studying a religion."

"*You?* You, George? Why, you were always so antireligion, so . . . well, so *nothing.*"

"I know." We were driving to the ballroom. "I have a book with me, *the* book with me, and while we're working, during the intermissions, I usually come out to the car and read it. I just thought you might like to look at it." He handed me a small book. It was *Science and Health with Key to the Scriptures,* by Mary Baker Eddy.

"Why, that's the woman who doesn't believe in doctors!" I gasped. My Cincinnati upbringing had taught me that she was a sort of witch and that Christian Science was some kind of crazy ritual which caused you to end up sick and dying because you were forbidden to see a doctor. My first thought was, Oh, my God, if George is into this then that's the end of him. But then I thought, No, there must be something to it, because look how he has changed; how impressed I am with these qualities I see in him now that weren't there before.

So I said, "Yes, I'd like to look at the book."

"Only if you would *really* like to," he said. "I mean, don't do it just to please me. They don't like us just to hand the book around. That isn't the style of the people in this religion. It's very quiet. Very low-key."

"I'd like to read it," I said, "if for no other reason than to see what has brought about such a great change in you."

George went into the ballroom while I stayed in the car and started to read *Science and Health*. The first thing I came to was a little poem by Mary Baker Eddy:

> Oh! Thou hast heard my prayer;
>   And I am blest!
> This is Thy high behest:—
>   Thou here, and *everywhere.*

101

Something about its simplicity, its directness touched me. Then I read the first line of the text: "To those leaning on the sustaining infinite, to-day is big with blessings." This was such a far cry from the Latin and obscurity of Catholicism. It was aimed directly at me, simple language peeled down to the truth.

During intermissions George came out to the car. I asked him what "infinite" was, as used by Mrs. Eddy.

"That's God, or whatever you want to call God. The Maker, our Source. Something or someone had to create all of this around us. Whatever it is, that is what is sustaining. If you lean on that and know God and make your contact and come to know that oneness, you are automatically blessed."

I spent all that evening reading Mrs. Eddy's book, and during the weekend George and I discussed what I was reading. It was a weekend I shall never forget. For it brought spirituality into my life, a sense of real believing, an inner citadel. It was destined to change me even more than it had changed George, in the sense that I would find a spiritual purpose in my existence and in everything that exists around me. "There is no life, truth, intelligence, nor substance in matter," I read. "All is infinite Mind and its infinite manifestation, for God is All-in-all. Spirit is immortal Truth; matter is mortal error. Spirit is the real and eternal; matter is the unreal and temporal. Spirit is God, and man is His image and likeness. Therefore man is not material; he is spiritual."

They were words of gleaming light that I did not fully understand, but they were to become beacons that would lead me to a spirituality of my own. A spirituality that would sustain me through some very dark times in the years ahead.

The only sad thing that happened during this period was that I had to give up my dear friend and agent, Al Levy. No one had ever cared more about my well-being. There was nothing Al wouldn't do for me; he had an unshakable belief in my talent and my future, and I was very fond of him.

Al was one of those men who looked older than he was. Baldish but with beautiful white-flecked hair at his temples, splendid clear eyes, expansive white-toothed smile. Lovely sense of humor. Never married, he said his job was his wife. When *Romance on the High Seas* was shooting, he was on the set every day. We had dinner a couple nights a week. Al got me a car through a friend of his and helped me look for a house. He was always willing to discuss my problems with me, and to offer solace when I was blue and weepy.

So I was truly nonplussed when Curtiz called me into his office one day during the shooting of *Romance* and asked, "What does Al Levy mean to you?"

"Why, he's my dearest friend—why do you ask?"

"Well, I'm telling you something you probably don't know. When he comes to studio he comes onto set through side door and goes up on catwalk and watches you from up there. The crew members have seen him up there many times. Then later he makes regular entrance to set."

"Well, maybe he just likes to watch from that angle—"

"I don't think so. Al know you are seeing Jack Carson?"

"Of course, of *course* he does. Oh, Al's like a father to me."

"Okay. Just so you know. Me, I like Al very much. But maybe you keep the eyes open, all right?"

Not long after that, when I came into the lobby of my hotel one night after a date with Hal March, I noticed, among the people sitting in the lobby, a man with a newspaper in front of his face who was unmistakably Al Levy. I could tell from the shoes, hands, clothes that it was Al, but he was obviously trying to hide so I pretended not to notice him.

From then on, every time I came into the lobby, I looked for him; and often I spotted him, hiding behind his newspaper, obviously spying on me. It was just too embarrassing a situation to mention to him. But then one evening it all came to a head in a most unpleasant way. I had gone to dinner with Al, and afterward he was to drive me to a friend's house for the weekend, a woman named Lee Levine, who shared my beginning interest in Christian Science. Al drove me back to the hotel so I could pick up my bag, but instead of waiting in the lobby, as he always did, this time he got into the elevator with me. He followed me into my room, closed the door, turned off the lights, and pulled me onto the bed. He desperately thrust himself on top of me as if he were some unknown rapist and I were an anonymous victim.

It was a frightening moment for me, trying to overcome this berserk attack by someone I liked. I kept pleading with him, trying to reach him, saying what I had to say; and finally he heard and rolled away from me, sobbing.

"This is a very unfair thing to do," I told him. "I don't need an-

103

other trauma in my life. I really don't. You know what I've been through. If you want to talk about something, talk, but I don't need this physical rough stuff. Look at the position you put me in."

After a long pause he said, "I love you, you must know how much I love you and I just . . . well, couldn't handle it anymore. I want to marry you, Doris. I didn't mean for it to come out this way, but that you prefer to spend a weekend with a girl friend instead of me . . ."

I told him that there was no hope of any such relationship with him. I made it as strong as I could, but all the way to Lee's he kept saying, "There's no chance? Are you sure? Maybe if you slept with me you'd feel different. I won't give up. I can't. You're all I think about. The way I care about you . . . you'll never get a husband like me."

I was desolate because obviously our relationship was ruined, and Al had been an important person in my life. Not just as an agent, but as a person. Over the next few weeks, I began receiving anonymous letters on blue stationery, written by a woman who told me what a fool I was not to marry Al. When Al was in New York on business, I received letters from this anonymous woman telling me that Al had met some young beauty but that if I really went after him it was still not too late.

Al continued to spy on me—in the lobby, at the studio, even in restaurants where I'd be having dinner with a date. Finally, I went to his partners at Century Artists, Dick Dorso and Marty Melcher, and I told them why it was impossible for me to continue a client-agent relationship with Al. They said the situation was going to solve itself since Al was being sent to New York to run their office there, and Marty would become my agent. Marty Melcher was then married to Patty Andrews of the Andrews Sisters. I had seen him on occasion and found him to be a bright, affable man who seemed organized and competent.

George was traveling with the Stan Kenton band but I saw him quite often on his frequent returns to Los Angeles, where the band was based. We liked each other and had a fine time together and George began to talk about how our relationship had changed. "We could have now what we couldn't achieve before," he said. "I had so much pride then, and I was jealous, I guess, of the success I knew you were going to have, just afraid of being swallowed up by all that. But all that false insecure stuff like pride has gone out of me. I am learning the meaning of love—spiritual love. Before, love was purely a physical thing, materialistic like everything else. Now, if we were married, I really think it would work."

For me, however, although there was still a strong physical attraction and I enjoyed sleeping with George, I no longer had the kind of feelings toward him that would have made for a marriage. Something was over. That phase of my life was finished. There had been a wrenching, a tearing, a healing, from which I had learned a great deal about myself. Now it was time to move on. "I really think that we should stay just as we are," I told him. "No reason we can't go on seeing each other. We enjoy that. You're traveling and I'm busy with my work. Soon my child will be here with me. I like you, George —maybe I still love you, but I don't think we have the makings of a marriage anymore."

Five

〰〰〰〰〰〰〰〰〰〰〰〰〰〰〰〰〰〰〰〰〰〰〰〰〰〰〰〰〰〰〰〰〰〰

IN between my first and second pictures at Warners, I put in a couple of tours of duty as a member of Bob Hope's concert and radio troupe. It was a frightening, educational, exhausting, enjoyable, depressing experience.

Over a six-week period, the concert tour took us, by a United Air Lines DC-6, to a different city every night—and sometimes, when we played a matinee, to two cities in a single day. This was in the winter of 1948 and we often flew through storms and turbulence that had me praying more than once. We made landings where I couldn't see the airfield until I was on the ground; sometimes the pilot had to circle a few times to find the landing strip.

Then when we thankfully got off the plane, there would invariably be a mob of people waiting at the bottom of the steps. Bob was first off and I was in back of him with my hands full of traveling gear; as his fans moved in and mobbed Bob, I'd always get clobbered by the backwash of his faithful, virtually shoved off the steps, and an hour or so later, still spooked by the harrowing airplane ride and the clobbering fans, I'd have to go out on the stage of whatever mammoth auditorium we were playing with my pipes in good condition and my personality bubbling. I really learned what the expression "tough it like a trouper" means. By the time I finished my second fifteen-thousand-mile concert tour with Bob, I had developed a chronic fear of flying that haunts me to this day.

On the positive side, I learned a great deal from performing skits with Bob, who is the undisputed master of timing and delivery, which are the very essence of comedy. We were very good together, and I must admit there is something peculiarly rewarding about generating laughs from a live audience. Bob himself was a joyous man to be around. He radiated good cheer and he's very funny on his own—in fact, funnier than when he's restricted to his writers' material. There's something quite pixie about him, his mischievous face, the way his teeth take over his face when he smiles. And the way he swaggers across the stage, kind of sideways, beaming at the audience, spreading good cheer. Good cheer is a part of Bob whether on stage or off; just watching him work makes you feel good. Someone once wrote that about me, that I spread good cheer, and I think it's the nicest thing ever written about me. Of course, the way my life went I was crying a lot of the time, but if I somehow managed to perform cheerfully, and that came across, so much the better.

When the tour ended, we did a weekly radio show out of Hollywood, sponsored by Lever Brothers Swan soap. My overriding memory of those shows was how much time I spent in the toilet. I had by then developed a real aversion to live radio, and before every performance one end of me or the other would erupt. Bob would be out on the stage warming up the audience and I would be flat out in my dressing room, moaning to my agent and the producer that I couldn't go on, that I had to be taken off the show, that I couldn't do it, that I couldn't go out there and face all those people—and *sing!* Going out and reading the lines in a skit was easy, at least for me, but to sing when you're upset and nervous—that's a whole other thing, because you don't have the control and dominance over your voice that you must have, and you don't sing well.

The pattern of the radio show was that I would sing a song, usually a ballad like "Someone Like You" or "It's Magic," and then Bob and I would play a sketch. The sketches were only intermittently funny and it was primarily Bob's comedy skill and the eagerness of the studio audience to laugh that brought them off. This sketch we performed on a March 22, 1949, broadcast, is a pretty good sample of what constituted big-time radio humor of its day:

DORIS:	I'm certainly surprised to see you here in Palm Springs at the Racquet Club, Bob. Are you a member?
HOPE:	No, I used to be, but I was thrown out in disgrace . . . it was over gambling.
DORIS:	You mean you were cheating at cards?
HOPE:	No . . . they caught me playing Ping-Pong with a loaded Ping. But it's nice here by the pool, isn't it?
DORIS:	Yes, Bob, but at a fashionable place like this, don't

	you think you should wear a more modern bathing suit?
HOPE:	I have had this quite a long time.
DORIS:	Bob, in a suit like that how can you get a tan?
HOPE:	Oh, you'd be surprised how much sun filters through those buttonholes. It still fits me pretty good.
DORIS:	Yes, but what causes all that lumpiness in the back?
HOPE:	My street clothes . . . they charge a dollar here for a locker. I don't care whether I'm in style or not . . . if I say so myself, I'll compare physiques with anybody . . . just look at the hair on my chest.
DORIS:	Where?
HOPE:	Right there . . .
DORIS:	Yes, they do make a lovely couple.
HOPE:	Well, I had three, but the wind was awfully strong yesterday. Gee, I love staying here at the Racquet Club, Doris . . . I've been here four days now and it hasn't cost me a penny.
DORIS:	I don't see why you didn't register like the other celebrities do . . . Look at Clark Gable. He's got a seventy-five-dollar-a-day suite . . . Van Johnson has a cabana that costs fifty dollars a day . . .
HOPE:	What about it?
DORIS:	Well, sooner or later they're going to find out that you're living under the kitchen window in a wigwam.
HOPE:	I'm just trying to save a little money.
DORIS:	I don't mind your saving money, but aren't you carrying it too far . . . painting your face with Mercurochrome and selling beaded moccasins?
HOPE:	They're going like hot cakes . . . and Doris, that thing I'm living in is not a wigwam . . . it's a tent . . . I made it myself.
DORIS:	Well, it's the funniest-looking tent I ever saw.
HOPE:	That's because I didn't have much to work with . . . just Gary Cooper's hat rack, and a suit of Sydney Greenstreet's underwear . . . but it's nice . . . on a clear day I can see Catalina through the flap.
DORIS:	Oh, look, Bob, there's a waiter with some hors d'oeuvres . . . let's have some.
HOPE:	Wait a minute, Doris . . . it might cost something . . . and everything around here is so high-priced . . .
DORIS:	Who cares? [up] Oh, waiter . . .
HY AVERBACK:	[British] Did you wish some hors d'oeuvres, Miss?
DORIS:	Yes . . . what do you have there?
HY:	Well, I have some delicious sturgeon eggs . . . they're twelve dollars . . . and these little anchovy

	tails are six dollars . . . and here's a special delicacy we have today for only fifteen dollars . . . they're sardines' ears.
HOPE:	What makes them so expensive?
HY:	Well, after we cut the ears off the sardines, they become deaf so naturally we have to buy them those little hearing aids.
HOPE:	I don't think we care for anything right now.
HY:	By the way, sir, if you'll pardon my saying so . . . haven't I seen you someplace before?
HOPE:	Well, it's possible . . . I'm quite a globe-trotter . . . was it the famous Flamingo Club on the French Riviera? . . . Or perhaps the Singapore Spa in the English section of Bombay?
HY:	No, now I remember—you sold me some moccasins under the kitchen window.

Now it's pretty apparent that that is not a particularly funny script, but after each of those broadcasts, some good, some bad, Bob's staff would circle around him and tell him what a dynamite show it was. Week after week they'd squeal with delight after every show and Bob preened in the glow of their hyperbole.

It taught me a lesson I never forgot. I knew very well that some of those shows were quite awful. Allegedly funny lines that weren't funny at all. And I couldn't believe that Bob, wise about show business as he is, didn't know it—but I guess it was easier for him to defer his judgment to the uncritical accolades of his aides. But when I got to the point in my career where I had some say-so about my movie scripts, and particularly later on when I had my own television show, I listened only to my own inner voice and never to those around me who used nothing but superlatives. I never needed that kind of reassurance. Nobody can make me believe what I don't feel. What's good registers "up" inside me, and what's bad registers "down"—that's the reality I've always dealt with.

BOB HOPE

When I think about all the performers I've been associated with over the course of my fifty-odd years on the stage, on radio and television, in the movies, whatever, when I think about *natural talent* I'd have to rate ladies at the forefront—Doris Day and Judy Garland. When Doris first came to work with me, her background was very limited—a gal who had sung in front of a band—but she acted in sketches like she'd been doing it all her life. Great comedy timing, one of the difficult accomplishments in show business—and it came to Doris as easy and natural as that great smile of hers.

I consider Doris one of the great singers, and to put across a ballad, which is a dramatic story with music, believe me, anybody who can do that like Doris did has a great sense of timing. I've watched singers all my life, I've worked with most of the good ones, and I found that the ones who can put across a ballad can also perform without the music. Bing Crosby is another example of someone who could do it all. But what knocked me out was that in the second year she was with me, Marty Melcher came to me and announced that Doris would sing no more ballads on my radio show. Only bouncy numbers. Apparently he had decided that he could get a better price for Doris if she had a bouncy image. It broke my heart—she was so great with ballads—but there was no way to make Melcher change his mind. I always had a feeling, when Melcher was around, that he wasn't looking out for Doris as much as he was looking out for himself. Needless to say, he wasn't one of my favorite characters.

But Doris was and still is one of my favorite people. I used to call her "Jut-Butt"—I'd say, "You know, J.B., we could play a nice game of bridge on your ass." A truly great body and she was wonderful about taking my kidding. I always called her "J. B." on the radio show but only the band knew what the initials stood for. We had our moments on those tours. Fifty towns in fifty days, with a few hair-raisers along the way. I'll never forget coming into Pittsburgh on instruments with no visibility, and as we got down to where the runway was supposed to be, there wasn't any runway! The pilot gunned our plane for all it was worth and just pulled us out of there in the nick of time. He made it on the second try. I had just made a movie, *Paleface,* and I said to Doris, "You want to see a real paleface—take a look."

There was the time we played Oklahoma City when it was hit by a severe snow storm. Doris had a thing about snow. A passion. She made me promise to go for a sleigh ride after the show. And, by George, when we left the stage door that night there was a huge sleigh with horses, and we all piled on, the entire band, everyone, and we went right down the main drag of Oklahoma City. Never a dull moment with J. B.

Another time, we came into Little Rock and the advance man met us at the airport and asked us to perform for a hospital before we did our regular show. Just Doris and I went to the hospital. They had everybody in the auditorium and I came out and started my routine, sure-fire jokes, but I was getting no response. None. I took a closer look at the audience and saw that there were attendants sitting next to the patients. From my experience I realized that this was a mental hospital and that the patients were so far down into depression that they couldn't relate to jokes. So I introduced Doris in a hurry, knowing that if anyone could lift an audience, she could. And she did. A couple of songs and she had turned those patients into an audience at the Paramount.

It's a crying shame that Doris has this thing about not appearing before live audiences, because on a stage, I can tell you, she lights up the house. She has that rare quality of making people feel good by just walking on—whatever she radiates lifts them. And when she sings a ballad, and you're there, she can break your heart.

Six

~~~~~~

IN the course of the seven years I was under contract to Warner Brothers, from 1948 to 1955, I made a total of seventeen pictures, all but two of them musicals. In between pictures and the publicity tours they required, I somehow managed to squeeze in time to prepare and record a steady output of singles and albums.

I can assure you that this hectic schedule was not of my doing. In those days, a contract performer was subject to the demands of the studio, and if there was a new script waiting for you the day you finished shooting your current one, then into your new picture you went without stopping to draw breath. There were no such things as rehearsals, and location shooting was very rare. It was simply a question of going from one sound stage to another, from one contract director to another. Four of my pictures were directed by Michael Curtiz, six by David Butler, three by Roy Del Ruth, and these men went from one picture to the next with no more time to prepare than I had.

With pictures assigned to me one after the other, I found myself performing with the same Warner Brothers actors over and over again. Three pictures with Jack Carson, five with Gordon MacRae, two with Ronald Reagan, four with Gene Nelson, and so on. A major studio was really a big repertory company that constantly shuffled its employees around so as to keep them busy as much of the time as possible. Jack Warner did not like to pay an actress for two weeks while she basked beside her pool waiting for the sets to be built. Producers were kept on the treadmill along with everyone else—six of my films were produced by William Jacobs, and two each by Alex Gottlieb, Jerry Wald, and Henry Blanke. When a performer was handed a script it was already in production, and that precluded any of today's refine-

111

ments such as rewriting lines and scenes that certainly needed it. One made do with whatever one had been given; studio control (a euphemism for the spy system) was such that if a contract actor wanted a line improved, he had to ask his contract director, who, if he agreed with the needed improvement, had to call in his contract producer, who knew that if he allowed the director to allow the actor to substitute words he could manage to speak for the tongue twisters that were in the script, the producer could expect to be summoned to Jack Warner's office within ten minutes of his misdemeanor. It was well-known that Mr. Warner registered violent objection to any tampering with a script that he had approved, so all things considered, the producer would tell the director to tell the tongue-tied actor to do the best he could with the words at hand.

Of course, in the beginning it never occurred to me to do anything but perform the script as written and as directed. It was fortunate for me that my first three movies, *Romance on the High Seas, My Dream Is Yours,* and *It's a Great Feeling,* were with Jack Carson; he helped me enormously with my technical indoctrination into movie acting. He taught me dozens of tricks about how to move to precise camera marks without actually looking for them, how to handle myself in close-ups so that my face or profile rather than the back of my head would be in a shot, how to sustain the evenness of a performed scene so that when I repeated it for various angle takes, each succeeding performance would precisely match what I had done in the master shot. There were so many little things that Jack patiently explained to me, demonstrated, rehearsed with me. Since we were going together, we'd often discuss some of these things in the evening, and there's no doubt that my relationship with Jack helped me considerably in my early going. Not just for the movie technique I learned from him, but Jack helped assuage my loneliness, my feeling of being an outsider, and thanks to him I was more able to cope with the strenuous new demands being made on me.

It's a Great Feeling wasn't much of a picture, as I dimly recall it, but it had a great ending, which is the one thing about it I remember very well. I played a hayseed girl from remote Gurkey's Corners who comes to Hollywood to become a star—at that time the All-American dream of every girl in the country. I get a job at Warner Brothers as a waitress in the Commissary, and the picture is preoccupied by my attempts to get some big shot at the studio to give me my big chance. Jack Carson and Dennis Morgan, who played themselves, are the primary targets of my pursuit. I work at various studio jobs like running the elevator, trying to catch someone's eye, but after much effort, primarily focused on Jack, I am finally convinced that no one is going to come through for me. My only alternative is to pack my bags and go back to Gurkey's Corners and marry my local fiancé, Jeffrey Bushfinkle.

But unbeknownst to me, Jack has been working on my behalf and has finally gotten an okay for me to appear with him in a picture —but of course when he comes looking for me, he discovers that I have packed up and gone off to my dreary fate of becoming Mrs. Jeffrey Bushfinkle. At that point, Jack grabs a plane and rushes to Gurkey's Corners to head off my marriage, but he arrives at the church just as I am at the altar with Jeffrey Bushfinkle and we are saying our "I do's". Our backs are to the camera. Jack is looking in the church window. We turn to face each other as Jeffrey raises my veil to kiss me. Jack falls out of the window as the camera moves in on Jeffrey Bushfinkle, who is Errol Flynn.

As I said, after only a few pictures I came to realize that in movie acting I had found my niche—that which came naturally. It wasn't just the pleasure of being a lunch-bucket lady with regular daytime hours—it was that I felt very real in the make-believe parts I had to play. I felt what the script asked me to feel. I enjoyed playing and singing for the cameras and I guess that enjoyment came through on the screen, somehow communicated itself to the audience and made them feel good too. I had never felt "myself" on a bandstand singing for a ballroom full of dancers; or standing in front of a radio mike singing "Sentimental Journey" for the five thousandth time. But acting for the camera was an immediate love affair. When the camera turned, instead of suffering the agonies that always preceded radio and stage appearances, I easily and rather happily responded to whatever was demanded of me; I had no inhibitions, no doubts, no hang-ups.

I enjoyed singing for films because it wasn't the impromptu business of standing in front of a ballroom band or a radio audience and hoping that that one shot, despite all its distractions, would approximate my best effort. Although a movie song is filmed on the set during its performance, the song itself is prerecorded in a recording studio under ideal conditions before the picture ever starts. In the solitude of a room with perfect acoustics, I could record a song as many times as necessary to get it right. Of course, when you film a song it is necessary to sing the song in perfect synchronization with

113

the way you previously recorded it so that your lips move at precisely the right time. Later on in my career, I often recorded without an orchestra. This was achieved by having the orchestra put its accompaniment on a track; then, alone in the studio, by means of a headset, I would sing to that prerecorded accompaniment. I like that method for films and albums best of all because of the flexibility it gives me in allowing me to record on a day of my choosing, when I know my voice is in good shape. But every artist, including me, does her best work when she can feel the band's presence.

But there was a time I shook up a studio by asking that a song be recorded as I was performing it before the camera. This is virtually never done because it's extremely difficult to get a decent sound quality on an overhead boom mike while a performer is moving around a stage. But in 1957, in *Pajama Game*, I had to sing "Hey, There!" while crying, and in a manner that was so involved with the action (I felt it was more of a scene than just a song) that I thought it could not be properly synched if it were prerecorded in the studio in the usual way. There was the expected studio resistance to this innovation but I insisted (my seven-year indenture to Warner Brothers had ended and I had some clout by then), and from the way the song turned out in the picture, I was very glad I did.

Toward the end of 1949, I was assigned to a picture, *Young Man with a Horn,* which was a significant change from the first ones I had made. Although a musical, it was a realistic depiction of the life of the great trumpet player Bix Biederbecke. This was not cheerful comedy but a strong drama played against the background of nightclubs and one-night stands. Kirk Douglas and Lauren Bacall were in the cast, and I keenly anticipated performing with them, but it turned out to be a very upsetting experience for me since it carried me back into the band world, and the sets and dialogue stirred up memories I was trying to forget. The realistic scenes with Kirk as Biederbecke, the trumpet player, brought the ghost of Al Jorden into my life again, and many nights during that picture I went home depressed and miserable. I even found it painful to sing some of the old songs I had sung in my early band days.

But the picture itself was successful, and the album that I cut for Warner Brothers records which bore the name of the picture was also successful. One of the few pleasures connected with that picture was that I got to know Hoagy Carmichael, who played the part of a piano player in the nightclub where I worked. The composer of "Stardust" and other great standards, Hoagy had always been someone I had admired, and getting to meet him and perform with him was a pleasure—a sweet, low-key, unassuming, amusing man.

Happily, my *Young Man with a Horn* depression was quickly dispelled by my next picture, a lighthearted musical called *Tea for Two* which was as enjoyable as any picture I ever made. It was my first movie with Gordon MacRae and Gene Nelson, two cheerful, amusing men, and with a funny, warmhearted man who was destined to become a close friend, the marvelous comic Billy De Wolfe. One day on the set, Billy announced that Doris Day was not suitable as a name for me and promptly christened me Clara Bixby, which is what a lot of my friends call me to this day. Billy said I was much more a Clara Bixby than a Doris Day, and he was right.

Also in *Tea for Two* was a fat, lovable, Viennese character actor named S. Z. Sakall, who had been in my first two pictures. He had three chins (or perhaps four, depending on the tilt of his head), a belly that jiggled outrageously when he laughed, and more acting tricks than a dog act in a Viennese circus. Everyone called him Cuddles, and rightly so. Every day his wife came to the set to have lunch with him. She brought a huge wicker hamper from which emerged the most elegant repast you ever saw—snowy-white damask linen, polished silver, vintage wine, and five or six courses that would have made the *Michelin* sit up and take notice.

Cuddles was a delight to work with, but he did cause a major disturbance every morning that he was on the set. I'd be in my dressing room when suddenly a chorus of protesting voices would rend the studio air and I would laugh, knowing that Cuddles had arrived and was in makeup. The cries of distress emanated from the makeup people as they chased Cuddles around the set, trying to corner him to finish his makeup. They rarely succeded for, fat as he was, Cuddles was an artful dodger who had had a lot of practice over the years evading makeup men. Cuddles did not mind having his face made up, but he reared up and bolted at any attempt to put makeup on his neck or ears. Neck makeup, he explained to me, imperiled his shirt collar, and he was convinced that makeup in his ear would somehow seep into the auditory canal and make him hard of hearing.

The makeup department, on the other hand, was in just as big a sweat to swab his neck and ears, for they knew only too well how Jack Warner felt on the subject. In fact, there were three things guaranteed to bring down the wrath of J.W.—bow ties, yawns, and no

115

makeup on the neck or inside the ear. It was said that Jack cared more about a ring around the neck than about a performance. Certainly the quickest way for an actor to get his option dropped would have been to appear on screen in a bow tie, yawning and with a circle of white in the center of his ear. But somehow Cuddles never got nailed. Probably the camouflage of all those chins.

In my years at Warners, I only had one serious encounter with Jack Warner. I had been to a few parties at his house and had seen him casually on the lot, but the only time we had a confrontation was over a script I had been given that I thought was pretty bad. It was the custom at Warners that when an actress was given a script she didn't want to do, she simply refused to work and took a suspension on her contract. She couldn't work for any other company and she was off salary, but sooner or later the studio relented and gave her another picture to do. I didn't want to do this—I felt that my contract obliged me to perform, but I asked my agents to tell Jack Warner how I felt about the script.

As a result they took me to see Jack Warner, the only time I can remember being in his cavernous, rococo office. I no sooner mentioned the script than he took off on me. "So you're a big star already," he shouted in that gruff voice of his. "She's made a coupla pictures and already she's telling the front office how to run the studio."

"Now, Mr. Warner, that's not fair, it's just that I want to do my best and this script—"

"Listen to who's an expert on scripts! I've got people here I pay five times what you're getting and they've okayed this script and you're coming in here and telling me how to run my business, that it? Where do you think you get off? Every nickel actor on the lot wants to come in here and tell me how to run my business."

I tried to say something but he wouldn't let me get a word in edgewise. By now it was just a humiliating harangue and I was reduced to tears. I have never thought of myself as a star. I'm a working lady who tries to be as good as she can at what she does. But "star" is a hokey word. I don't know what it means. If I'm a star then the expert upholsterer who does my couch is a star.

"You just do what you're told to do," Jack Warner raved, "and let those of us who know the movie business take care of things, you understand?"

There are things about Marty Melcher, Doris's third husband, that she doesn't understand to this day.

With Kirk Douglas in *Young Man with a Horn*.

Ginger Rogers was Doris's idol, and appearing with her in *Storm Warning* was a dream come true.

Once established at Warners, Doris bought a house and for the first time was able to live with Terry.

Cuddles Sakall, shown here in *Lullaby of Broadway,* appeared in four movies with Doris, with defiantly white ears.

Billy de Wolfe changed Dori name to Clara Bixby and, over t years, became one of her deare friends.

Doris had not danced since her train accident, but Gene Nelson got her going again.

"The guys who look at Doris on the screen," James Garner says, "and think she's the girl next door would love to ravage her but they wouldn't dare admit it."

For a while Doris dated Ronald Reagan, shown here in *The Winning Team*. He liked to take her dancing, she liked the view from his apartment.

When Danny Thomas sang "Pretty Baby" to Doris at her maternity bedside in *I'll See You In My Dreams,* it triggered a weepy emotional response out of Doris's own life.

Doris and Ray Bolger got along fine in *April in Paris,* but Bolger and the director were something else.

Doris made a series of nostalgic musicals—this one is *On Moonlight Bay*—that undoubtedly contributed to her image as Miss Goody Two-Shoes, America's Virgin.

I carried my tears out of there, blaming my agents more than Jack Warner. They must have known about him. They should never have subjected me to that, and I told them so. As a matter of fact, as the years went on and I got to know Jack Warner, I realized that the gruff, rough, snapping exterior was mainly a facade and that he was a pleasant, amusing man. But it was an experience that taught me something. After that, whenever I encountered a Jack Warner, I turned on my heel and left. I never suffered rudeness again.

In those Warner Brothers years, the pictures I enjoyed the most (not the scripts but the fun I had making them) were the nostalgic musicals—*Tea for Two, Lullaby of Broadway, On Moonlight Bay, I'll See You in My Dreams, By the Light of the Silvery Moon, Calamity Jane.* I liked the old songs, and the good old times that those films captured. I guess I'm really an old-fashioned girl at heart, even though I look so contemporary that I always seemed misplaced in those period costumes.

My guess is that it was this succession of cheerful, period musicals, plus Oscar Levant's widely publicized remark about my virginity, that contributed to what has been called my "image," which is a word that baffles me. There was never any intent on my part either in my acting or in my private life to create any such thing as an image, but I suppose that whatever there is of me that shines through on the screen looks wholesome and virgin-y. I don't think anybody would have believed me if I had been cast in the role of the mistress whore Mildred (the Bette Davis role) in *Of Human Bondage.* Just as I don't think an audience would ever have accepted Gary Cooper as a bad guy. A producer could have put bad-guy words in Coop's mouth, plunked a black hat on his head, and put him on a black horse but nobody would have *believed* him as the villain. Just as nobody would believe Jack Palance with a white hat on a white horse with good-guy words coming out of *his* mouth. I think that Marlon Brando is one of the few actors who can play good guy or bad guy, whereas George Scott can play drunks or angry misfits and yet he always comes through on the good guy side of the fence.

What I am trying to say is that as actors we put ourselves into the guise of a role we are called upon to play, and we perform it as honestly as we possibly can; but we have no control over whatever the result of that acting projects upon an audience—if we did try to

117

exercise this kind of control, the result, I am sure, would be artificial. I never think about what the public expects of me; I am only concerned with what I expect of myself.

So much for my image.

Not all of my Warners pictures were cheerful nostalgia. In 1951, the producer Jerry Wald came to me with a script called *Storm Warning* and asked me if I thought I could play a serious dramatic part. *Storm Warning* already had Ginger Rogers, Ronald Reagan, and Steve Cochran in the cast. Ginger Rogers! My idol from my Cincinnati movie days. The part offered to me was that of Ginger's kid sister in a drama about the Ku Klux Klan in a small southern town, a hard-hitting indictment of the Klan's savage bigotry. I didn't hesitate in accepting it.

What intrigued me most about Ginger Rogers was the assured way in which she handled herself. She was one of the top stars in Hollywood at that time, and unlike performers under contract, she was under no compunction to keep her feelings under wraps. She arrived at the stage door in her chauffeur-driven limousine with her secretary at her side, but there was nothing grand about her manner or her attitude toward the cast and crew. However, from the moment she set foot on the set, she really ran the show. She was very knowledgeable about the script and she sent for the writers quite often to have conferences with them in her dressing room. I could see that it was one thing for Jack Warner to chastise an indentured neophyte like me for having criticized a script, but quite another when a superstar was involved.

As far as the picture itself was concerned, I found that playing a serious dramatic role (I was a waitress whose truck-driver husband, unbeknownst to her, was a muscleman for the Klan) was no more difficult than playing a comedy role in a musical; if there was a difference, it was perhaps that in the musicals I played a bit more broadly.

Once we got to know each other, Ginger and I had a good time doing the picture—she's a laugher, as am I. Also, she was a devout Christian Scientist who always had a copy of the *Sentinel* in her hand when she wasn't on camera. My blossoming interest in Christian Science gave me a certain feeling of kinship with her.

Shortly after *Storm Warning* was released, I was coerced into going to the kind of splashy Hollywood party that I usually avoided. I am really not very good at parties—shyness, I guess. Whatever it is, I usually drift off to a corner, where I stay until it's time to go home.

And that's what I did at this one. Snug in a corner, gratefully over-looked, not having to talk to anyone, until slowly, painfully, I realized that there had been standing in the corner beside me, as immobile as I, Mr. Alfred Hitchcock, the noted director. I had heard he was the shyest man in L.A. but after we stood there silently for a while, I think he realized that in me he had met his match.

"You are Doris Day, are you not?" he said in that precise English way of his, and I almost fainted. He turned his head to look at me. "You can act," he said, quite forcefully. Long pause while I tried to think of something to say, but couldn't.

"I saw you in *Storm Warning*. Good, very good. I hope to use you in one of my pictures." I think I muttered "Thank you" as he moved off to an unoccupied corner. I didn't again hear from Mr. Hitchcock for almost six years, but his pronouncement in the corner that evening was one that I treasured. And the movie we eventually made, *The Man Who Knew Too Much*, with "Que Sera, Sera" as its theme song, was well worth the wait.

Seven

〰〰〰〰〰〰〰〰〰〰〰〰〰〰〰〰〰〰〰〰〰〰〰〰〰〰〰〰〰

ON April 3, 1951, my twenty-seventh birthday, I married Marty Melcher, my agent. After Marty had taken over when Al Levy had been eased to New York, for a long time our relationship was strictly that of client and agent. Marty was married to Patty Andrews, of the Andrews Sisters, and I was seeing several men—Jack Carson, occasionally my ex-husband, George Weidler, when his band was in town, and Ronald Reagan, with whom I made two movies, *Storm Warning* and, later on, *The Winning Team,* in which Ronnie portrayed Grover Cleveland Alexander, the great pitcher for the 1926 St. Louis Cardinals, and I played his wife.

During *Romance on the High Seas,* I had become good friends with my hairdresser at the studio, and she suggested that it would be more pleasant for me to leave my hotel room and go to live with her and her husband while I was looking for a house. By curious coincidence, her house was located directly in back of Marty Melcher's house. She and I often went over to Marty's to play volleyball on Sunday morning, but, as I say, although I saw a lot of Marty, it was strictly business. He had negotiated my movie and record salaries up to around two thousand a week, and he was a very sympathetic listener during those long stretches when I felt lonely and depressed. My career was going well, of course, but I never cared as much about my career as I have about my private life—and that was going nowhere. I brooded about my two failed marriages, and I spent hours ruminating on how I could have messed up such a long, important span of my life. And I still didn't have Terry with me.

I wanted a solid home for him, but I knew that a home without a man in it who was a good husband for me, and a good substitute father for Terry, would not be very solid. And I also knew that none of the men I was seeing at the time could be taken seriously. I have already discussed how it was with Jack, sweet, funny Jack who drank too much and couldn't communicate; I'm a talker and a sharer and I would wither with a man with whom I couldn't establish a communicating relationship. I certainly didn't have it with Al Jorden. Nor did I have it with George Weidler, although now that he was into Christian Science he was certainly someone I could talk to and relate to; but although I liked to see George, and enjoyed sleeping with him, the marriage part of it was over for me and there was no turning back.

I had met Ronald Reagan through mutual friends from New York who had come out to Los Angeles to live. Ronnie had recently been divorced from Jane Wyman, and he lived alone in an apartment high above Sunset Strip. There were two things about Ronnie that impressed me: how much he liked to dance and how much he liked to talk. Ronnie is really the only man I've ever known who loved dancing. There was a little place on La Cienega that had a small band and a small dance floor where he often took me. He danced well and he had a pleasant personality, so I invariably enjoyed going out with Ronnie.

When he wasn't dancing, he was talking. It really wasn't conversation, it was rather talking at you, sort of long discourses on subjects that interested him. I remember telling him that he should be touring the country making speeches. He was very good at it. He *believed,* or at least he made you think he believed, which, for a politician, I suppose, is just as good. Ronnie was a very aggressive liberal Democrat at that time, and I approved of most of what he said. He wasn't actually in politics, of course, but he had what I would call a political personality—engaging, strong, and very voluble.

One night we went up to his apartment, and it was the first time I had seen the view from high up there in the Hollywood hills, with the lights of the city spread out below. I thought it was lovely, and I decided that that was the area where I wanted to live, high above the city lights with that celestial view; but in all the years I have lived in Los Angeles, I have never had a place high up with a view. I wonder why.

Where I wound up living at that time was in a house at Toluca Lake, which was near Warner Brothers. I bought it for $28,000, furniture and all, and for the first time since his birth, I had a home in which to live with Terry. Marty helped me with the purchase and

121

all the problems of moving in, and he took an immediate shine to Terry, who was a freckle-nosed, outgoing, ebullient little boy. For eight years Terry had led a rather nomadic life, but now, finally, we had a home of our own where we would likely stay put for a long time.

Warners required a lot of publicity appearances, which in my case consisted primarily of late-night visits to disk jockeys to promote songs from my pictures; Marty would take me to the radio stations, and afterward, when he took me home, we would often sit in the car and talk for hours. Rather, I talked (about my busted marriages, my growing involvement with Christian Science, about whatever was bothering me that day) and he listened.

One such night, I was holding forth as usual.

"The fact is, Marty, I'm a failure."

"A failure? Why, you're at the beginning of a great career."

"I'm not talking about that. I've failed at the only thing that matters to me—being a good wife, having a happy marriage—"

"Now, Doris, you've got to stop getting on yourself about those marriages of yours. You're young, you're on your way, give yourself time, you'll meet someone and everything will fall in place. The trouble with you is, you think you're the only person in the world who's had a marriage flop. You think everybody else has it made. Well, it's not so—it's just not so. There are an awful lot of people in your boat."

He was right about that. I really did regard myself as a unique failure in the land of milk and marriage.

"Well, let me tell you something," Marty went on. "I'm having a pretty rough time in my own marriage. It's been going downhill for a long time. Patty and I just aren't getting along anymore."

"Oh, I'm sorry to hear that, Marty. You always seem so—well, you know, all right when you're together."

"Well, as you know, you can't judge a marriage by what's out in the open."

He never mentioned his marriage again, but it wasn't long afterward that he moved out of his house and took an apartment by himself. At the time a lot of people jumped to the conclusion that his leaving Patty was motivated by an affair he was having with me. Not so. There was absolutely nothing between us when Marty left Patty. But I heard that Patty was very angry for a while, and that Al Levy became convinced that I had been having a secret affair with Marty and that was why I had turned Al aside when he confessed his love for me.

After his separation Marty and I did start to see each other regularly. Marty had no children with Patty, and the more he was around the house, the more he became involved with Terry, who responded to him wholeheartedly. Marty was a tall (6 feet, 3 inches), well-built man with brown hair, gentle brown eyes, even features, and a good smile with good teeth. His easygoing, amusing manner enchanted Terry, who obviously saw in Marty the father figure he had never known. Terry called Marty his "manager," figuring, I guess, that what was good enough for me was good enough for him. Marty, on the other hand, seemed to find in Terry the child he had wanted but never had with Patty.

I felt bad about Patty. I liked her very much and I knew she still loved Marty but I also knew that no third person ever breaks up a marriage. A person does not leave a good marriage for someone else. But I heard that Patty suspected that Marty and I were having an affair and that that was why he moved out. I never saw her after that, until years later, so there was no chance to discuss it with her. Anyway, what is there to discuss? No amount of denial by "the other woman" can ever allay the angry suspicions of a wife. But I did feel very bad about Patty.

Marty became a constant visitor to the house. My mother liked him and, as I said, Terry adored him. I found him to be an amusing companion who gave the house some substance when he was around. Marty was really quite funny and a very good mimic—especially his imitation of President Roosevelt, which never failed to convulse me. My involvement with Marty was a gradual one, a slow-gathering, amiable relationship which kind of snuck up on me. When we started sleeping together, it was good and satisfying—not overwhelming, but I guess I didn't want to be overwhelmed by a relationship anymore. I stopped seeing other men. I can't honestly say I was in love with Marty, because I had become very suspicious of love, of what it really was, of what it really demanded. I knew that if love was what there had been between Al Jorden and me I certainly didn't want any more of that. I suppose it was the low-key, undemanding nature of the relationship with Marty that attracted me to him as much as anything else.

Marty was Jewish. He came from an Orthodox Jewish family, New England background, father a shopkeeper, marginal existence.

123

Marty was not a religious person, in the sense that he went to the synagogue or even observed Jewish holidays. But I was told that when my relatives in Cincinnati heard that I was marrying a Jew they were shocked. Of course, there were no Jews in the neighborhood in which I grew up. My father would refer to them occasionally as "kikes" and "sheenies," but as a girl I had never met a real Jew whom I could balance against my father's bigotry. And the Catholic church, and the parochial schools I attended, although not as demonstrably bigoted as my father, did nothing to equalize non-Catholics. By the time I entered high school I had rejected this superior attitude. The woman who did our ironing, Millie, was a black Baptist, whom I adored, a sweet, funny woman who was called nigger by my father and, as a Baptist, put down by the church as a virtual infidel. Well, I was offended by that, for I felt that Millie had better credentials for getting into heaven than my bigoted Catholic father. So by the time I left home I had no "anti" feelings about anyone. It just never occurred to me that a person was Jewish or Protestant or black—none of these things entered my feelings, really.

So that Marty was Jewish or anything else made absolutely no difference to me. Nor to my mother, who was also surprisingly free of the Cincinnati prejudices. She had endured my father's bigotry, but had not condoned it. She has an openness of spirit and of heart that embraces everyone she likes—and the people she's liked have been all manner of races and religions. She is *some* lady, Alma Kappelhoff, *some* lady.

My deepening interest in Christian Science aroused the curiosity of Marty, who began to read some of the Mary Baker Eddy books which I had assembled. He seemed to be even more enthusiastic than I had been when the power of her words first struck me. He began going to meetings with me, and we spent a lot of time reading aloud to each other and discussing the meaning of what we read. We both stopped smoking and drinking, which Christian Science demands, and we both felt better for it. Not just physically better, which we did, of course, but spiritually better for clearing our senses of those artificial stimuli, and letting the natural stimulus of ideas take their place.

I have no recollection of when or how the subject of getting married came up—Marty once said that Terry suggested it. The peculiar thing is that I have vivid recall of the day I took my first step but I draw a blank on such things as getting married.

We were married at the Burbank City Hall by Justice of the Peace Leonard Hammer. (I certainly had a succession of glamorous weddings, didn't I?) We didn't have a witness so Marty scouted around and found a young man who was willing to oblige us. It was about as low-key and uneventful as a marriage could be. That suited me fine. I didn't want to make a big thing out of it; it was almost as though, in the light of my two previous failures, I wanted to keep this marriage suppressed, not expect too much of it. But that does not mean that I was not hopeful and optimistic about this marriage with Marty. It is my nature to persist in the positive. I may brood about a past failure but I am an optimist about what's to be.

So when Marty and I walked out of Judge Hammer's office I felt good and hopeful about being Mrs. Marty Melcher. We were supposed to take off on a motor trip to the Grand Canyon, but I first wanted to go to an upholstery shop way out on Ventura Boulevard to check on a chair I had there. I remember Marty standing there in the shop while I discussed fabrics with the owner, shaking his head and muttering, "I don't really believe this is happening on my wedding day." I just didn't want to make a big deal out of getting married.

When we returned from our motor trip—motels, deli sandwiches in the car, hitting the hay early every night—Marty and I moved into the Toluca Lake house we had bought for forty-thousand-dollars from Martha Raye. Shortly afterward my mother found a small apartment for herself nearby. I seemed to have found the solid, serene life I had been seeking. And for many years that illusion persisted. I say "illusion" because I lived with Marty Melcher for seventeen years, until the day he died in 1968, but not until then did I discover that this man who had slept with me, adopted my son, managed my career and business life, was indeed an enigma. He may have been a charlatan, he may simply have been a dupe, he was certainly secretly venal and devious. But that day in 1951 when we returned from our wedding trip to the neat house in Toluca Lake, Terry excitedly running to the car, Alma in the kitchen preparing a welcome-home dinner, that day I thought he was the answer to what I had prayed for.

SAM WEISS

When I first met Marty Melcher I was in charge of Warner Brothers music, and Melcher came to see me in my office on Hollywood Boulevard.

He had a letter of introduction from Lou Levy, who was a friend of mine who was a music publisher. Melcher asked me if I could help him get started and I said, "Sure, just let me know what I can do for you."

Well, Melcher went out to the waiting room that adjoined my office and hung out there for the rest of the day. There were a lot of people coming and going, a lot of name singers and others connected with our business who had appointments with some of the men working with me. As these people walked in Melcher would grab them and try to persuade them to leave us and join his outfit. My secretary told me what he was doing, so I went out and told him to cut it out, but he still hung around the waiting room, soliciting our people as they came in. Finally, I had all of him I could take. I grabbed him by his collar and the seat of his pants and bodily ran him out of the office and down the hall and pitched him through the front door. He was a lot bigger than I was but he was not the kind of man who, if you showed him any muscle, would give you any trouble.

The next I knew of Melcher he had joined Century Artists and had married one of their clients, Patty Andrews. Patty was just as nice a gal as you'd ever want to meet, great gal, everybody loved her, but Marty stepped all over her, got everything he could out of her, and when he had a chance to better himself with a new client, Doris Day, who was starting to be big stuff at Warners, Marty couldn't get rid of Patty fast enough.

I knew Doris very well from my band connections, long before she came to Hollywood. So it was inevitable that I wound up being a close friend of hers, and that meant seeing a lot of Marty once he moved in on Doris. There were some rough times about that. I got a call from Doris's mother one night. "Sam," she said, "I'm scared to death. I'm alone in the house and Patty Andrews is at the door yelling that she wants to get in to get at Marty. She's mad as hell."

"Hold on, Alma," I said, "don't open the door, I'll be there right away."

"She's going to kill somebody," Alma said. "She's yelling terrible things."

"Don't open the door."

I parked about a block from the house and snuck around through the backyard to have a look. Patty was on the porch with someone, and she had a baseball bat in her hand. She was spitting fire. There was no doubt, from the way she was swinging that club, that she meant to use it. I snuck away and phoned Alma from the corner drugstore.

"Where's Doris?" I asked.

"She went with Marty Melcher for some publicity thing."

"Well, just be quiet and don't do a thing. Sooner or later she'll go home."

"Sam, I've never been so frightened in my life."

"Don't worry—I'll hang around, but I don't want her to see me."

Patty left after an hour or so, and it was true that Marty and Doris were on a legitimate publicity mission, but the fact was that the only thing Marty loved was money. He loved Patty's money until Doris's money came along and then, because there was more of it, he loved Doris's money more.

Eight

THE ultimate yardstick of achievement in Hollywood has been the annual poll of the theater owners of America. To be voted by them into the top ten is to enter the celluloid sanctum sanctorum. Shortly after my marriage, I received a call early one morning from Bob Thomas of the Associated Press, telling me that I had made the hallowed ten. At this point I had made only nine pictures, and Thomas complimented me on so remarkable an achievement after so relatively few movies.

The picture I was then working on was *I'll See You in My Dreams,* a musical biography of the song writer Gus Kahn, played by Danny Thomas. I think this was the first film for Danny, who had been performing in nightclubs. I played Mrs. Gus Kahn, struggling up the musical ladder of fame at the side of my talented husband.

There was one scene in that picture that comes vividly to mind. I am pregnant, and Gus is away writing a song somewhere when the time comes for me to go to the hospital. Word is sent to him but he gets to the hospital too late, and when he comes into my room I have already had the baby. He sits on the bed beside me, holds my hands, and, full of tenderness and love, sings "Pretty Baby," a song he had just written. In the way Danny played the scene, there was a sense of his remorse in having not been with me when the baby came. When Danny started his song, I couldn't help but cry, for what came to mind was the birth of my own baby, how Al Jorden had not been with me, and how alone and unfulfilled I had felt. I also felt how different it was, Danny singing to me so tenderly, in contrast to the rather cold, offhand way Al had been when he finally did come to the hospital. We did quite a few takes of that scene, and every time it moved me to tears.

127

In 1953 I made a lavish musical with Ray Bolger called *April in Paris*. It was one of two movies I made at Warners that had trouble on the set. I didn't like the movie and I certainly didn't enjoy making it. I had never met Ray before, and we got along very well, but not long into the shooting there was a flare-up between Ray and the director, David Butler. This was my fourth picture with David, who was an urbane, considerate, witty man who had never been anything but genial and understanding in his dealings with his actors. But unbeknownst to me, David and Ray had been having a disagreement which suddenly erupted on the set one day.

"Ray," David said, as he stopped the cameras in the middle of a scene I was playing with Ray, "you're upstaging Doris again."

"I'm doing no such thing."

"I've warned you about that."

"I don't give a damn what you've warned."

"Well, you may as well play it straight because I can always take care of things in the cutting room."

"And I can take care of *you* with Jack Warner."

Although this was my twelfth picture, I was still a neophyte when it came to involved technical matters like upstaging in a film shot. I asked around the set and found that many of the technical people agreed with David that Ray was a master at scene stealing, which is much more difficult in film making than it is on the live stage. Even in tight shots, Ray was doing something that gave him favorable camera position. I don't know what it was that he was doing. To this day I wouldn't know how to cheat in a shot so that I could block out another actor or achieve a more favorable camera angle. But whatever Ray was doing during the shooting of *April in Paris* had succeeded in rousing the dander of Butler. The coolness between the two men certainly made filming for all of us something less than enjoyable.

I also had to deal with the problem of who was going to choreograph the film. There was quite a bit of dancing, and by now I knew how vital it was to have someone with bright, fresh ideas working on the routines. Leroy Prince, the venerable resident Warner Brothers dance director, had been assigned to the picture, but Leroy Prince didn't dance any more than Bud Westmore, who was always given makeup credit, did the makeup. These men put their names on the film credits, but the actual work was done by underlings. Leroy Prince had a nice, easygoing brother named Eddie, who actually did the work on musical films. But I wanted more than what Eddie Prince would bring to this picture. *April in Paris* was a dancing musical that needed well-planned, bright dance numbers.

I had made two previous musicals that required considerable dancing, *Tea for Two* and *Lullaby of Broadway,* both choreographed by Gene Nelson, who was super. His wife, Miriam, was an excellent dancer who helped him with the choreography and who was absolutely marvelous to me. When we first met, during the filming of *Tea for Two,* I confessed to Miriam my fears and doubts about being able to dance well enough to satisfy the sharp eye of the camera. Of course, I knew that my leg was all right, but since I don't like to do anything that I can't do very well, I had my doubts that my best would be good enough. Miriam took my hand and said, "Clara, I'm going to work with you, we'll have all the time we need, and I will see to it, I *promise* you, that I won't let anything go by that isn't first-rate. I'll watch you like a hawk. That's going to be my job, just to watch you. Gene will do the overall choreography, but I will be your personal choreographer. Please don't worry. Trust me."

Miriam was true to her word, but, oh, God, was it difficult! I never worked harder at anything than I did at the dances in my films. Hours and hours and hours. A film dancer does not have the freedom of a stage dancer. She must dance precisely to a mark. Her turns must be exact. She must face precisely in the camera direction required while executing very difficult steps. And to learn those steps! It is not easy to recommence anything that you have laid off of for many years, and the stretch between my automobile accident and *Tea for Two* had me stiff and rusty. Miriam worked with me for endless hours, striving for the fluidity and verve that are the hallmark of the professional dancer. And Gene invented and adapted routines for me that were beautifully suited to my abilities.

I would drag myself home at night, too tired to move another step, but I kept practicing—in my head. It was a trick I learned early on that was of great help to me. I could rehearse a dance routine in my head, watching myself perform, and that did me almost as much good as getting up on my feet and doing it. I rehearsed songs that way too. Not just the lyrics, but the actual rendition of the song, the phrasing, breathing, all of it, without singing a note.

My most difficult dance routines were in *Lullaby of Broadway.* There was one spectacular number that required me to dance up and down a steep flight of stairs while wearing a long dress. I'll never forget that dress. Gold lamé and my hair was up on top of my head —I looked like Whistler's mother. I had to do this number with Gene Nelson, in tails, who danced it as well as choreographed it. Of course, Gene was a marvelous dancer and that was a help, but when I walked on that set in my gold-lamé ball gown and looked up at that Mount Everest of stairs, I put on the brakes. "You've got to be out of your minds!" I said, in a loud, clear voice which I hoped carried up to Jack Warner. "I can't even *walk* up and down those stairs!"

Miriam was right at my side. "Now, Clara," she said, "it's like skiing—it looks difficult, but once you start down it's all right."

"Yeah, once you start down it's a busted leg."

"Now, Clara, why don't we—"

"You know, I think we should have the ski patrol standing by, because if you ever want to see a casualty in the making, you're looking at her."

Somehow Miriam induced me to dance on those steps. Up, down, spins, turns—you've seen Astaire do it but it was not something I had learned in Hessler's dancing school in Cincinnati. For a climax, Gene devised a fast series of full, spinning turns, down and then up and then down again. I would have preferred a dive off the Golden Gate Bridge. But somehow, some way, black and blue of shin and calf, skinned of knee, and dizzy of head, we got that dance in the can. Then and only then did Miriam make a confession to me.

"Now I can tell you, Clara, you did something I can't do."

"What do you mean?"

"Thank God you didn't notice that when I was demonstrating the routine on those turns, I never actually did them for you—just indicated where the turns came with my hand. Doing turns up and down stairs is too tough for me. Never was able to do it. I guess because it's so dangerous. But you were absolutely super."

Despite this inexcusable treason, when the time came to face the *April in Paris* dances, I wanted Miriam and Gene on the picture and not Leroy Prince's brother. It was the first time since my early run-in with Jack Warner that I had made a request. By then I had made twelve successful pictures for Warners and I was number two in the box-office ratings, so I had reason to believe that this time I'd be listened to. I was wrong. Eddie Prince did the choreography, which was as banal as the script.

I had but one year to go on my seven-year contract and no

prisoner ever awaited deliverance day more eagerly than I anticipated being sprung from Warners. I just wanted the privilege of being able to say no. It was a word that had been banished from my vocabulary and I meant to put it back where it belonged.

In 1953 I made one of my favorite musicals, *Calamity Jane,* not realizing that on its completion I would be starting the run of Calamity Doris. There were no storm warnings. I had just completed a routine but charming period musical with Gordon MacRae, *By the Light of the Silvery Moon.* Marty had left Century Artists and was devoting himself full-time to managing my affairs and a music company which we had established to handle not only my songs and records but general music publishing as well. Terry was reveling in his new and complete home life. Marty had legally adopted him in 1952, when he was ten, and Terry was proud to be Terry Melcher. My mother was well settled and happy with her life and newfound friends. My brother, Paul, had moved out to Los Angeles with his wife and children and gone to work for our company, which we called Arwin Productions. My earnings were now in the neighborhood of five thousand a week, and for whatever it was worth I was near the top in both the movie and music polls.

But that's when I became unstuck and fell apart.

Calamity Jane was a demanding picture but no more so than a few others I had done. I loved portraying Calamity Jane, who was a rambunctious, pistol-packing prairie girl (I lowered my voice and stuck out my chin a little). I can't say that the physical high jinks of jumping on horses, bars, wagons, and belligerent men or doing pratfalls in muddy streams seemed to be particularly exhausting while I was doing the picture. I had a great working relation with my costar, Howard Keel, and absolutely first-rate songs to sing (by Sammy Fain and Paul Webster), one of which, "Secret Love," became my third million-plus recording and won that year's Academy Award.

The picture was a rousing success, establishing some sort of record at Radio City Music Hall. But shortly after finishing my work on it, I was laid low by a strange and frightening affliction. I first became aware of my condition on a hot Sunday when Marty and I were driving to Irvine Park, where Terry had been participating in a week-long Boy Scout jamboree. Marty was driving and suddenly, while sitting there in the front seat looking out the window, I began to have trouble breathing. I tried to take a full breath but I couldn't.

131

Short gasps were all I could manage. I felt a rise of panic. I kept my face averted so that Marty couldn't see what trouble I was having. I really felt that I was going to suffocate.

"What are you doing over there?" Marty asked.

"Oh, nothing. Nothing. Why?" I was so short of breath it was difficult to talk.

"You're practically hanging out the window."

"I'm okay."

I thought we'd never get there. But it was even worse trying to get through the afternoon in hot, dusty Irvine Park. I was positively gasping. I could barely manage to walk around. I was perspiring, more from fear than from the heat. Every short breath was a conscious effort. I desperately tried to pull air into my lungs but my breathing apparatus seemed to be choked off and what little air I was able to inhale I had to consciously force into myself.

The days and weeks that followed were a hideous nightmare. Not only was I plagued by this inability to breathe, but I also began experiencing terrible heart palpitations. Often I could feel my heart pounding in my throat and chest, twice its normal rate. I found myself taking my pulse every few minutes all day long. I was convinced that I had tuberculosis or some other lung affliction that had caused my lungs to collapse. The palpitations, I felt, were caused by the extra strain my deficient breathing apparatus was putting on my heart, and I lived in fear that these palpitating seizures were preludes to a heart attack.

As if this weren't enough, I also discovered at this time that I had a small lump in my left breast. I decided that the lump denoted a cancerous condition which somehow was tied to my afflicted breathing and heart trouble.

I tried to keep it all from Marty. I managed to hold myself together in the morning at breakfast, but as soon as he left for the office I was flat out, back in bed. I seemed to feel a little more comfortable when I was in bed and my breathing, although forced and consciously monitored, was somewhat easier. The only person in the house with me was my wonderful housekeeper, Katie, who had been with me for years.

"Missus," she would say, seeing me in bed, "you all right?"

"Yes, Katie, I just feel kind of tired. I'm just going to stay in bed for a while."

"You want me to call Mister?"

132

"No, no, Katie, I'm all right—you just go about your work and I'll call if I need you."

The only person whom I did call, and in whom I confided, was my Christian Science Practitioner, Martin Broones. I had first tried to help myself by reading *Science and Health* but relevant passages on which I concentrated did not have any noticeable effect on my condition. "The physical affirmation of disease should always be met with the mental negation" was one of Mrs. Eddy's precepts. "Whatever benefit is produced on the body, must be expressed mentally, and thought should be held fast to this ideal. If you believe in inflamed and weak nerves, you are liable to an attack from that source. You will call it neuralgia, but we call it a belief. . . . If you decide that climate or atmosphere is unhealthy, it will be so to you. Your decisions will master you, whichever direction they take." I understood this, and I concentrated on its message, but my hideous days and tortured nights continued.

Martin Broones was the husband of that marvelous English comedienne Charlotte Greenwood, who was also a devout Christian Scientist. He was a warm, sensible, compassionate man with whom I had become great friends. He had never dealt with anyone with a breathing problem like mine, but he felt that he could help me overcome my physical problems by concentrating on certain fundamental precepts in *Science and Health,* which, as I have previously explained, contains Mrs. Eddy's fundamental truths. " 'The cause of all disease is mental,' " Mr. Broones read aloud, and I closed my eyes in concentration. " 'A mortal fear, a mistaken belief or conviction of the necessity and power of ill-health; also a fear that Mind is helpless to defend the life of man and incompetent to control it. Without this ignorant human belief, any circumstance is of itself powerless to produce suffering. It is latent belief in disease, as well as the fear of disease, which associates sickness with certain circumstances and causes the two to appear conjoined, even as poetry and music are reproduced in union by human memory. Disease has no intelligence. Unwittingly you sentence yourself to suffer. The understanding of this will enable you to commute this self-sentence, and meet every circumstance with truth. Disease is less than mind, and Mind can control it.' "

But not *my* mind. At night I lay in bed beside Marty, sleepless, my heart pounding, my eyes riveted on the ceiling, monitoring every gasping breath as I repeated and repeated Mrs. Eddy's words—to

133

no avail. Of course, by now I had told Marty about my maladies, and often he would wake in the night and read to me from *Science and Health*. Contrary to popular belief, Christian Science does permit a visit to a doctor if the person, after conscientious effort, cannot rid himself of the mental condition that is causing his physical problems. But I am a disciplined person who abides by the rules. If I were indeed a true Christian Scientist, then by golly I should be steadfast and stick with it. I was being put to the test, I felt, and I wanted to measure up. And Marty, having embraced Christian Science even more avidly than I, certainly shared my point of view.

I became a virtual recluse, not going out of the house for days on end. The starting date was approaching for a new picture at Warners, *Lucky Me,* with Robert Cummings and Phil Silvers, but I postponed all my preproduction meetings, such as costume fittings. I didn't speak to my friends and I canceled all recording dates, interviews, and other publicity activities. My only concern was survival. I lost weight rapidly. My depression was so deep, so numbing, that often I stayed in bed from morning till night.

I was alone in the house one afternoon when the phone rang. I hadn't spoken to anyone for days, but the phone didn't stop ringing. Finally, to get it off my nerves, I answered. The caller was a clerk who worked in one of the stores where I made purchases. His voice was clearly manic and he had no sooner identified himself than he began an insane attack on me, threatening me with every conceivable sexual assault. His language was horribly explicit and mostly concerned with sadistic sexual suggestions. I was so horrified that the receiver seemed to freeze against my ear. Then, as his madness escalated, I finally threw the phone away from me and ran to my room and locked the door. I was too distraught to go for help, and too fearful of the phone now to attempt to call anyone. My inability to breathe was worse than ever. I threw myself on the bed, gasping, desperately trying to get air inside me.

A few minutes later, I heard someone on the porch outside the front door. A pause, then the bell. I was petrified. Again the bell. I went to the door; it was securely bolted.

"Who's there?"

A man's heavy voice: "Western Union."

I trembled, terror-stricken, and ran back to my room. When Marty came home, about an hour later, I threw myself in his arms and sobbed uncontrollably. When I could control myself, I told him what had happened. He reached in his pocket and took out a telegram.

"This was stuck in the door," he said. "You're invited to a premiere."

For several more weeks I continued to see Mr. Broones every day, desperately trying to improve my deteriorating condition. But not only did I not get better, I had to face a new affliction—an inability to swallow, even my saliva. I never brought up with Mr. Broones the advisability of going to a doctor. I felt that he wouldn't have approved. I tried very hard to gather, from *Science and Health,* the spiritual and mental strength that could overcome the physical maladies that were consuming me. "Man is never sick," Mrs. Eddy said, "for Mind is not sick and matter cannot be. A false belief is both the tempter and the tempted, the sin and the sinner, the disease and its cause. It is well to be calm in sickness; to be hopeful is still better; but to understand that sickness is not real and that Truth can destroy its seeming reality, is best of all, for this understanding is the universal and perfect remedy."

I tried, I desperately tried but there was no way for me to alleviate, let alone eliminate, my fear. I was afraid that one of my lungs had collapsed. I was afraid that I had cancer of the breast. I was afraid I had tuberculosis. I was afraid that that threatening voice on the telephone would materialize.

It all came to a climax at two o'clock one morning. I was lying awake as usual, my heart beating so heavy and fast that I was sure I was on the verge of the long-expected heart attack. My breathing was tortured.

"Marty, are you awake?"

"Yes, of course."

"Would you please call Mr. Broones and ask him to come over."

"But it's two o'clock in the morning."

"I know. I'm sorry. I wouldn't ask him if I weren't desperate."

Mr. Broones came right over. He sat by my bed and read to me and talked to me and tried to calm me. I got up to go to the bathroom. Halfway across the room, I collapsed in a dead faint.

I don't know who made the decision to call the doctor, but when I came to, Dr. Hearn, who lived nearby, was there. As he examined me I rattled off my ailments.

"Look, Dr. Hearn," I said, "I don't want you to try to spare my feelings. I know I'm dying so you may as well level with me."

He put away his stethoscope and called Marty into the room. "Do you have a paper bag?" he asked.

"A paper . . . ?

"Yes, a small brown paper bag."

Marty looked at him as if he were nuts and went to find a paper bag. "Now, listen, doctor," I said, "don't play games with me. I just want the truth. I'm a very realistic person."

"Doris," he said, "I'm going to give it to you straight—you're hyperventilating."

"I'm . . . what?"

"Overbreathing."

"Well, that doesn't sound very serious."

"It isn't."

"You mean all these months, this absolute hell, and all I am is breathing too much?"

"Did you do a film recently?"

"I'm always doing a film recently."

"Were you tired?"

"I was exhausted."

"That's when it started. A very common affliction among people who are high-strung, exhausted—it's a nervous condition that can be brought on by stress, overwork, being overly tired, or being anxious. The tendency is to breathe too much, take too much oxygen into the body, and expend too much carbon dioxide. That makes you short of breath, which induces you to try to breathe in even more oxygen, and when finally you get too much oxygen into you, and too little carbon dioxide, you faint. Are you yawning a lot?"

"All the time. I'm a chain yawner."

"Every yawn is a gulp of oxygen. Do you know that a friend of mine has a racehorse he can't race because she hyperventilates? She takes in so much oxygen she faints—as you did—sometimes in the middle of a race."

Marty came in with a small brown paper bag. Dr. Hearn gathered the mouth of the bag into a small opening and handed it to me. "Now put your lips to this," he said, "and start to breathe in and out, don't take your lips away, just breathe in the air you breathe into the bag. That way you'll get some carbon dioxide into you."

I did as he instructed and after a while I began to feel a little

136

better. He gave me a sedative. "I've reserved a room at St. Joseph's Hospital for you," he said. "We've got to put you back together again."

"What about the lump in my breast?"

"I think it's benign but we've got to make sure."

"When shall I check in?"

"Now."

"You mean . . . but it's three o'clock in the morning."

"They're open."

Dr. Hearn was right about my physical condition; after two days of tests, they found nothing wrong with me, and as for the lump in my breast, as Dr. Hearn had predicted, it proved to be benign, and the cyst was removed with simple minor surgery. I felt somewhat relieved, but I was still a nervous wreck. Dr. Hearn was aware of this. He came in with Marty for a consultation.

"You have been so worried—so full of fear and anxiety—for such a long period," Dr. Hearn said, "that your nerves are shattered. I've suggested to Mr. Melcher that we bring in a neuropsychiatric specialist to treat you—to talk to you."

"You mean a psychiatrist?"

"Well, no, he's not exactly that. He's someone who will deal with your immediate psychiatric problems as they relate to your physical problems. You see, you are presently caught in a revolving problem. The more afflictions you have had, the more frightened you have become, and the more frightened you became, the more nervous it made you, and the more nervous you got, the more depressed you were. That's why I want you to see a specialist—we've got to break this insidious pattern."

I readily consented, for I was painfully aware that I was on the verge of or over the verge of a nervous breakdown. My nerves felt as if they were exposed on the surface of my skin. The specialist was Dr. Karl von Hagen, and when he came into my hospital room the following day I burst into tears. Buckets. I couldn't stop crying. Poor man, hadn't even sat down, and there I was consumed with tears. I finally pulled myself together and started to tell him about my life. I thought that that's what I was supposed to do. I went back to my failed marriages, and then to my childhood, the divorce of my parents. Eventually he stopped me. "I'm not really that kind of doctor," he said. "I don't want you to go into those previous events in your life. You are terribly nervous and I want to concentrate on

137

your recent fears and anxieties which have induced this nervousness. Now I want you to tell me everything that bothers you about your health, so that we can discuss it fully. If your heart starts palpitating, I'll tell you why. If your vision seems cloudy, I'll explain it to you. It's all nerves. In each instance, I want you to understand the connection. I want you to keep a diary of every physical manifestation that bothers you, and we'll go into them every day."

"But that's really not much different from what I was trying to do through Christian Science—make my mind overcome its fear so that it wouldn't impose bad reactions in my body."

"Yes, in a sense, that's true."

"But I wasn't able to do it. What makes you think you can succeed where Mrs. Eddy has failed? Or, I should say, where I failed Mrs. Eddy?"

"Well, we're going to use some physical medicine, like sedatives, and we're going to deal *specifically* with your physical problems. Christian Science is a *general* application of the philosophy of the dominance of mind over matter. Medical approach is the *specific* application of knowledge to a specific bodily malfunction. We have given you a very thorough physical checkup. These tests show there is absolutely nothing wrong with you. And yet you suffer. You have told me about your inability to breathe properly, your heart palpitations, the occasional blurriness of your vision when you move your eyes, the prickly feeling in your right arm, the recurring headaches, your occasional inability to swallow, and the way at times your left leg twitches uncontrollably. All these, plus the fear related to discovering that lump in your breast, have added fear upon fear about what is happening to you. And these accumulating, escalating fears have made a massive assault upon your nerves. Well, the nerves are like rubber bands. They have great resiliency, but pulled too far and too often they begin to lose that resiliency, and that is what has happened to you. Your nerves have lost their elasticity. As we alleviate fear, we will little by little restore that resiliency—but it won't happen overnight. We have a lot of ground to cover."

The doctor gave me a note pad on which I was to keep track of every physical thing that bothered me, along with what I was thinking as it bothered me. He allowed me to go home but put me on a strict program of rehabilitation. No newspapers or news programs. No telephone calls. No entertaining—the fewer people I saw, the better. As much quiet and tranquillity in the house as possible. No discussion about work. As little talk as possible, because talking caused overbreathing. As much reading as possible, but only "positive" books that were uplifting. I was forbidden to read any movie scripts. Dr. von Hagen put me on a regimen of swimming three times a day, with particular emphasis on the dead man's float. He said swimming was a complete relaxant that affected the whole body, and that the dead man's float was one of the best ways to remove tension from the body.

He gave me a liquid sedative called Butisol, I think, to take at night before going to sleep, but he said he wanted me to stay away from drugs as much as possible so as not to impede the restoration of my natural functions.

During Dr. von Hagen's daily visits, as I went over my diary with him, I began to have the feeling that I was getting on top of my problems, but as soon as he left the house, I began to backslide. Nights were the worst times. I knew that my fear that I was terminally ill had been proved to be unfounded, but knowing that did not completely remove the fear. (One knows, I told myself, how often doctors have been proved wrong.) For I still had attacks during the night, although breathing into the paper bag which I kept on my night table did help when I began gasping for air. I knew, of course, that whatever was going on in my head was the sole cause of my sickness, and that I was making myself sick. How often I repeated Mrs. Eddy's definition of fear: "false evidence appearing real." Everything that was happening to me was false evidence, appearing terribly real. But I discovered that true as that insight was, the false evidence persevered. When I could not swallow, and would lie there for hours, desperately trying to swallow, in a panic because I could not swallow, choking and gagging in my attempts, I would remind myself that it was false evidence, that I *could* swallow, that there was nothing wrong with my throat or esophagus or anything else—but telling myself that did not help me to swallow.

One thing about me, in all circumstances I am an *organized* lady, and I followed the routine Dr. von Hagen had prescribed for me to a T. The thing that seemed to help me the most was the dead man's float. I could literally feel the tension drain out of me into the warm water of the pool. And afterward I felt less depressed, less bleak, less set upon by my afflictions.

I was also helped by the daily discussion with Dr. von Hagen. He would take up each complaint on my list and give me a complete physiological explanation of the cause of my backache or blurred vision. Every nerve, muscle, bone, organ, canal was charted and explained. I could have passed a freshman medical-school exam. As I came to understand just how nervous tension and fear exercised their control over physical areas of the body, my suffering from these physical ills began to diminish.

During those weeks of recuperation, I leaned heavily on *Science and Health.* "Oh! Thou hast heard my prayer; And I am blest! This is Thy high behest:—Thou here, and *everywhere."* That had such power for me. Not "Oh, please hear my prayer! Help me!" but "Thou hast heard my prayer and I am blest." An accomplished fact. Not praying to a God somewhere out there or up there or wherever. In other words, there's no duality. Everything is one. So you don't have to go anywhere or pray to anything but just go inside yourself, for that is where God is. John said, "Ye shall know the truth and the truth shall make you free." And Shakespeare said, "There is nothing either good or bad, but thinking makes it so." These are quotations in the front of *Science and Health* and I thought about them a lot during my long recuperation. What is good in one person's mind may be bad in another. We see a play. I think it is good, you think it is bad— what is it?

I have never read reviews of my pictures because the praise or damnation is simply one man's reaction and is therefore infinitesimal. I have always done the best I know how without thought to how I will be judged. I have never felt competitive. Never. With whom? There is nobody like me, just as there is nobody just like you. From our fingerprints to our noses, from our speech to the way we walk, we are all one of a kind. As an actress I certainly wasn't competing with Judy Garland or Marilyn Monroe. Being a number in a poll in no way made me feel competitive. The studio calling excitedly, "Doris, you're number two in the international ratings!" That was nice to know, and it was even nicer to hear, a few years later, that I had become number one. But when I was first informed, a few years after I had started making pictures, that I had landed in the top ten, I remember thinking, Oh, they've got to be kidding—it's a mistake. I'm just learning. And I was amused at finding myself a number. Actually, in a way it's a little depressing to become number one because the only place you can go from there is down.

But what I was thinking about all this, during my convalescence, was that no matter what you achieve you really can't take credit for any of it. God, the Creator, whatever you want to call Him, has put you here to fulfill a function, everything in you predestined, and you perform as ordained and that's all there is to it. If you were destined to be an actress and you achieve a certain prominence with whatever talents you have been given, fine, but there's no reason to get pompous and overbearing about that.

Also, I read again and again Shakespeare's wise observation that there is nothing either good or bad, but thinking makes it so. I began to look at my past marriages in a different light. My first marriage was, in many ways, horrendous, but something very good did come of it—my son. And I certainly came out of it with more strength and determination than when I went into it.

So too with my second marriage. Its dissolution was sad and debilitating, to lose a man I thought I loved, unable to comprehend what had brought the marriage to such an abrupt end, but the good that came of it was that I matured and found out a great deal about myself as a result of the long days and nights I suffered. Also, I found a sense of religion as a result of my indoctrination into Christian Science, thanks to George Weidler. Christian Science, as it turned out, was not, for me, the stopping place, but it was an important plateau that led me to the very personal, gratifying religion which is so important to my life today. I feel that God is my very being and God is the life of everything around me. So I don't have to seek God. He's right here. I don't pray. I just realize God.

Nine

CALAMITY JANE was released across the country during my convalescence, and I was amused to think that the silver screen's two-fisted, back-slapping, pistol-toting Doris Day was in reality a basket case doing dead man's floats. The image and the reality. That's what it's all about, isn't it?

There was a heavy demand for interviews in connection with the picture, but I turned down all requests. Since I had always been very cooperative in the past, the media people interpreted these turn-downs as an indication that I had become snooty, a movie queen aloof on her throne. There was a lot about that in the papers and magazines, and many columnists put me down for not appearing at the Academy Awards to sing "Secret Love," the *Calamity Jane* song that won the Award that year. Although I was not reading papers and magazines, I nevertheless found out how the press had turned on me, even to the extent that the Hollywood Women's Press Club gave me their annual Sour Apple Award as the most uncooperative actress in films. That upset me very much.

Warners was getting very insistent about the start of my next picture, *Lucky Me;* when Dr. von Hagen finally gave me the green light to go back to work, I read the script and was dismayed at how bad it was. Robert Cummings, Phil Silvers, Nancy Walker, and Eddie Foy, Jr., were all talented, funny people, but I knew by now that no amount of talent can overcome an inferior script, especially if it is a comedy. What I didn't want to do, after the rough time I had had, was to get involved in a project for which I had no enthusiasm. I also knew that the only way not to do a film that had a poor script was to take a suspension.

I discussed this with Martin Broones, whom I was seeing on a regular basis during my recuperation.

"Do you have a contract with Warner Brothers?" he asked.

"Yes," I said, "for seven years. With options. They can drop me whenever they want to but I can't drop them."

"That contract stipulates that you are to perform for them in pictures assigned to you, at a regular weekly salary, right?"

"Yes."

"Then that is the only right thing to do—honor your word and your commitment."

"But, Martin, I know it isn't exactly right to take a suspension but everyone on the lot does it to avoid being put in a bad picture."

"Doris, once you make a deal, the ethical thing to do is to abide by it. It is better to live by a set of principles than by opportunistic expediencies."

"But they want to put me in a bad film."

"Why would they want to do that? It would be a waste of money, wouldn't it? They really think this is a *good* film, or else why would they do it? They have spent a lot of time and money writing it and putting it together. They are counting on you to perform in it and do the best you can with the script and songs they give you. That's all you have to worry about. Doing your best. Believe me, nothing is going to hurt you. If you go into everything you do with that thought—that you're about your Father's business, and you're going to stick to it—then you'll be all right. A deal is a deal, that's the principle, and every time you deviate from a principle, you diminish yourself."

"You're right, Martin. I'll always remember that." And I always have. There were some pictures I had made that I didn't like at all. I couldn't sit through them for any amount of money. But many people have been entertained by them and don't share my feelings. So there it is again—nothing is good or bad.

Lucky Me was anything but lucky. I can't remember much about the picture. We were a vaudeville troupe touring Florida, I think, and I remember one good song, "I Speak to the Stars," which I sang to Robert Cummings while strolling on the beach. Whereas I had always been able to get into a part with effortless vitality, now it was all I could do to get myself up to a performing level. Dr. von Hagen had warned me to take it easy, to be less self-demanding, and I at-

143

tempted to do this by resting in my dressing room as much as I could, avoiding all interviews, and closing the set to visitors. Some days, if the shooting schedule was too long, I asked the director to shorten it. Judy Garland was on the lot at the same time, making *A Star Is Born;* she was being difficult and erratic about her hours and the press lumped us together as the Warner Brothers prima donnas. I tried not to let that bother me. My primary obligation was to keep myself well enough to finish the picture. Nothing else really mattered.

My memory of working on *Lucky Me* is very fuzzy but I do recall that by the time it was over I felt strong enough to make a conciliatory move toward the press. I invited the press corps to my home for an open interview. Marty was there beside me. I felt very nervous and ill at ease about facing them but it was something I simply had to do.

There was a large turnout. I planned to tell them the truth about myself, which was, of course, an unpleasant task, but being outspoken is the only way I know to operate. As the questions started, Marty tried to answer for me but neither the journalists nor I felt that was satisfactory. I told them frankly that I had had what was tantamount to a nervous breakdown, that I had had a very bad time of it, but that I was all right now. I apologized for avoiding them, but hoped they would understand how I had needed to be alone until I could get myself together again.

My ability to face all those press people, and to deal candidly with my condition, was the turning point in my recovery. It was not long after that event that I began feeling like my old self again. Or, perhaps more accurately, like my new self. For out of the holocaust of those abysmal days and nights had come some truthful realities that were destined to sustain me in the much more trying times that lay ahead.

My last picture at Warners was *Young at Heart,* a remake of a previously successful picture called *Four Daughters.* There were some lovely new songs, and a first-rate cast that included Gig Young, Ethel Barrymore, Dorothy Malone, and Frank Sinatra in the part previously acted by John Garfield. This was the only movie in which I worked with Frank; but years before, just after I made *Romance on the High Seas,* I had been on "Your Hit Parade" radio show with him. Frank was the star of the show.

I had hated every minute of it. Not because of Frank—we got

144

along fine—but because I really disliked that kind of big-time radio program, performed live before a big audience in a big theater. I also disliked living in New York. I stayed with Joy Hodges and her husband, Paul Dudley, who were friends of Ronald Reagan and who had a pleasant East Side apartment, but I felt inhibited and cheerless in the city. Of course, it was not a very good time for me, and I'm sure that had something to do with it. But I was primarily depressed by having to get up there in front of that audience every week and sing—usually a song I had sung the week before in a slightly different arrangement.

I was on the show for twenty weeks, and during that time I saw a lot of Alex Stordahl, who was the musical conductor and a long-time Sinatra crony. Alex, who was an excellent yachtsman, had a fine boat that he kept moored in the East River yacht basin, and one of the few pleasures I had during my "Hit Parade" tenure was when Alex took me out on the boat. He said I was a very good sailor, probably because I'd bundle up in my hat and pea jacket and go out in all kinds of weather without getting sick.

I can't say that I got to know Frank, even though we were together at rehearsals and performances every week, for Frank is a reserved, self-protective person and that was a time in my life when I was anything but outgoing. We had a pleasant, easygoing relationship, however, and even though Frank was the star of the show and I was just an extra added attraction, Frank was never condescending or overbearing in his attitude toward me.

Our reunion on *Young at Heart* was the first time I had seen Frank since those "Hit Parade" days. He seemed a bit more querulous now, more reactive to his situation, less inclined to accept things as they were. In *Four Daughters* John Garfield had died at the end, giving his performance and the film a sharp poignancy, but Sinatra refused to die. He put his refusal on a take-me-or-leave-me basis, so after many hectic conferences, the producers caved in and changed the ending to satisfy Frank. I thought it was a mistake, because there was an inevitability about that character's death that would have given more dimension to Sinatra's performance. And enhanced the film.

Although this picture was produced by Warners, our company, Arwin Productions, with Marty as its representative, was involved in the production end of it. It was the first time we had actually participated in producing one of my pictures. Preproduction meetings

145

were held in Marty's office on the lot, but from the very beginning Frank displayed an open hostility toward Marty. I remember one meeting that Frank attended during which he sat with a newspaper in front of his face, reading, for the entire time. I was the only person he talked to. He read through the paper at that meeting, rustling the pages as he turned them, never taking the paper away from his face, and when he finished it he got up and left without a word to anyone.

Before the picture started, Frank sent word that he would not step onto the set if Marty Melcher was anywhere on the lot. I really have no idea what caused Frank to be so hostile toward Marty. There must have been some basis for it. Marty said he didn't know. That they'd never had a quarrel. Perhaps someone like Sam Weiss would know better than I. Sam was a music publisher, still is, a dear friend who was very close to Frank and also knew Marty from the time he first came to Hollywood. Sam would probably know what set Frank off against Marty. At any rate, Marty had no choice but to abide by Frank's ultimatum. It was either that or throw Frank off the picture, and Marty certainly didn't have that kind of clout.

The irony of this was that several years before, when Frank's fortunes had dipped and he was working the nightclubs, Marty had urged me to go to the Cocoanut Grove one evening to hear Frank sing. "Frank is down," Marty had said. "And when a performer is down, that's when he needs your support—not when he's on top of the world." The Cocoanut Grove was a cavernous place and when it was only a third filled, as it was that evening, it had a melancholy air. Frank's voice had changed. He wasn't singing the way he had sung before or the way he sings now. He seemed uncertain. I suppose when you fall on hard times, your confidence is shaken to the point at which you can't do the things you always had under control. Of course, Frank still had the basic quality of his voice. The sound is always there. That never leaves a singer. The tone, the sound, the style—that's what God gives out, what you come in with. You can't learn sound from a teacher. You can learn flexibility, phrasing, breathing, those things that enhance sound and tone, but that's as close as you can get.

Frank came over to our table and sat with Marty and me for a while and had a drink. He knew he wasn't singing the way he wanted to. Of course, we didn't talk about that, but he seemed a little em-

146

barrassed. About the small turnout too. Now here he was, a few years later, throwing Marty off the set.

No sooner had the picture started than Frank had a new grievance: the cameraman. Charles Lang was the cameraman, one of the top men in his profession, but Frank stopped in the middle of a scene and announced that he would not go on unless Lang was dismissed and a new cameraman brought on the picture. Again, I haven't the remotest idea what triggered Frank's outburst, but he held up his hand and said, "Okay, hold it, that's it, we don't go any further until Lang is off this picture." It may be that Lang took too long in his setups for Frank's tastes. Lang was a very careful, methodical man who was very fussy about lighting, and it might have been that Frank, who is a very impatient, impulsive actor, couldn't abide the long waits between takes. Frank didn't like to rehearse. He didn't like doing a scene over and over. He liked to come on, do one take, and have it printed. That was all right with me. I think that repeating a scene makes a performance mechanical. There is something more alive and creative when you do a scene for the first time with all your juices flowing.

After Frank made his point about Charles Lang, he walked off the set. The message was clear: it was either Lang or Sinatra. Of course, Frank had no right to do what he did but when a picture is in production with all of its overhead in operation, there is no right and wrong; there is only that old devil, expediency. I don't recall who came in to replace Lang but whoever it was never had a minute's trouble with Frank.

〰〰〰〰〰〰〰〰〰〰〰〰〰〰〰〰〰〰〰〰〰〰〰〰〰

SAM WEISS

When Doris made *Young at Heart* with Sinatra, the picture almost shut down because of Melcher. I was close to Sinatra and visited him on the set quite regularly. Marty tried some hustle having to do with some of the songs in the show—Marty was always trying to work little angles for himself—and whatever pitch Melcher made to Sinatra, it was something that really set Frank off. Frank threw Melcher out of his dressing room, and then he put out an order that if Melcher was anywhere on the studio lot—and the studio was nine miles long—he, Sinatra, would walk off the movie.

The producer, Henry Blanke, put in a call to Jack Warner, who was down on the set in two minutes flat.

"What the hell's going on down here?" Warner demanded.

147

"What's going on is I refuse to work on this picture," Sinatra said, "if that creep Melcher is anywhere on the Warners lot. I've heard too many rotten things about him and I don't want him around. Now I'm just as much to this picture as Doris and if she can't get along without him then I walk."

Jack Warner put up his hand in a stop signal and picked up the phone. We were in Frank's dressing room and I was standing right beside the phone.

"Now here's an order and I want you to get it straight," Warner announced in that traffic-cop voice of his. "Frank Sinatra does not want Marty Melcher around, and I want you to find the lousy bum and run him off the lot and be sure he *stays* off until this picture is in the can. That's it, period! An order. You got it?"

⬛⬛⬛⬛⬛⬛⬛⬛⬛⬛⬛⬛⬛⬛⬛⬛⬛⬛⬛⬛⬛

Another thing about Sinatra that caused some trouble on the film was his tardiness. The production of a picture, needless to say, is a large, expensive, immediate undertaking that thrives on or suffers from its ability to stick to its schedule. There were many mornings when Frank came late, hours late, and there were some days when he missed his morning schedule altogether and didn't show until the afternoon.

I was in my knitting period so I stayed in my dressing room and concentrated on that, having learned somewhere along the line the futility of getting all steamed up because I was in makeup and waiting for some miscreant actor who couldn't get himself together. I was of two minds about Frank's tardiness. On the one hand, I sympathized that perhaps he was feeling down, hungover perhaps, or just plain not feeling up to the demands of the camera that day; perhaps he looked in the mirror and didn't like what he saw there. I have days like that. On the other hand, I am a compulsive performer. I am too aware of all the people on the set whose jobs rely on my being there on time. I think most actors share my feeling. (Paul Newman tells me he has been late on a set only once in his life. And in most other respects Paul is a disorganized, blithe spirit who is frequently late.)

I don't think Frank was concerned with what his absence meant to the other people on the picture. It caused the director, Gordon Douglas, some anguish, and Harry Blanke, the producer, fretted and fumed, but as for me, despite Frank's sure and rather cocky exterior, I always felt there was a sad vulnerability about him. Perhaps that's why I always had understanding and compassion for

148

By the Light of the Silvery Moon, with Gordon MacRae, and *Calamity Jane,* one of Doris's favorites, were also steeped in nostalgia.

Getting prepared for her big mud scene in *Calamity Jane*.

After her nervous breakdown, Doris had a tough time returning to action in *Lucky Me* with Phil Silvers.

Judy and Doris were great friends who often crossed the country together and who also had breakdowns at about the same time on the Warners lot.

Doris and Frank had an amiable relationship in *Young at Heart,* but Frank threw Doris's husband off the lot.

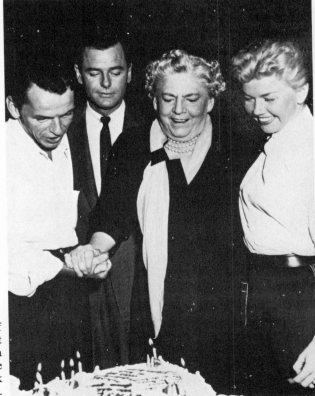

A lovely moment on the set of *Young at Heart,* when the great Ethel Barrymore, old and in a wheelchair, was given a surprise birthday party by Sinatra. The look on Ethel's face tells the whole story.

what he did. I liked him. We had a fine relationship. There were many lovely things about him that I admired.

During the shooting of the picture, Ethel Barrymore, the *grande dame* of American actresses, had a birthday, and Frank gave her a surprise party on the set. She was a very old lady who spent most of her time between takes in a wheelchair. She wasn't crippled but she was fragile, as the old get fragile. But I had to marvel at her transformation when she was assisted from her wheelchair to play a scene. Suddenly from deep within her a kind of dynamism arose, her body became erect, and, great actress that she was, for the moment that the camera required she was able to produce that special kind of grandeur that was the hallmark of the Barrymores.

She was very touched by her birthday remembrance. Sinatra proposed a toast to her and she kissed him on the cheek. I knew that it was entirely possible that this might be her last birthday, and my emotions being what they are, my eyes filled with tears. She came over and hugged me as if to thank me for my tears.

"Hey!" somebody called out. "Doris needs a Kleenex!"

From across the set, someone threw a box of Kleenex to me. I didn't see it coming and the box struck me in the forehead. It stung a little and I gasped, more in surprise than pain. Frank sprang at the man who had flipped the box at me and grabbed the front of his shirt, pulling the fabric up tight under his chin.

"Don't you ever do that!" he shouted at the man. "You don't throw things at a lady, you understand?"

"It's all right, Frank," I said. "I'm not hurt—"

"That's beside the point! You bring the box, you creep, and you *offer* a Kleenex—you got that? You *offer* a Kleenex!"

Frank let the man go and came over to me to be sure that I was all right. Often, over the years, whenever I pulled a Kleenex out of a box, I thought of Frank.

TERRY MELCHER

My first and only memory of my father, Al Jorden, was in his living room in Cincinnati when I set my hair on fire with his cigarette lighter. I was five, I guess, and I had gone to spend the afternoon with him and his new wife. It was the only time I remember seeing my father.

Strangely, I recall seeing my mother only once before I came to

149

Hollywood to live with her, when I was seven. My grandmother, with whom I lived, had brought me to Hollywood for a visit and my memory is of an evening at the Palladium, where my mother was working, and I remember that because I had an avocado for the first time. The fact is, I wasn't quite sure who my mother was until I came to live with her. "Mother" was just a word, without meaning. My grandmother was my total parent. I knew my mother was on the road, that she was a singer, my grandmother told me all that, but it didn't make her real for me.

The next time I heard about my father, after that incendiary incident in his living room, was when he pulled up his automobile at a stoplight, took a gun out of the glove compartment, and blew his head off.

The way I figure it, Al Jorden was my mother's one romance, and I think, because of him, sex and violence in her mind are one and the same. She's never told me that, we've never discussed it, but that's what I think. I figure a young girl of seventeen, married for the first time—the guy's obviously a passionate man. From what I'm told, he was a hell of a good musician, but his success was affected by his passion, which got in the way of his work.

After his death I was really sorry that I had never seen him. I don't even know what he looked like. No one has a picture of him. His name was never mentioned around the house. All I know about him is what I've learned from my grandmother since Marty Melcher died. Since Marty died, we all three talk openly about a lot of things that used to be taboo.

In my memory, it seems that I met my mother and Marty at the same time. When I came out to Hollywood to live with my mother, Marty was around the house, and a couple of years later he adopted me and gave me his name. It was good between us in those early years, but when I became a teen-ager, Marty couldn't handle it. He became hell-bent on making me feel guilty and in trying to run my life like a Marine drill sergeant. He was all holier-than-thou in his Christian Science uniform, ushering on Sundays, and proverbs came out of him at me like machine-gun bullets. Every occasion, no matter what I did, he had a proverb. "Do as I say, not as I do," which means, I get my ass kicked for something he also does but he doesn't get his ass kicked because he told me not to do it. Fine, great—just what a teen-ager wants to hear.

He threw Christian Science at me every way he could. Sunday school, a C. S. grammar school for six years, and a C. S. college for a year. During my growing-up years, I only saw as much of my mother as Marty would permit—and he didn't permit much. Marty was the agent, the manager, the coproducer, the potentate, who let me see her if we took a weekend vacation, but Marty didn't like my mother and me to get too close. He didn't want me to talk to her. He was afraid I might say something that would upset her. He treated her like a patient of some sort. The number-one standing order, before "God is love" or anything else, was "Don't upset your mother"—which, translated, means, If you've got a problem, don't tell your mother or it's your ass, just tell me—and it will be your ass anyway.

When I was in the ninth grade, Marty sent me to a military school that was only fifteen minutes from our house. Said I needed discipline. Some discipline. They kicked my ass every day because my mother was a movie star. I'd come home weekends and say, "Hey, listen, these crazy seniors are beating the hell out of me, and my roommate got stabbed with

150

a saber by a twelfth-grade little kid who is an officer, and the officers wear their swords all the time—to class, to breakfast, to lunch, to dinner, to bed for all I know—and this is some crazy place that I want out of." Ninety percent of the kids in that school lived in Los Angeles and had been sent there, as I had been, just to get us out of the house. So they were full of bitterness and resentment and by the time they became seniors they took out all that frustration on the freshmen—Tom Brown's school days, forget it. It was our necks all the time.

The next year Marty tried to ship me farther away so I couldn't even appear on weekends. I mean really away—Gstaad, Switzerland— but my mother wouldn't hear of it. So that's how I wound up at Beverly Hills High School. I went there for two years. The principal called me into his office one day and said, "You know, Terry, your situation is really unique—half the kids come to this school in limos, most of the parents are power-mad egomaniacs, nouveaux who just made it last week, and my hands are really tied, because if I tried to discipline one of these kids I'd have fifteen lawyers on my neck. I can't do a thing because of the parents—don't touch my kid, you rotten creep, how much do you make, how much are you worth, I could buy and sell you ten times over, that's what I have to contend with. But your father came in here and said, 'Any time you want to lower the boom on my kid, Terry Melcher, go right ahead.'" Here was the principal of the school calling me in to tell me that he was flabbergasted. "I've never encountered this before," he said. "What kind of a man is your father?"

I hadn't done anything wrong, mind you—Marty was just making sure that when I did do something wrong, I'd get my ass kicked. Toward the end of my senior year I did get in trouble. Beverly Hills High was a really *boring* school, and I had worked out a system for cutting class with my friend Craig Martin, Dean's oldest son. I had discovered that the woman in charge of absentees was a big fan of my mother's, so Craig and I used to cut school together at least three times a week and it was cool, I'd lay a Doris Day album on the woman once in a while, give her some signed Doris Day photos, and all I'd have to do every week was turn in a few excuses on which I had signed Marty's name. I had her in my pocket. But one day the principal happened to be in her office just as Craig and I were checking in—we usually showed up around two in the afternoon after we had played golf or been to the beach. The principal dug out our records and in no time flat he sized up all those forged signatures—eight months of forgeries. He hauled us into his office and called Dean Martin to tell him about Craig, but then he looked at me and said, "Well, I guess I won't call your father because there's no telling what he might do to you." So help me, got off scot-free because Marty had been so paranoid with the principal.

After I graduated from high school, Marty made it painfully clear that my choice of college was strictly limited to Principia College in St. Louis, a Christian Science institution. I went there under protest and barely lasted the first year. There was no point in trying to go around Marty and talk to my mother about college because she would have just deferred to him and then it would have been my ass for having gone around him. I just wasn't strong enough yet to take him on.

Principia was an unofficial theological seminary for C. S., designed to turn out Practitioners. The student-body president, when I was there,

151

was a guy named Egil "Bud" Krogh, who recently went to jail in the Watergate mess. I had occasion to go to Krogh when a friend of mine, a senior whom I knew from Hollywood, was stoolied on by some creep who was out on a zoology field trip with his field glasses and had seen my friend in a field somewhere fucking his girl friend. This stoolie reported this sinful event to Krogh, and I went to see Krogh before he turned in a report to the president of the faculty. I said, "Listen, Krogh, show a little compassion—all my friend did is make love to his girl, and if you turn him in he'll get kicked out of school and here it is only two weeks before his graduation."

"Geez," Krogh, said, "I'd like to help the poor fellow but the rules are the rules . . ."

"It's up to you, to your discretion—nothing says you've *got* to turn in this report. Be a good guy and bury it."

"I'm sorry, Melcher," Krogh said, straightening his back, "rules are rules and laws are laws and I must do my duty."

They kicked out my friend, not quietly but with a lot of fanfare, like that television show that opened every week with a guy having his brass buttons ripped off his uniform, his sword busted in two, and him put on a donkey and ridden out. And why? He made love to his girl in a field of daisies. (Krogh also blew the whistle on the girl, who got booted out of her school.) When Krogh got busted over Watergate and thrown in the slammer I felt good for a week. One time I visited a whorehouse in East St. Louis with about thirty Principia guys. The place was raided and all of us were rounded up along with the hookers. I got one of the cops aside and explained that we were from Principia and we would all probably get kicked out if they booked us. The cop thought about that and then he let us go. So the point is, an ordinary cop had more compassion than Krogh.

152

Ten

LIBERATION from Warner Brothers brought with it, for the first time, the inalienable right to say no—but I found that in some ways my newfound freedom made life more difficult, not easier. For now a great variety of scripts were offered to me and I had to make judgments that I had never had to make before. Whether to choose Script A over Scripts B, C, and D. Whether this director would be better than that director. It was certainly easier to be in peonage at Warners, where there were no choices.

One of the scripts that intrigued me was a dramatization of the life of Ruth Etting, the torch singer of the Twenties who got her start through gangland connections. The picture, called *Love Me Or Leave Me,* had a veteran producer, Joe Pasternak, a first-rate script by Isobelle Lennart, a very competent director, Charles Vidor, and Jimmy Cagney already cast in the role of Marty Snyder, "the Gimp"—a small-time hood who devoted his life and fierce ambition to furthering Ruth Etting's career. Etting was an important singer of her day, and the relationship between her and the crippled, hard-driving Snyder was an unusual and compelling one, but Ruth Etting was a kept woman who clawed her way up from seamy Chicago nightclubs to the Ziegfeld Follies, and I wondered whether audiences would believe me in a part like that.

As I previously said, there is something about a performer's own personality that forms the base of every character she plays, and it is only within that framework that she is believable. This is particularly true of so-called stars because it is their strong basic personality shining through their roles that has made them stars, a personality that audiences want to see in every part they play. That's why I hesitated doing *Love Me Or Leave Me*—not that I was worried

153

about my image (that word!) but only if an audience would accept me, *believe* me, for believability is the essence of every performance.

I had several discussions with Joe Pasternak about that. The part would require me to drink, to wear scant, sexy costumes, to string along a man I didn't love in order to further my career. There was a vulgarity about Ruth Etting that I didn't want to play.

"That's just the point," Pasternak said. "It will be in the playing —that's why I want you for the part. You will play Ruth Etting in a way that will give her some dignity, that will play away from the vulgarity. Besides, there's all that great music that will do a lot to affect the characterization."

It was a great score, all right, but I think what finally induced me to do the picture was the opportunity of performing with Cagney. Actually, I had already been in a film with Jimmy, *The West Point Story,* made in 1950, early on at Warners, but that was a real idiot picture in which almost all of my scenes were with Gordon MacRae, and Jimmy's scenes were with Virginia Mayo. I couldn't possibly tell you anything about the plot. Zero. Gordon was a cadet and Jimmy was a Broadway hoofer. End of my memory.

But in *Love Me Or Leave Me,* the relationship between Jimmy and me was marvelously detailed, combative, involved; the Gimp was a difficult and demanding role that would bring out all of Jimmy's fire, and the prospect of performing with Jimmy at the top of his form was my primary reason for doing the picture.

I prepared for the role by listening to all the Ruth Etting records. She had a quiet way of speaking and singing. It was not my intention to mimic her, but to suggest her style with little inflections and shadings that I picked up from the recordings.

It was a picture that worked at every level. I don't go to rushes (I had a policy of *never* looking at rushes and only going to premieres when absolutely forced to) but I knew after each day's work that we were doing something special. The most dramatic scene in the picture involved a confrontation in my New York hotel room. I was the star of the Follies. I had captured the success for which I had been striving all those hard years. Marty Snyder was now an embarrassment and an encumbrance. My real love was my accompanist and arranger, played by Cameron Mitchell. In this scene I tell Marty that it's all over between us, that I am not going to be his woman anymore, and that I want him out of my life. He attacks me savagely; and the way Cagney played it, believe me, it was savage.

He slammed me against the wall, ripped off my dress, my beads flying, and after a tempestuous struggle, in which I tried to fight him off with every realistic ounce of strength I had, he threw me on the bed and raped me. It was a scene that took a lot out of me but it was one of the most fully realized physical scenes I have ever played. As I said, I don't look at rushes, so it wasn't until I saw the movie in its release that I became aware that most of that scene had been cut. I was told that it couldn't get by "the Code," but that excuse was often standard cop-out for not wanting to fight for something. It was my only disappointment in the picture. I was particularly pleased with the sound of the songs I sang. A new process called Perspecta Stereophonic Sound brought rich, full tones into the theater.

JAMES CAGNEY

The first time I saw Doris perform, it affected me as I had only been affected twice before in my life. The first time was when Spencer Tracy and I went east together by train. He phoned me at my hotel the day after we arrived in New York and said I had to drop everything and get tickets to see an actress named Laurette Taylor in a new play called *The Glass Menagerie*. I went and what I saw was a performance that was pure art from beginning to end. The lady made not one false turn. I met Spence after the show and we discussed her performance for hours. Laurette Taylor.

The second time was when I saw Pauline Lord in the Eugene O'Neill play *Anna Christie*. Doris has the same qualities those two ladies had—same capacity, same understanding of what's required and how to communicate it. The touchstone is simplicity, the simple line of performance, directly to you, uncluttered. That's true of everything—writing, painting, music—that's the rare thing, to strip away all that is fake and artificial. Not a trace of ham. Someone asked me to define "ham" and I said when you overlard something, whatever way you overlard it—whether a thing is overpainted, overworded, whatever. So what Doris has, and all the good ones have, is the ability to project the simple, direct statement of a simple, direct idea without cluttering it.

That's what she brought to *Love Me Or Leave Me*, which is a movie that I rate among the top five of the sixty-two pictures that I made. I played Marty Snyder, the crippled, small-time hood who sponsored and managed Ruth Etting's career. I knew the Marty Snyders of the world from the tough New York neighborhood in which I grew up. Hard-bitten, aggressive little guys, self-assertive, driven to compensate for their poverty and, in this case, for the handicap of a crippled leg. The director had some kind of iron device that he wanted to clamp on my leg to achieve the crippled effect, but I said it would only get in the way, I much preferred to play crippled as I felt it. I didn't want to imitate the real Marty Snyder any more than Doris tried to mimic Ruth Etting. It's my

155

feeling that impersonation gets in the way of a performance and takes over. I prefer to interpret rather than imitate.

The producer, Joe Pasternak, said he had a hell of a time persuading Doris to play the part because she had doubts that she could play a dramatic part of such intensity. That was as it should be—there should always be some doubt. I operate on the simple premise that as soon as you're sure, you're through. Always doubt, always butterflies. You just work like hell and hope that the job gets done. I told that to a cocksure director one time—as soon as you think you've got all the answers, get ready to go down the road. The best stage director I ever worked with, George Kelly, who was also a great playwright and actor who could have played all the parts in that play better than any of us, asked us to make as many suggestions as we wanted because he certainly didn't have all the answers. Of course, we never suggested a thing, so good was he, but he never once gave us the impression that he knew everything.

I suppose the most curious aspect of *Love Me Or Leave Me* was the parallel relationships of Ruth Etting and Marty Snyder, and Doris Day and Marty Melcher. It was as if the picture was a prediction of Doris's own life. Snyder lived vicariously through Etting, as Melcher did through Doris. A man named Albert Knock, a long time ago in a movie called *Reminiscences of a Superfluous Man,* said, "If self-preservation is the first law of nature, then exploitation is certainly the second." Life sometimes imitates art, doesn't it?

Doris and I have both had long careers in films, and I'm sometimes asked how to account for this longevity. Not easy. A lot of very talented people have very short careers. One factor is certainly timing. I came along during a tough time when gangsters and prohibition had captured the front pages, and had become a kind of romantic aspect of those times. Doris came along when we were beginning the postwar era, and there was something about her that caught the mood and fancy of those times. It could very well have been that if I had come along a couple of years later than I did, I would never have made my way. And the same holds true for Doris. Who knows?

One thing I do know, though, is that none of us should take any credit for our initial endowments over which we had no control. Doris and I certainly agree on that. You work on what you've got, but what you've got was given to you by the Great Provider. But the other element about longevity is this: no matter how good your acting skills, the essential person comes through—you simply can't fool that camera. The Barrymores were perfect examples. Brilliant people, all of them, but absolutely no guile, not a vestige of guile in them; they were wide open, innocence itself in spite of the kind of lives they led. And it was that quality, coupled with their great talents, that kept them up there at the top for so long.

My feeling is that shrewdness is not a very happy quality; it photographs, cuts right through everything, and if anything gives a performer a short run, that's it. Well, Doris is the epitome of guilelessness. An almost naïve quality of innocence and trust. As an actress, she perfectly illustrates my definition of good acting: just plant yourself, look the other actor in the eye, and tell him the truth. That's what she does, all right. Sometimes when we finished an emotional scene that went well on the first take, she'd say, "Oh, that's a good one, just look how the hair has risen on my wrists!"

In one of the key scenes in *Love Me*, we have a slam-bang argument that culminates with me slapping Doris. We rehearsed the scene a couple of times for the camera, but each time I only feigned slapping her, stopping my hand just short of her face. That's a common movie technique, with the sound of the slap dubbed in later. But when we were playing the scene, and I felt it was going just right, I didn't pull my slap but I really whacked Doris across the cheek. I didn't want to fake anything about that scene. She was stunned, more surprised than hurt, although the slap was sharp enough to have given her face a sting—she looked at me with a stricken look on her face and tears welled in her eyes and the surprise was 100 percent genuine.

And so is Doris.

The only unpleasant aspect of *Love Me Or Leave Me* was some of the fan reaction I received. I was deluged with mail attacking me for drinking, for playing a lewd woman, for the scant costumes I wore in the nightclub scenes. I suppose many Christian Scientists were disappointed and in some cases angry that I, a Christian Scientist, was up there on the screen drinking and smoking. What's involved in this kind of protest is the movie realism that made me hesitate to play the role in the first place. On the screen I am not Doris Day playing a part, I *am* that part. They may call me Ruth Etting in the movie but to the audience I am Doris Day and I shouldn't be doing those dreadful things on the screen. I answered every piece of mail, explaining this as best I could, for I feel a performer has the same responsibility to his public that a politician has to the electorate. It was a beautifully made picture about which I had no regrets, but I cared very much about people who were disturbed by my characterization. It was a picture that could not have been made at Warners, where musicals were done as quickly and cheaply as possible. The time, money, and expertise that MGM devoted to the film were what gave it its look of quality. My first adventure in the free world was certainly a rewarding one.

There is one other aspect to *Love Me Or Leave Me* that didn't really register with me until some years later, and that is the parallel, in some respects, between Marty Snyder and Marty Melcher—and I don't just mean the coincidence of their names. I will go into this later on, when I discuss my relationship with Marty Melcher as it developed over the years; I hadn't yet realized, in 1955, how much Ruth Etting and I had in common.

SAM WEISS

I am maybe the only man alive who personally knew both Ruth Etting and Marty Snyder, and Doris Day and Marty Melcher, and I can vouch for how similar their relationships were. I worked with Lennie Hayton when he was musical director on the Ruth Etting radio show in New York. Snyder used to come to rehearsals to make pronouncements about the music and to give orders to Hayton, but Snyder knew no more about music than Melcher did. What irony that Doris wound up playing Ruth Etting! The only difference between the two Martys was that Snyder had a limp, but when Melcher started to act like he knew something about music and began to choose theme songs for Doris's pictures and all that, I nicknamed him the Gimp and it stuck. I don't know if Melcher resented it or not. He'd laugh when we called him that, but he was such a namby-pamby, such a coward, that there's no telling how the nickname really affected him.

Alfred Hitchcock redeemed his six-year-old promise to me with *The Man Who Knew Too Much*. I was as tentative about doing it as I had been about *Love Me Or Leave Me* but for a totally different reason. Hitchcock was going to film most of the picture in London and Marrakesh. I had never been out of the United States, and with my uneasiness about air travel being what it was and is, I thought maybe I'd pass up this Hitchcock for the next one. I had never gone abroad with Bob Hope or Les Brown, but it was Hope's domestic tours through impenetrable winter weather that had spooked me off the airplane.

Marty would have none of my protests. "Now, Doris, this is a fine picture that you want to do with Hitchcock and Jimmy Stewart and you simply can't back out just because you have to travel. You're not going alone—I'll be with you and we'll take Terry and we'll all go by train and boat. It will be *fun*."

"What about the dogs?" I had two big standard poodles to whom I was devoted (and vice versa).

"Well, we have a housekeeper, haven't we, and we'll ask your mother to move in and look after them while we're gone. Now, Do-Do, stop making excuses—you're going to have *fun*."

The first time I saw Hitchcock I was with Edith Head, talking about my costumes. Hitchcock came in, wanting to see the sketches and discuss them; he is a very thorough man who gets involved in every aspect of a picture he's doing. On that day he threw out some

158

of the sketches and was very precise about exactly what he wanted for my wardrobe. Hitch's office on the Paramount lot was right next to Wardrobe so he'd often drop in during my fittings to keep an eye on just what they were creating for me.

There was a song-writing team under contract at Paramount, Livingston and Evans, to whom Hitchcock had assigned the task of composing a song for me to sing as a lullaby to my little son in the picture. Jay Livingston and Ray Evans had written "Buttons and Bows" and many of the songs for the Hope and Crosby pictures. One afternoon when I was in Wardrobe having a fitting, Ray Evans came in and asked me whether I'd like to hear the new song for the picture, which had just been approved by Hitchcock. We went to their music studio, where they played "Que Sera, Sera" for me. I thought it was fine for the spot in the picture where it was needed, but later, when I saw Marty, I expressed my disappointment that it did not have a broader appeal.

"What do you mean?" Marty asked.

"Well, it's a kiddie song. It's sweet, and perfect for where I sing it in the film, but I was hoping it would be more than that. You know —'whatever will be, will be'—that's not really my kind of lyric."

"I think you're dead wrong. Hitchcock and I both think it's going to be a big hit. You'll see."

Of course, I've never been wronger about anything than I was about "Que Sera." I recorded it for Columbia and for the movie album and it became the most popular of all my songs. Also, although I did not know Jay Livingston or Ray Evans, they had by pure chance hit upon a philosophy in "Que Sera" that was my theme song. Whatever will be, will be. As I previously mentioned, I strongly believe in the inevitability of everyone's life pattern. Our destinies are born with us. They are predestined to happen and the best one can do is to ride out the storms and bask in the glories. I don't believe in luck, good or bad. There is no such thing. I would hate to think that my life was a life of chance. There are those who believe that their career happened because they had the good fortune of being at the right place at the right time. Nonsense. It was meant to happen. Of course, there has to be a beginning, but I don't for one minute believe that luck has anything to do with it. The "lucky" one was meant to be there, that's all. The talent that was given to him, or the business acumen, or the scholarship was predestined to be recognized. The actual occurrence of recognition is an immaterial event.

159

And whoever, or whatever, is in charge of this force, this creative planning, *that* is God.

> When I was just a little girl,
> I asked my mother, "What will I be?
> Will I be pretty?
> Will I be rich?"
> Here's what she said to me:
>
> "*Que sera, sera,*
> Whatever will be, will be;
> The future's not ours to see.
> *Que sera, sera,*
> What will be will be."

"Que Sera" turned out to be not only a kiddie song but also an everyone song. Whether because of its utter simplicity, which made it so easy to remember and easy to sing, or because its philosophy hit a universally responsive chord, after the picture's release it was sung by everyone, everywhere I went. It was an overwhelming winner at that year's Academy Awards.

Contrary to my expectations, I really enjoyed the trip to London. We boarded the Santa Fe Super Chief on a Friday evening, had dinner, slept on the train two nights, and arrived in Chicago on Sunday. The Super Chief was a luxurious train that had marvelous service, a good dining room, excellent compartments—a first-class hotel on wheels with some of the world's prettiest scenery passing by the windows. On Sunday we had lunch in the Ambassador Hotel's Pump Room, then boarded the Broadway Limited that evening, again a luxury train, and arrived in New York on Monday morning.

We went straight to the *Queen Elizabeth,* which put to sea that evening. It was my first experience on a big liner and I loved every minute of it. I could have stayed aboard for a month. Above all, I liked the quiet of being on deck on the open sea. I'm a very quiet person, a very private person, and I found that everything about the crossing suited me, from having breakfast served on a tray in bed to sitting bundled up on a deck chair. I read, and ate marvelously, and went to the movies, and swam in the ship's pool, and dined at the captain's table, and nobody butted in on my privacy.

Terry made friends with a woman on board whom I knew slightly—she was a writer at MGM—and they did all the ship's events together. Terry asked me if he could play Bingo. I gave him five dollars and told him that that was all he would be allowed to lose. By the time we got off the boat in Southampton he had amassed four hundred dollars in Bingo winnings.

There was a car waiting for us in Southampton that drove us to London, where we were booked at the Claridge. It was a pleasant drive but as we got near Claridge's, we had trouble moving down the street. There were great crowds of people along the sidewalks and at the edges of the streets, and traffic was at a virtual standstill.

"How nice," I said to Marty, "there's going to be a parade. Maybe this road goes to the Palace." I leaned forward to speak to the driver. "Who are they waiting for?" I asked. The crowds had now spilled into the street and we were at a standstill.

The driver turned around and said, "I think you, ma'am." I roared with laughter, but then somebody on the street shouted, "There she is!" I turned around to look out the rear window, expecting to see the Queen's limousine or carriage, but suddenly the crowd surged against our car and they started to rock it from side to side! It was really spooky. What was happening was so unbelievable—that this was London and that this mob of people had turned out because they had found out I was due at the hotel. I had the sensation that it was a scene staged for a picture I was in. It was only with police assistance that we were able to move the car to the hotel entrance, and even with the help of the police it was extremely difficult to get from the car to the hotel lobby. Even though my fan mail from England had always been extremely heavy, this reception was totally unexpected. I found a devotion and loyalty there that was embarrassing. (There is to this day a very active Doris Day Society in London that, among other things, publishes a Doris Day magazine.) My English friends told me that of all the signs of the zodiac, Aries rules England, and that's my sign. I love the English. Their simplicity. The beauty of their parks. If I didn't have my family of dogs, I would seriously consider living there.

We were virtual prisoners at Claridge's. We had a lovely suite but there were so many flowers we could barely move around. It was as if someone were laid out in the living room. I've been to funeral parlors with fewer flowers. It was eerie—and a little depressing. Hordes of people camped outside the hotel entrance and on the back lawn beneath our windows. We couldn't leave the hotel. Terry thought it was all a marvelous lark. A publicity man from Paramount brought us a batch of pictures and Terry set himself up at the windows, filling requests from below. "Hey, Mom," he'd say, "this one's for Sidney." I'd autograph it and he'd sail it out the window.

It was inevitable and understandable that the management asked us to move. The manager was very polite about it and I thought he was absolutely right to ask us to leave out of consideration for the hotel's other guests.

We snuck out of the hotel through the service entrance at four in the morning and flew to Paris. One of Edith Head's assistants was there to work on some of my wardrobe, and I met some of the other people who would be working on the film—Brenda De Banzie, Bernard Miles, Daniel Gélin, Christopher Olsen—who were also there for wardrobe. We stayed with friends in a remote *quartier,* ate in small, unfashionable, but delicious restaurants, rented a car, and drove to the south of France. Terry sat up front with the driver and practiced his French, while Marty and I gawked at the beautiful towns and countryside. We stopped in little villages and stayed in small inns with good restaurants, and the loveliest part of the trip was that nobody knew who I was. I know it's a cliché for stars (oh, how I hate that word!) to exult in momentary anonymity, but that was a particularly pleasant respite after the London madness. Of course the proliferation of television and movies has eliminated anonymity, but back then the south of France was still unspoiled. People were pleasant to you and outgoing because they liked you for yourself, not because you had a face they recognized.

Our only mistake was that we wound up in Cannes. If anyone doesn't belong in Cannes it's I, especially when the Film Festival is on, which, unhappily, it was. We stayed at the Carlton, which was full of Americans. The beach was so shockingly narrow and small as to be almost (to a Californian) nonexistent. The photographers were all running around looking for starlets and the starlets were all running around in sequined bikinis, and less, looking for the photographers. I couldn't believe that I had had the misfortune of arriving at the Riviera during the Film Festival. The only bright spot was that my dear friend Van Johnson was in the hotel. Van is one of the funniest, liveliest people I know; we all went to dinners and screenings together and thanks to Van, we had fun—except for the night there was a screening of a new film Van had made with Deborah Kerr. To put it generously, the film was not a hit. People in the audience got quite ugly about it, and Van, who was moaning and groaning more than anyone else, finally got physically sick from what he was seeing on the screen and went running from the viewing room. He ran all the way back to his room at the Carlton and got in bed and stayed there for twenty-four hours.

I went up to see him. He lay motionless in bed. He looked as if he had just had a major operation. "I don't think it was all that bad," I said.

He sat up and screamed at me. "Are you crazy, Clara Bixby? It wasn't bad—that's right—it was rotten! Rotten, rotten, rotten! It's the worst film that ever came out of Hollywood's rear end. Don't ever mention it again! Promise? As long as you live."

With a great sigh he lowered himself into the covers and seemed to expire.

One afternoon Peter Ustinov and his wife invited us to join them and some friends for a picnic on the beach. They had found a remote stretch where we had a lovely lunch that Peter had arranged with a nearby restaurant. Toward the end of the lunch, we became aware of a man who had appeared on the road above the beach and was now walking by us on his way to the water. As he passed, and I got a good look at him, I almost fell off my beach chair, for he was wearing clear plastic trunks. Clear, see-through plastic trunks! We all got hysterical. Van was there (recovered by now) and he got some good pictures of the mystery bather as he left the water. For me, that plastic-trunked bather epitomized the Cannes Film Festival.

We drove from Cannes to Marseilles, where we boarded a small boat, the *Djenne,* that took us to Morocco. We stopped first in Tangiers to off-load some cargo, and the captain urged us to take a tour of the picturesque native section, which certainly did not seem picturesque to me, for all I saw was the poverty and starvation of the people and the animals. I couldn't wait to get back on the boat.

There was a car to meet us when we put in at Casablanca, and it took us directly to Marrakesh, where, to my horror, the poverty and starvation were even worse than in Tangiers. The good hotel, the Mamooneah, was closed for the summer, but our quarters at La Menara were perfectly all right. But it was difficult for me to go out on the balcony of my suite and see the emaciated animals and people on the streets. I am not one who finds poverty and malnutrition very quaint, no matter what the setting. A few rich people in Marrakesh had everything, and the rest of the people, and the animals, had nothing. Marty was standing on the balcony beside me and I told him that what I was seeing made me sick, physically sick, and I didn't want to stay there and do the picture.

"Oh, now, Doris," Marty said.

"No, I'm serious. I want you to tell Mr. Hitchcock."

"We begin photography tomorrow—"

"Well, you tell Mr. Hitchcock to call Grace Kelly. Let Grace Kelly do it."

"I'll tell him," Marty said, in a tone that I recognized.

"I'm serious."

"I know you are."

"I'll bet Grace Kelly would love to do this picture."

"Doris, come in out of the sun."

"The sun has nothing to do with it! Just look at those animals! They're all skin and bones. Maybe it won't bother Grace Kelly."

Of course, Marty did not pass my suggestion along to Hitchcock, but when photography started, I went on the warpath about the animals being used in the scenes. It was one of the few times in my life that I pulled rank. I said I would not appear in any scenes with animals unless they were properly fed. I wouldn't get in the *keop* and allow the horses to pull me unless they were fed. As a result, the company set up a feeding station where all the goats, lambs, horses, cows, dogs, cats, burros, and other animals were brought to be fed. I couldn't provide for the feeding of the entire undernourished population of Marrakesh, but by the time our photography was finished I had succeeded in fattening up the animals used in the picture.

I only wish I could have fed myself as easily as the horses and goats. From the moment we arrived in Marrakesh, my stomach rebelled at the sight of the local cuisine. Almost everything was served out of community pots. Our first night there we were invited to some palace where the diners filled their plates from a community pot *with their hands!* Well, D. Day is a lady of rather simple, hygienic eating habits and there was no way I was going to dig into the couscous or anything else. From then on, I lived on eggs in the shell and I only ate those if I opened them myself at the table. Occasionally, Hitchcock would invite us to a dinner he had had flown in from Paris or London, and I suppose that's what kept me alive. Jimmy Stewart and his wife, Gloria, Marty, Terry, and everyone else ate the local cooking and tried to convince me that their survivals were endorsements of the food, but I tend to be emotional about what I eat and Marrakesh cooking simply zapped my gastric juices.

However, I was less concerned about the food than I was about Alfred Hitchcock. He didn't direct. He didn't say a word. He just sat next to the camera, with an interpreter on either side of him (French and Arabic), and all he did was start and stop the camera. Jimmy and I were left to our own devices. Hitch never spoke to me before a scene to tell me how he wanted it played, and he never spoke to me afterward. On those evenings when we all had dinner, he was chatty and entertaining but we never spoke a word about the picture we were doing. Jimmy knew Hitch very well, of course, having made *Rear Window* and *Rope* with him, but all Jimmy would say, when I asked about Hitchcock's behavior, was "Well, that's the way he is."

I finally became so upset, broiling in that summer sun for a director whom obviously I wasn't pleasing, that I again told Marty I wanted out. "I mean it, Marty. Hitchcock will probably be relieved. I'm obviously not pleasing him and he'll welcome an opportunity to get someone else. Why don't you suggest Grace Kelly?" I really don't know why I was so set on getting employment for Grace that summer—I suppose, because of her roles in *Rear Window* and *To Catch a Thief*, I jealously thought of her as a Hitchcock alumna who had pleased him on former occasions.

"You'll be all right when we get back to London," Marty said.

"Don't humor me! I will *not* be all right in London unless Alfred Hitchcock *relates* to me. I'm a lost soul!"

"Oh, Doris, he's just preoccupied—"

"I don't think he likes me."

"Maybe he's nervous—all those hundreds of extras and those crazy interpreters yelling at everyone."

"I want to go home."

"You *can't* go home. You made a deal, and that's that." Of course, Marty was right—I couldn't walk off this picture any more than I could have turned down an assignment at Warner Brothers. I was in the Marrakesh soup and that's all there was to it.

That night, crotchety and frustrated, I fell off the Christian Science wagon with a Tom Collins. One strong Tom Collins in that desert heat on an empty stomach (boy, was it empty!) and I got staggeringly drunk. We were all having dinner in the courtyard of

165

La Menara beside a large fountain, and Terry had to help his tipsy mother get up from the table and, holding her firmly around waist and shoulders to keep her upright, he walked her round and round the fountain. She wept a little, his tipsy mother, and muttered to herself and finally went back to her room and passed out on the bed.

When our Marrakesh shooting was finished and it was time to go to London for location work there, they told me I had to fly because they were behind schedule, half expecting me to put up a protest. What they didn't know was that I would have taken a balloon, so anxious was I to get out of there. I served food and drinks in the plane all the way over to get my mind off of where I was and how high up.

This time we stayed at the Savoy, with pretty much the same disturbing results. Mobs out front, mobs on the rear lawn that runs from the hotel down to the Thames. Some people pitched tents and stayed out there overnight. In the morning they would chant "We want Doris!" or "We love Doris" to bring me to the window. Clifton Webb and his mother were living in a suite directly above us and they were furious. You can imagine Clifton's cold fury. Spirals of smoke from his ears. Bobbies were constantly in evidence, looking for young people whose parents had called Scotland Yard to report them missing. On my day off, we would get in the car for a quiet day in the country but a whole retinue of cars would zoom after us, filled with cameras and autograph books.

We filmed in Brixton, where, between takes, the charming towns-people invited us in for tea, at Albert Hall and at the American Embassy, but not once, in any situation, did A. Hitchcock say a word to me that would have indicated that he was a director and I was an actress. I had an eerie feeling that I wasn't even being recorded on the film—that when the rushes were shown all there would be was Jimmy Stewart and some invisible presence who moved glasses around and opened doors, like Topper.

The first thing I did on getting back to Hollywood was to call my agent, Arthur Park. (Marty was my business manager but it was Arthur Park who was concerned with my relationships with the people I worked with.) I told Arthur that I wanted to have a heart-to-heart talk with Hitchcock before we started the difficult scenes that were scheduled for interior sets on the Paramount lot.

The meeting took place in Hitch's office with Arthur Park present. "I wanted to have a frank talk with you about the picture," I told Hitchcock. "I don't know why it is. I've gotten to know you pretty well and I like you so much, but I really feel like I'm not pleasing you."

"What makes you say that, my dear?"

"Well, you're not telling me what to do and what not to do and I just feel like I've been thrown into the ring and left to my own devices. We have all of our big scenes coming up and I want to please you, and do my best, but I just want you to feel free to say whatever you want to say to me because I want us to have a good rapport so that we can make a good movie."

"But, dear Doris, you've done nothing to elicit comment from me."

"What do you mean?"

"I mean that you have been doing what I felt was right for the film and that's why I haven't told you anything."

"Gosh, I wish you had told me that—it would have made all the difference. You see, I'm kind of, well, frightened of you in a way, and insecure."

"Everyone's frightened."

"Don't tell me you are."

"Oh, yes, I am. I'm always frightened. When I walk into the dining room at Paramount I'm as insecure as everybody else."

"Honestly?"

"Everybody's frightened and insecure, and the ones who appear not to be are just appearing not to be. Deep down, they're as frightened as the next fellow, maybe even more so."

"Well, Hitch, I'm not frightened anymore and I feel that you and I can talk about anything. And if I'm not giving you what you want in a scene—"

"Of course I'll tell you—you'll be the first to know!"

From then on, I never had an uneasy moment. My imagination had done me in—I had been reacting instead of acting.

The most difficult scene in the picture was the one in which Jimmy, who played my husband, a doctor, came to our hotel room to tell me that our son had been kidnapped. In the scene he first gives me some pills to sedate me, then, as the pills start to have an effect on me, he tells me about our boy. I want to rush out to try to find him but the pills are making me groggy. Jimmy restrains me but I try to fight him off. As the pills take hold, I grow progressively weaker until I can't fight them anymore and they overcome me.

"I think we should simply walk through the scene," Hitch said, "then right after lunch we'll try to get it in a single take."

I was all for that. I like to get up as high as I can for scenes that require heavy emotion, and give it everything I've got, holding back nothing. During lunch I would get myself ready, doing the whole scene, every detail, every line of dialogue in my head, which is the only place I like to rehearse. Before breaking, Jimmy and I walked through our moves for the camera and I covered our actions with a running monologue. "I will come in here, and Jimmy will come in here—I will be packing at the bed with the bags open, and he'll turn me around and say that he has something to tell me and he wants me to sit down, and I get up and say what is it, and he sits me down, and I get up again and then he tells me, and then we have the tussle, and I end up on the bed." All the time we were walking our moves for the cameras.

After lunch we assembled on the set and with no further preparation Hitch started the cameras and we did the whole scene in one take. Just like that. I've seen movies where an entire day, even more, is spent on a scene like that. But I always have confidence that I can walk on and deliver out of myself precisely what I want, for I firmly believe that whatever I really need—not *want* but need—will be there when necessary. I don't know what you would call that. I've heard it labeled "technique." I don't really know if I have technique in that sense. "Technique" suggests something rather mechanical that is imposed on a performance by an actress. What happened to me in that scene seemed very real to me; I actually *experienced* losing my little son to a kidnapper. I was living that ordeal, and when the cameras started to roll I was confident that whatever there is in me that makes me an actress would rise up and take command.

The Man Who Knew Too Much was very successful, destined to be one of the enduring Hitchcock films. Although he had verbally communicated very little to me, somehow, by some mystical process, I had learned some important things about Hitchcock movie-making that were to serve me well in the future. Certainly a lesson about confidence. And about the camera—Hitch used the camera differently from and more effectively than anyone I had worked with before. He was the most even-tempered, most organized director in my experience. Altogether a lovely man. I have had very little experience with genius but there is something about those who are touched with it that exalts everyone they work with, and I was no exception.

JAMES STEWART

Doris surprised a lot of people with her acting in *The Man Who Knew Too Much,* but she didn't surprise Hitch, who knew what to expect from her. A singer's talent for phrasing, the ability to put heart in a piece of music, is not too far removed from acting, in which the aim is to give life and believability to what's on paper. It all has to do with the center of thrust—the ability to find that which can make a song, or a scene, work.

I knew Hitch pretty well, from having made *Rear Window* and *Rope* with him. He didn't believe in rehearsals. He preferred to let the actor figure things out for himself. He refers to his method as "planned spontaneity." Of course, this is confusing to an actor who is accustomed to a director who "participates" in the scene. In the beginning, it certainly threw Doris for a loop. Hitchcock believes that if you sit down with an actor and analyze a scene you run the danger that the actor will act that scene with his head rather than his heart, or guts.

Another thing about Hitch: he is a very visual person. An old-school fellow. He feels that if you can't tell a story visually without a lot of dialogue, you are not using the film medium properly. In *The Man Who Knew Too Much,* Doris and I had a long scene in Albert Hall. The scene took place in the back of the hall with the London Symphony Orchestra on stage performing a symphony. An assassination was about to take place at the moment in the orchestral score when cymbals were crashed together. While the orchestra played, Doris and I had dialogue to explain what was happening and what might happen afterward. In the midst of the scene, Hitchcock appeared and said to us, "You two are talking so much I can't enjoy the symphony. Cut all the dialogue and act out the scene." Doris thought he had suddenly gone bananas, but we did the scene as he suggested, with the result that the scene was twice as effective as it had been with all that dialogue. And Hitch was able to enjoy the symphony without interruption.

Eleven

E VER since my release from Warner Brothers, Marty had been trying to find a property he could produce on his own; *Julie* was what he turned up with. It was a heavily dramatic script in which I played an airline hostess who was bedeviled by a rabidly jealous husband. I didn't want to do it. It wasn't a bad script, but playing the part of a woman victimized by a jealous husband washed back the reality of the insane jealousy of Al Jorden, the bizarre jealousy of Al Levy, and George Weidler's jealousy of my career. I had had more than enough real jealousy to contend with in my life. I didn't want to act in a film in which I played a woman whose husband was so jealous of her he was trying to kill her. That kind of sick film never has appealed to me and I told Marty so.

"That's the trouble with you, Doris," he said, "you just want to keep doing the same thing."

"Now that's not true, Marty. I've just done a dramatic picture for Hitchcock, and *Love Me Or Leave Me* before that."

"They had music. This will be different. A straight dramatic role. You'll be great in it."

"Look, Marty, the part doesn't appeal to me—"

"I've got a great deal all set with MGM—a budget of one million six with a fifty-fifty split of the profits. Everything is set to go. I've even got Jerry Rosenthal looking into a tax shelter for us."

"Well, you should have shown me the script before you went so far—"

"Don't you think I know a good script when I see one?" Marty was beginning to lose his temper.

"Marty, take it easy, I didn't say it wasn't a good script—"

170

"Then stop worrying. This is Oscar material. Would I put you into something I didn't *know* was going to be a big hit?"

"It's just the part, Marty—a jealous husband trying to kill—"

"And would MGM set me up to produce the film if they didn't believe in it?"

"I'm not saying it won't do well at the box office—"

"Then what more can you ask? Just do this one for me and the next one we'll get you a nice, easy musical."

This discussion lasted for the better part of two days but finally, as I always did with Marty, I gave in, albeit reluctantly. The Jerry Rosenthal whom Marty mentioned was a lawyer whose offices adjoined that of Arwin Productions, our company. (Marty made up the name and I have no idea what "Arwin" refers to.) Rosenthal worked very closely with Marty on deals, contracts, and tax matters, and at that time he was considered *the* Hollywood specialist on tax shelters. He had an impressive list of film clients. I am underlining his presence at that time because he was destined to become an oppressively evil force in my life.

Julie was a terrible ordeal, from start to finish—not the movie itself as much as the events that surrounded it. To begin with, I had to take flying lessons so that I could realistically handle the controls of a disabled airliner which, at the picture's climax, I had to land in an emergency. Marty, Terry, and I were driving to the airfield for my lesson in the new Cadillac which Marty had just given to me when we were hit broadside by a young man in a hot rod who had run a red light. The impact of the crash was just in back of my seat. The Cadillac was demolished. Marty, Terry, and the hot-rod driver were uninjured, but I was taken to the hospital for X rays and observation. Luckily the X rays revealed that my bumps and bruises did not involve any broken bones.

Marty later told me that he had been concerned that the accident might have set off the hyperventilating and other nervous disorders that I had suffered after *Calamity Jane,* but actually I took the accident right in stride.

Other events, though, were not so easy to take. Almost all of *Julie* was shot on location in Carmel, which is a lovely resort town on the coast a little south of San Francisco. My costar was Louis Jourdan, whom I liked very much. An amiable man, very gentle, very much interested in the people around him; we had a good rapport and I found talking with him a joy. I think that Frenchmen are much better at conversation than Americans. They *like* to talk. They are reflective and responsive. I don't know why the "strong, silent" American specimen is held in such esteem. There's nothing like an evening with a guy with bulging muscles and a vocabulary of twelve words. No, give me a skinny, chatty Frenchman every time. Louis and I had long talks about our problems, about life in Hollywood, about Paris, about our children, about Life in the larger sense. We would take long walks on the beautiful Carmel beach, chatting by the hour. There was nothing going on between us. We were not having an affair, but Marty became very jealous of Louis. He suspected we were having an affair but he was also jealous of how much I enjoyed our walks and talks. Marty and I had a compatible relationship but Marty was not a conversationalist. He liked to talk about pictures and albums and grosses, the usual Hollywood conversation, and he liked to discuss our Christian Science lessons, but he never really talked about us.

But he should have talked about us, for our relationship was changing. Marty's relationship with Terry, which had been so good at first, was also changing. As Terry got older, Marty's easygoing manner turned increasingly more tyrannical. And up there in Carmel, as producer of the picture, he was also showing a tyrannical side of himself. I can frankly say that I enjoyed being with Louis much more than with Marty. Of course Marty sensed this, and that too was part of his jealousy. But what irony, that during the making of this picture about a jealous husband, I should be beset with a real-life one.

We were about two weeks into the picture when another upsetting event occurred: I began to hemorrhage. Quite heavily. I told Marty about it and proposed that I go back to Los Angeles to see my gynecologist, but he suggested that we call our Practitioner, Martin Broones.

"I think it's best," Marty said, "to find out what Martin Broones suggests we read in the book. We'll concentrate on that and maybe by morning you'll be better."

I was trying to be a good Christian Scientist so I agreed to try to put into practice what I knew and had studied.

But the hemorrhaging got worse. I was losing quite a lot of blood, and there was a constant, rather intense stabbing pain in my abdomen. I spoke to Broones every day but it didn't affect the hemorrhaging. I begged Marty to let me go back to Los Angeles, but I was in virtually every scene and it meant shutting down the film. Marty wouldn't hear of it. "You're not *concentrating,* that's all that's wrong with you," he said. "Instead of thinking about running to a doctor, you should be working on your lessons and conquering whatever is causing the bleeding."

"But, Marty, there's this pain, and I feel so darn weak."

"All mental. In between setups, instead of spending your time gabbing with that Frenchman, you should lie down in your trailer and study *Science and Health.* You are what you think you are. You can think yourself well, and you know it. You better get hold of yourself or next thing you know you'll be hyperventilating."

Somehow, despite the bleeding, the pain, the loss of energy and weight, I got through the picture. Marty had been concerned about me—I don't want to give the impression that he wasn't. And, in all fairness, his concern had been about *me,* not just about whether I could finish the picture. Naturally he was concerned about that too, but I think that his main motivation for keeping me away from a doctor and concentrated on getting help from Christian Science was his own fear of doctors and the intensity of his conversion to C. S. I don't really know why Marty feared doctors. Whatever caused it was something far back in his life. That's why Christian Science came as such a godsend to him—a tailor-made religion for a man who was concerned about his health and well-being but fearful and distrustful of medical men.

The day I returned from Carmel, I drove straight to the office of my gynecologist, Dr. Willard Crosley. I had spent weeks in Carmel trying, as a good Christian Scientist, to "demonstrate what I knew" (C. S. terminology for putting theory into practice) but, obviously, from the amount of blood I was passing, as a demonstrator I was a flop.

Dr. Crosley poked around on my belly a few times and said, "Can you go to the hospital now?"

"Pardon me?"

"I've got to get you into the hospital immediately. I'd prefer right now—but I can wait until morning if necessary."

"Well, I've just come in from Carmel and I'd like to go home and see my mother and my dogs. What's wrong that it's such an emergency?"

"You have a tumor in there the size of a grapefruit, an endometriotic tumor growing into your intestines. It's quite bad. We've got to get it out—*immediately.*"

173

"Can you tell if it's malignant?"

"I'd say most likely not. Ninety percent. But even if benign it can cause a lot of damage."

The operation at Glendale Memorial lasted four hours. It was not only a hysterectomy, but (and this is the reason Dr. Crosley was so concerned) my intestines had to be surgically rebuilt to repair the damage the giant tumor had done to them.

I was in the hospital for ten days, which was recuperative procedure then, with the result that when I finally got out of bed and tried to walk I looked like Groucho Marx. The stitches had all solidified and I felt as gathered in my insides as a ruffle. I thought I'd never be able to stand up straight again. The slightest movement was an agony of pain, as if I were being prepared for shish kebob. Today a patient having that same operation probably gets out of bed and starts to move around after a day or so.

While I lay there in the hospital for those ten days, letting my stitches congeal, it dawned on me that I had lost the possibility of having another child. My life had been too crowded for childbearing, but I had intermittently thought about how I had been deprived of Terry's very young years and how nice it would be to have a baby that could be with me all the time. I was only thirty-two and although we never really discussed it, I felt Marty would have adored the experience of fatherhood. Well, that was gone now, the possibility ripped out of me, and thinking about that—the finality of it—threw me into a terrible depression. I burst out crying at the strangest times, and continued to do so long after I was out of the hospital. I had a lovely nurse who helped me during those dark fits, and who came home with me and stayed with me while I convalesced.

The sudden crying jags disturbed me. "I have no reason to cry," I'd blubber to the nurse.

"Cry—go ahead and cry. What difference if you do or don't have a reason?"

"But you can't cry when there's nothing to cry about, for Pete's sake!" I was sobbing so hard I could scarcely talk.

"Oh, yes, you can. They've just taken some woman things away from you, some very vital things, and your whole being is aware of that loss. That's more than enough to cry about. It *is* sad, and it's perfectly proper for you to shed tears over it."

As I said, the making of *Julie* was something of an ordeal.

But after my recovery some sunny events helped dispel the

gloom. First and foremost was the fact that we bought a new house on North Crescent Drive in Beverly Hills, the home I now live in. It was a single story house, and even though it cost around $150,000 it was rather modest by Beverly Hills standards. What I liked most about the house was the enormous, graceful old sycamore tree whose copious branches formed a canopy over the house and patio. (I have a deep feeling about trees, akin to my feeling about dogs, but what I'd like to be in my next life is a bird.)

I really enjoyed working on the interior decoration for the house. I love doing interiors. In fact, if I ever give up performing, that's what I'll be—an interior decorator. Nothing gives me more pleasure.

I used lots of prints and yellows to brighten the new house and give it a warm look. I chose comfortable, conservative furniture. No austere modern for me. My motto is "Better to please the fanny than the eye." I wanted to do some remodeling, such as redoing the living-room ceiling, which looked like it belonged in a dentist's waiting room, but Marty would not let me spend money on such projects. I had just signed a recording contract with Columbia Records for $1,050,000, the biggest contract of its time, but Marty wouldn't spend money on a new ceiling.

"We need all our surplus money for Rosenthal's investment program" was Marty's explanation. "Without tax shelters we'll be turning over everything we earn to the government." Oh, how I wish I had put it all in my ceilings!

DICK DORSO

Marty Melcher was a partner of mine in Century Artists long before he married Doris. He came from Massachusetts, immigrant parents, Orthodox Jews. He had a wonderful, dry sense of humor. When his father, who owned a hardware store in the little Massachusetts town where Marty was born, was coming to Hollywood for his first visit, Marty came into my office with a worried look on his face. "Listen, Dick," he said, "my dad is suspicious about the business I'm in, since there's no inventory, we don't own anything, and a goy is at the head of it. So when he's here and he comes in to meet you, please look a little worried, will you?"

What you've got to realize, to understand Marty, is that he worshiped money. It was his god, and it was all that he was really focused on, it was the only thing his immigrant parents understood. To accumulate money was Marty's drive, from the moment he hit Hollywood until the day he died.

Al Levy, our other partner, also had one big overriding need, and

175

that was to be loved. That was *his* motivation in everything he did. He tried to buy love with lavish presents to people who were startled to get them. Of course, you can't get people to love you that way, either you engender it or you don't, but Al never understood that. But this terrible need in him is what made him such a good agent, wanting his clients to love him for what he did for them. Al was a short man who was witty and urbane, and he came from a family with money. I think Doris was the first big love in his life, in the man-woman sense of love. Al didn't really know how to express that kind of love and it hurt him terribly when Doris rejected him.

When the split-up in our partnership occurred, there were hard feelings between Al and Marty. Al went to New York, where soon afterward he married a girl from the chorus line at the Copacabana. It was a very peculiar marriage. Al moved back to Hollywood with her, to make her a star, but she didn't want any part of it—or any part of Al. She went off for weeks at a time and had a life of her own, but Al seemed content to have it that way right up to the time he died.

When Levy left our firm, Marty and I had to buy him out. We were supposed to split his share along the same lines as our percentage of ownership—65 percent for me, 35 for Marty—but I waived that advantage and made it 50–50. Marty was terribly appreciative of that and said, "Dick, I'll never forget your generosity." And he didn't. Years later, when Doris went into television, I was no longer employed in the industry and Marty proposed me as coproducer of "The Doris Day Show." But CBS didn't like me because of previous dealings and turned me down. Marty went right to the CBS brass and told them, "Let's get this straight—either Dorso is the producer or I'll pull the series." That certainly shows Marty's integrity and loyalty—after all those years, Marty was paying me back.

After our agency became successful, we had a pretty wild time of it—parties, girls, every night a ball—but I finally came to realize that this was not a very constructive way to live and I decided to try analysis to get myself straightened out. After six months or so I felt it was working for me, so I recommended it to Marty. He went for a couple of months but it was not his kind of thing. That's when he began to get interested in Christian Science. It suited him better than analysis.

Because *Julie* was Marty's debut as a producer, I consented to participate in an all-out razzle-dazzle premiere—something I had always tried to avoid. MGM's plan was to open the picture in Cincinnati with a week of hoopla leading up to a gala premiere in the downtown Albee. I hadn't been back to Cincinnati in all those years, so it was the good old tried-and-true formula of hometown girl returning in cinematic glory to be hailed by the proud natives. Governor Frank J. Lausche issued a proclamation making October 8–11 "Doris Day Week" throughout the state of Ohio, and the mayor of Cincinnati was poised to give me a key to the city. There was to be an endless round of civic functions and banquets. Of all things on God's green earth I detest, it's having to participate in mass functions like those. I know it's hard to believe that anyone who has sung with big bands, appeared before live radio audiences, and made scores of movies is painfully shy, but that's the case with me. When I have to appear at a public function I have to get up for the event and prepare myself as if I were playing a part in a movie.

There was a big crowd waiting to greet me at the Cincinnati railroad station when our train pulled in around ten o'clock at night. Marty, Terry, and Warren Cowen, who handled my public relations and was a good friend besides, were on board with me, as well as a retinue of MGM wardrobe mistresses, studio photographers, press agents, and executives. In these times of movie austerity it's hard to imagine the opulence with which premieres were staged in those days.

I was standing in the little vestibule of our car, waiting to get off the train, when a man's face appeared in the window. The man waved and smiled at me. He looked familiar, a face I had known but couldn't place. After I got off the train and had met the various local dignitaries who were there to greet me, I felt a hand on my arm and turned to face again the man I had seen in the window. Tears came to the man's eyes, and at that moment I realized it was my father. We embraced. He wept quite openly. He was gray now and had less hair and had put on some weight.

"How nice that you came to greet me," I said. "That's really nice."

"I'm so happy to see you," he said.

"I'm sorry that when you appeared in the window . . ."

"Oh, it's been many, many years and people change."

There was a great crush of people and it was difficult to talk. "Would you like to come to the hotel and have breakfast in the morning?" I asked.

"I'd love to."

"We're at the Plaza. Come around nine-thirty, ten o'clock. That will give us an hour before my first interview."

When I went to bed that night, I thought about my father, not having seen him for all those years, or really thought about him. I had heard from a relative that his second wife had died of cancer. And another relative had written that my father had bought some property in the black ghetto as an investment. It seemed ironical that a man so

177

bigoted about the blacks should buy black property as an investment; but he was probably exploiting them, as many white absentee owners do, and if so, that would go snug with his prejudice.

But that's about all I had heard about him. He had never written to me, nor I to him, although I did receive a glass jar from him as a wedding present. I didn't even have an address for him. My mother never mentioned his name. After he moved out I don't think my mother ever saw him again. Christmases had come and gone without word of him or from him. Now here he was, this man who had once been so important to me, whose departure had left me so bereft. Perhaps it was a feeling of guilt at having left us that had made him so uncommunicative. Perhaps the magnitude of my success had had something to do with it. I was certainly very glad he had come to the train. In the brief glimpse I had of him, it seemed to me that his whole aspect had changed. There was a warmth and softness about him that seemed to belie my childhood memory of him. When he had lived with us, it would have been inconceivable for him to have shed a tear. Now he had wept openly and unashamedly, and his tears had touched me very much. Yes, I was thinking as I fell asleep, I'm so glad I came back to Cincinnati, if for no other reason than this opportunity to see my father again.

When my father appeared at the hotel the following morning, he was nervous and ill at ease, but Marty had a friendly, loose quality about him that soon made my father relax. But it was difficult to have a decent talk because the phone was already busy ringing. I did manage to ask him about his teaching and choral groups.

"I've given that up," he said.

"You mean you don't do any music work?" This was incomprehensible to me. My father's entire life had revolved around music.

"No, not really."

"Well, what do you do? You're not retired, are you?"

Before he could answer, I was called to the phone. When I returned, my father said, "Listen, Doris, I see how busy you are. Why don't you and Marty come to my place—I'd love to show it to you. I'd like you to meet my friends. Do you think you'll have time?"

"Oh, sure. We'll *make* time, but we can't do it till the end of the day, after all the interviews."

"That's fine."

My father wrote down the address and gave it to Marty. I was dumbfounded at my father's having given up his life of music. "Well, you said he bought a big apartment building in the black section," Marty said, "with a bar and grill. You'd be surprised how much income a place like that generates."

"I can't believe that my father has retired."

"Well, he's getting along in years."

"He's just not the type."

Around five o'clock that afternoon, in a big, black MGM Cadillac, liveried chauffeur at the wheel, Marty, Warren Cowen, and I drove to the address my father had given us. It was in the heart of the black ghetto; in all the time I had lived in Cincinnati, I had never been through this section of town. It was my father who had warned me about the dangers that lurked there, about what "they" would do to a white girl who dared set foot in their preserve, and now here we were, at my father's behest, driving along these forbidden streets. Looking out the window at the terrible squalor and poverty around me, I winced at how we looked in our fancy limousine with its uniformed chauffeur, the two gentlemen in silky Sy Devore Hollywood suits, the woman decked out in finery designed by Irene of MGM.

The driver pulled up in front of a bar and grill. The sidewalk and street were crowded with black people. Bunting was strung across the face of the bar, and a small, hand-lettered sign above the door said "WELCOME DORIS." My father came out to greet us and to lead us into the bar, his bar, of which he was obviously proud. It was a charming German bar with beautiful wood in back of the bar itself, beveled mirrors, and beer steins all arranged in neat rows. He had obviously told all the neighborhood that I was coming. The jukebox had nothing but Doris Day recordings, which played all the time we were there.

The only word to describe that crowd and that evening is "joyous." The people there were really glad I had come and they obviously had a wonderful kind of affection for and rapport with my father, whom they all called "Mister Bill." My father had marvelous German beer on tap and, Christian Science to the contrary, there was no way I could have passed up the cold, overfoaming steins that were constantly thrust into my hand. Marty and Warren were also caught up in the spirit of the occasion.

My father worked behind the bar with two assistants, a black man who helped him with drinks, and a lovely black lady who handled the grill. There was a clamorous demand for the plump, steaming knock-

179

wursts which she served on hard rolls under a blanket of sauerkraut. It seemed that every person there wanted to shake my hand, clink my glass, and tell me how much they enjoyed some one of my movies and which of my songs were their favorites. They also invariably commented on my father, what a great guy he was, and what great times they had here in his bar.

I went behind the bar and helped my father draw beer—the crowd loved that. It also gave me a chance to talk to him.

"What a wonderful place you have," I said, "and oh, how they love you!"

"It's mutual," he said.

"But how did it happen?"

"Quite by accident. I had bought this property as an investment but had nothing to do with it, until one evening I got a call that the man who was running the bar had taken ill. I came down and took over the bar myself, and I tell you, Doris, it was an instant love affair with the people here. We just seemed to understand each other. From that day on, I've been here every night and loved every minute of it. In fact . . . I'd like you to meet Luvenia."

He led me over to the woman who was making the sandwiches, and introduced us. Her full name was Luvenia Williams and she had one of the sweetest smiles I ever saw.

"We're going to be married, Luvenia and I," my father said. I was totally at a loss for words. I simply smiled at her and shook her two hands, and—well, as always when I am moved by something, tears came to my eyes. I had drunk a lot of beer by then, and I felt totally enveloped by the warm glow of the beer, the loving, joyful people, and the beautiful change that had come over my father. People were constantly getting up on chairs and proposing a toast to me and we would clink glasses all around and down some beer. It was without doubt the best party I had ever been to.

In the car going back to the hotel, no one said a word. We just enjoyed the euphoria. Even the driver had been in there drinking beer and enjoying himself. I sat back and closed my eyes and thought about my father. It was as if the man I knew had died and been reincarnated as the man who was in that bar. I thought about how much hate and prejudice there had been in my father, and how now he had come all the way around to loving and marrying a black woman. And I thought about how happy he was with all those blacks who were truly his friends. What an unexpected good time I had had! It was by far the

The soda fountain period when tobacco and alcohol were banished from the house.

Out of Doris's own past came much of the understanding and verve with which she played Ruth Etting, the great vocalist of a previous generation, in *Love Me or Leave Me*.

Love Me or Leave Me with Cagney was in many ways
Doris's best film—and Jimmy's too.

With Jimmy Stewart and Hitchcock in Marrakesh during the filming of *The Man Who Knew Too Much.*

Doris's off-screen conduct with Louis Jourdan, her costar in *Julie,* aroused Marty Melcher's jealousy.

With John Raitt in *The Pajama Game*, and Clark Gable in *Teacher's Pet*.

A campy moment with Elisabeth Fraser and Gene Kelly who directed Doris in *The Tunnel of Love*.

With Jack Lemmon in *It Happen[ed]
to Jane,* which was a comedy n[o]
body came to see, and with Ro[ck]
Hudson in *Pillow Talk,* which w[as]
a comedy everyone came to see.

Midnight Lace started pleasantly enough—this is Doris's mother, Alma, and costar John Gavin—but there were scenes in that picture that almost destroyed Doris.

Doris's father, William Kappelhoff, at age 62, married Luvenia Williams Bennett, the black woman who helped him run his bar and grill. (AP Photo)

In this scene from *That Touch of Mink,* Doris is flanked by the improbable combination of Mickey Mantle and Cary Grant.

best time I had had in that city and the best time I ever had with my father.

I did not see my father again during the *Julie* week, but several years later, when my mother, Marty, and I were on our way to New York, we stopped in Cincinnati to visit Uncle Frank and Aunt Hilda. There was a lot of antiblack talk in their neighborhood because blacks were starting to move into the area. Everybody was talking about the "niggers" and what terrible things they were doing to the neighborhood. I cringed but I knew that no purpose would be served in attacking such deep-rooted prejudices. I could not change them and there would only be a big fight. Marty agreed. What I did do, when the subject came up, was to get on to something else.

I telephoned my father, whom I had not heard from since my *Julie* visit, and invited him to come to see us. I told him my mother was with me. He said he would drop by that afternoon. I had received several letters from my Cincinnati friends and relatives, registering horror at my father's marriage to a black; my relatives simply assumed that I shared their prejudice. I'm sure my father knew how they felt about his marriage.

But that afternoon, when he pulled up to the door, he had his wife and another black woman in the car with him. I was watching him through the living-room window. My heart sank at the prospect of the confrontation that was about to take place. But my father left the women in the car and came to the door by himself. I greeted him at the door and brought him into the living room. He said hello to my mother but he was very cool toward her and did not look at her or say anything further to her. They hadn't seen each other for twenty years and I had thought that there would at least be a kind of civility. But there wasn't. There wasn't anything. My mother stayed in the room for only a few minutes, then excused herself and left. My aunt and uncle sat with us and my aunt served some beer and cheese, but the conversation was very strained. Through the living-room window we could all see the two women sitting in the car, but neither my aunt nor my uncle invited my father to bring in his wife. I didn't know what to do. I was dying to invite the women to come in, but this wasn't my house, and there was so much terrible prejudice on the street that if they did come in, my aunt and uncle were sure to suffer for it at the hands of their neighbors.

So I did nothing. My father did not stay very long. When I took

181

him to the door and said good-bye, I came out on the porch and waved to the two women in the car. They waved back and I stood there until the car drove away. I don't know if my father felt humiliated. I would think that he did. Afterward I wished I had gone down to the car and spoken to the women. That wouldn't have compromised my aunt and uncle and it would have eased my father's departure. I regretted not having done that. Instead, I just stood there at a safe distance on the porch and watched them go. It was the last time I saw my father.

Nor did I ever hear from him again. When he died, I sent flowers to his funeral but I did not go. I never go to funerals. I mourn the passing of someone dear to me in my own private way. I don't approve of public grief.

I have never heard from my father's widow. I don't know where she is. But I hope that he had some happy years with her, and with all those lovely people who called him Mister Bill.

Twelve

I previously indicated that my relationship with Marty had begun to change. In the beginning we had a compatibility that seemed solid enough. Our son, Terry, our movie-music company, our new house in Beverly Hills, our religion, a lovely little house we bought on the Malibu beach, some very good friends, going to Dodger ball games— all those things fed our mutual enjoyment of life. And we had a good sex life too.

But eventually many of these very things that we had enjoyed together became problems for us. One of the most troublesome areas was in connection with my work and earnings, and how Marty was handling them. Marty's working arrangement with the lawyer, Jerry Rosenthal, became an increasingly dominant force, and irritant, in my life. As my earnings increased, Marty and Rosenthal increased my investments in oil wells, cattle, and big hotels. I felt I had no business in any of these high-risk ventures. Marty was constantly bringing home new investment papers for me to sign in connection with big-capital projects he had gotten into with Rosenthal, when what he should have been doing was producing the films I was making. But after *Julie,* Marty devised a producing arrangement much more to his liking. He let others produce the pictures, giving himself credit as coproducer or executive producer and putting himself in the budget for a fifty-thousand-dollar fee. Whether because he lacked confidence in his ability or because he wanted a more leisurely life, the fact was that Marty was happiest when his day consisted of going to the office, opening his mail, consulting with Rosenthal, going to his club for lunch, briefly visiting the set where I was working, and then spending the rest of the afternoon playing tennis at the Beverly Hills Tennis Club. He didn't like vacations or any other distraction that took him away from this Hollywood ritual.

Marty was much more gregarious than I, and in the evenings he wanted to go to the many parties, home screenings, and premieres to which we were invited. But I was invariably tired from a tough day's work at the studio, which had usually started at five or six in the morning. Besides, when I was working on a film, I was "dressed up" all day long, and when I came home in the evening the last thing I wanted to do was to get dressed up again to go to some party. I used to urge Marty to go without me, but he'd say that we were only invited because of me and that they certainly didn't want him if I wasn't along.

That always irritated me. Shades of George Weidler. "Now, that's really stupid, Marty," I'd say, "putting yourself down like that. You're fun at parties and they love having you for yourself."

But nothing I could say had any real effect on his reticence. Perhaps that was one of the reasons he was so intent on making a great fortune out of what I earned—to prove himself, what he could do on his own, as Marty Melcher. But I'm inclined to think, on the basis of the startling revelations which turned up after his death, that his fondness for money, his drive to amass it, was something that existed apart from me. It has been said by some people who knew Marty rather well that he was attracted to Patty Andrews because of her money, and that he quickly left her for me when he became aware of the size of my potential earnings. I really don't know about that, but it was certainly a fact that Marty had an enormous concern about money, a concern about not spending it and a concern about making as much of it as possible.

Of course, Marty had no money of his own, so he could nourish his hunger to be very, very rich only by using the money I earned. The fact that I have little interest in money per se suited Marty's purposes very well. But as I became aware of what Marty, through Rosenthal, was doing with my money, I became increasingly concerned. One of the worst fights Marty and I had was over a lavish hotel, the Palo Alto Cabana, which had been built with my money. Marty had power of attorney so he could sign my name to deals without my knowledge; thus it wasn't until after I had been contractually involved with two big hotels—the other one was in Texas—that I became aware that I was in the hotel business. I told Marty that I thought that was a stupid investment because neither he nor Rosenthal knew beans about the hotel business, especially luxury hotels like those—and *I* certainly knew nothing about hotel management, nor did I want to, and the last thing in the world I wanted to be involved with was a hotel.

"Now, Doris," Marty said, in that rather condescending tone he assumed at times like those, "do you trust me or don't you?" That was his favorite theme song—"Do you trust me, darling?"

"Marty," I said, "I trust you—but not in the hotel business."

"Honey, do you think Rosenthal would put us in hotels unless he knew it was a sure thing? Look who he represents—every big name in Hollywood, and he makes money for all of them."

"I'd like to know who has a hotel. I'll bet Rosenthal hasn't put Kirk Douglas into a hotel."

"Well, just wait till you see it. It's being built by the same guy who put up the Dallas Cabana."

"But it's Palo Alto, Marty! Who's going to stay at a hotel like that in Palo Alto—and without gambling?" Palo Alto is a short distance south of San Francisco.

"Honey, you either trust Rosenthal and me or you don't. There's going to be a gala opening next month and when you see—"

"I am not going to any gala opening in Palo Alto."

"You've *got* to go! You're the owner. How would it look if you weren't there?"

When the time came, Marty talked me into going. I've never gone anywhere with less enthusiasm in my entire life. As we drove through the industrial district along El Camino Real, the worst section of Palo Alto, I kept asking, "Why are we in this part of town? Is it near here?"

Marty said, "Not too far."

"Well, this is a terrible section. El Camino Real is a rotten street. Who do you think will come to a hotel in this part of town?"

"Traveling salesmen," Marty said.

As we came around a curve, there it was, one of the most garish, hideous places I have ever seen in my life. I burst into tears. I like to think I have pretty good taste, and it was an absolute insult that a place as awful as this would be associated with my name. As we drove up to the hotel, with terrible statues and fountains all around us, I started to shout at Marty through my tears. I don't often raise my voice but that was one occasion when I really let fly. "It's obscene!" I shouted. "I loathe it! I never want to come here again—ever! And I'm heading right back to L.A. How dare you get me into this kind of a business? You don't know a damn thing about running a hotel like this. Your friend Rosenthal ought to be put behind the reception desk for the rest of his life—it would serve him right. What in the hell were you thinking of? I've worked hard to build a certain reputation and to run my life with some dignity and you have to go and drag me down to this level. Are you crazy? I could throw up—right here in this fountain—with its statue of a Greek whore."

"That's a goddess."

"In front of this hotel—that's a whore."

"Now, honey, you'll feel better when the money starts rolling in."

Impossible as it may seem, the inside was worse than the outside. I got physically ill just walking through the lobby. I tried to avoid the gala but Marty was so insistent (and I was so numb by then) that I sat at our table for a short time. Rosenthal was at the next table with a bunch of rowdy celebrants he had brought from Hollywood. They were swilling free champagne, served courtesy of D. Day, *hôtelière*. Rosenthal waved at me and smiled but I just looked daggers at him, hoping one of them would pierce his gizzard. I got my only laugh of that evening when my mother and my favorite brother-in-law, Jack Melcher, entered the twist contest and won first prize.

What I wanted to do with the money I was earning was to buy paintings I liked, some lovely antiques for the house, and land that I was interested in, especially in the Valley in the area now called Woodland Hills. But Marty wouldn't allow any expenditure except as authorized by Rosenthal. I bought a little painting, a Vlaminck snow scene, for four hundred dollars and Marty made me return it. "We need every cent for Rosenthal's program," he said, "and Rosenthal doesn't approve of paintings." I was earning a million dollars on a picture and I couldn't buy a four-hundred-dollar painting.

Marty was so chintzy about our new house that after a while I lost interest in trying to fix it up. While I was working at the studio, he would countermand plans I had made with the workmen, and he either canceled things they were to do or substituted cheap stuff for what I had ordered. I admit that in the beginning I had made some mistakes, and bought some things for the house that didn't work out, but how else was I to learn what had to be learned before I could produce the desired result? I had started on the road when I was sixteen, and for years and years my life had been nothing but hotel rooms and buses and furnished efficiency apartments. I had bought Martha Raye's house with all its furnishings, so this was my first opportunity to express my own taste and feelings about outfitting a house. It took some hit and miss before I realized that what I really wanted to create was a feeling of warmth, expressed by color and pattern, and antiquity. But Marty was insensitive to what this house-furnishing experience meant to me. Marty was a devotee of the current Hollywood cliché—wall-to-wall carpets and Pasadena modern.

And yet Marty had very good taste about the way he dressed, and in many other areas. He loved classical music, especially opera, and although he didn't have much of a voice, he could sing most of the arias of the major operas. But, curiously, when it came to getting someone to compose a musical score for one of my pictures (this was his department because our music company always controlled all music rights in our pictures) he invariably suspended his own taste and standards and hired an inexpensive no-name composer. Quite often I argued with him about his choice. "Why don't we get Hank Mancini," I'd say, "or someone like Hank to do the title song? Put a good-sized fee in the budget and I'll record the song and the picture will get away to a good start." It never turned out that way. It was always some bargain writer. As much as he loved good music, Marty couldn't bring himself to pay Hank Mancini his fee. So we never had a decent song. All those pictures and nothing but mediocre, lackluster music.

I did arrange a couple of confrontations with Rosenthal to protest his investments, but his explanation of what he was doing and how it would benefit me as a tax shelter was too technical for my comprehension. He assured me that my oil investments were sound (several wells, he said, were gushing heavily) and that they were providing us with a healthy income and a very favorable tax position, whatever that meant. (When people mention tax shelters to me I always have a mental image of a little lean-to somewhere where you run to hide when the tax collector comes.)

Despite my occasional uneasiness and protestation, I did agree with Marty when he said that either you trust a husband or you don't. Although I didn't like being in oil wells and hotels, there was no question that I did trust Marty. Moreover, I don't want to give the impression that there weren't many good things about our marriage. I enjoyed Marty, his sense of humor, his warm concern about my well-being, our mutual love of our house at the beach. We had bought the house despite Rosenthal's objections, and Marty and I adored our weekends there. Marty loved to putter around with his tools, and I like nothing better than to scrub, clean, polish, and shine. When we weren't cleaning and puttering, we took long walks along that beautiful beach with our poodles, and those were some of the nicest hours I ever spent.

Marty did not share my enthusiasm, however, for a small, inexpensive house I found, several years after the beach house, high up on Lake Arrowhead. It was a great change of scenery for me, at a time when I was working very hard. There was a real change of seasons at Arrowhead—in the winter, snow and crisp mornings walking along a country road; in the summer, our own dock with its own little boat. I water-skied, hiked four miles to the village and back, and felt wonderful. But Marty didn't enjoy going there. He said he didn't feel well there. Perhaps it was the altitude. I'd sometimes take Terry and a couple of my girl friends, but Marty rarely went and urged me to let him sell it; finally I let the house go. Maybe Rosenthal wanted the money. I don't know. It was a dreamy little place. But I could understand that someone like Marty wasn't happy in the mountains.

As Marty gradually changed in his relation to me, so he changed too with Terry. As Terry got older and began to have a life of his own, Marty seemed either incapable of understanding this natural development or unwilling to allow it. As a result, Marty became more and more of a strict disciplinarian. The camaraderie that Terry and Marty had enjoyed began to dissolve into orders and resentments and punishments.

Terry was a high-spirited, mischievous boy, full of the old Nick, as we used to say in Cincinnati, but a loving, amusing boy, not difficult to handle. The problem was that early on Marty had convinced me that it would be best for the family if he was the one who dealt with Terry, so that there would be a single person in authority. Mr. Broones corroborated this theory. "I have seen problems in homes where there is a division of authority between father and mother," Mr. Broones said, "and when the house is divided it falls. Mother and father must keep a united front and that is achieved by having only one of them deal with the child."

Since I was working six days a week and preparing every Sunday for the week ahead, it was only natural for Marty to become the united parental front. That was certainly a mistake. I know now that there is no such thing as a formula for dealing with children within the home. I should have had an equal voice. As it was, Marty made the decision to take Terry out of the Christian Science school where he was going and send him to Harvard, a military school in Beverly Hills where he would be boarded. We lived in Toluca Lake then, and Marty objected to the friends Terry had made on our street. They were just high-spirited boys like Terry—as I recall they broke a streetlamp and that was the incident that set Marty off. Hooliganism, Marty called it. Of all the boys in the world, Terry was the last one to be sent to a military school, and I tried to convince Marty of that, but he got angry.

"Now, listen," he said, "I'm the one who's dealt with Terry all these years and I think I know him better than anyone. What Terry needs right now is a strict hand. Discipline. Schoolwork by the numbers. He's got to shape up or the next thing we know he'll be in trouble with the police."

"Oh, Marty, Terry's not that kind of boy—the police? You've got to be kidding."

"One of the kids Terry's hanging around with is a bad apple. That's all it takes to turn a young boy's head—one bad apple. So he'll board at school Monday through Thursday, and he'll spend Friday, Saturday, and Sunday with us. What's so bad about that?" (Terry's bad-apple pal is now a Beverly Hills policeman.)

Terry was dead set against going, but in the end I decided that the experience couldn't do him any harm. If I had it to do over, I would never have a work schedule like I had then. I would make no more than one picture a year, cut one album, and have the rest of my time for myself and my family. I'm not one of those women who feel unfulfilled being around the house. I adore keeping house. The more cleaning the better. But I probably would not have participated in afternoon treks to the kiddie park. I think it's a mistake for the mother and child to be together all the time. The child becomes overattached and the mother begins to feel like a warden. I would send my child to the kiddie park to play with other children and leave myself out of it.

Terry really resented the military school and complained bitterly about it. Marty should have known that Terry didn't have the temperament for a military school. One could not dictate to Terry. But one could achieve anything with love. However, love has never found its way into a military school.

Thirteen

~~~~~~

IT has been my good fortune that, at those times in my life when tragedy has struck, I have had to work. I think there is nothing worse for the grieving spirit of someone who has suffered death or disaster than to withdraw into her own shadows and cut herself off from all possibility of rehabilitating her morale. Life must go on, and it is only through the society of the living that one can overcome the despair that a death inflicts.

My brother, Paul, whom I adored, a lovely, gentle, amusing man, died suddenly, finally overtaken by the baseball injury of his youth. The drugs he had been taking all those years had kept his seizures under control, but apparently the drugs were not able to withstand this fatal attack. Paul had moved to Los Angeles with his wife and children, to work for our Arwin Productions, and he was very good at generating publicity for the music we published and the records and albums we produced. My mother and I felt his death very deeply, and I know I would have been laid low by it if I had not been committed to start photography on a picture with Clark Gable.

~~~~~~

SAM WEISS

I put up with Marty, and everybody else endured him, because of Doris. I don't know anybody who liked Marty. Not even his own family. But I loved Doris, and I loved her brother Paul, one of the nicest men I ever met. He moved his family from Cincinnati to work for Doris's company, and I honestly think that Marty was a factor in Paul's death. I don't want to be venomous, but the way I saw Marty treat Paul, ruin his spirit, his self-respect, treat him like shit, and there was Paul doing more work for Doris than Marty did in his whole life—well, the effect of all that has to be taken into account when a young man dies. Sure, I know Paul had a

kind of epilepsy from the baseball beaning, but that was just part of it.
Paul had a wife and two kids but Marty wouldn't pay him enough to live on. Doris adored Paul and if she had known the way Marty was treating him, starving him on the salary he paid Paul from money that Doris earned, well, I think Doris would have pitched Marty out on his ear. But Paul was not one to complain, and I always felt that an outsider shouldn't meddle in another family's affairs. But it broke my heart when Paul died, and afterward I felt remorseful that I hadn't spoken up.

I had just finished *The Pajama Game*, which had been an arduous assignment (I was the only one in the cast who had not played it on Broadway and I had to fit into a polished company that had been together for two years). I would have taken a few months off if the opportunity to perform with Gable hadn't presented itself. Gable was called "the King" and for good reason—no actor I ever performed with had such public appeal. He was the King when I was going to movies in Cincinnati and he was still the King when we made *Teacher's Pet*. He was as masculine as any man I've ever known, and as much a little boy as a grown man could be—it was this combination that had such a devastating effect on women.

When Clark came on the set in the morning, I could actually feel the magnetic force of his personality. He dressed in marvelous tweeds, which obviously had belonged to him for a long time, or in leather, and he wore heavy, thick-soled oxblood brogues that were always shined. He had very big hands, and a thick, large-boned physique that gave him great dimension. There was something very affirmative about him, and a directness that suggested great inner strength.

But there was nothing of the King about his personality. Just the opposite. Utter simplicity. Uncomplicated. A man who lived on a simple, down-to-earth scale. Very much like Cagney. Of course, I know Jimmy much better than I knew Gable, since I've seen him many times since we made *Love Me Or Leave Me* and we are good friends. But I'd say that Gable and Cagney had in common the fact that they were totally unaware of themselves. Totally unaware of Hollywood or the impact they had on people. In no sense, big-shot movie stars. Gable, like Cagney, steered clear of the Hollywood social whirl. He lived with his wife, Kay, out in Encino in the farmhouse where he had lived with Carole Lombard. Gable's close friend was his makeup man; they had been friends for years. At the end of a day's shooting, Gable would go to his dressing room and have a drink of Scotch with his makeup man, sometimes joined also by his stand-in. They'd shoot the breeze for a while, then Clark would head home. That was the only staff Gable had—those two men. Quite a contrast to Sinatra, who also has a kind of royal status in the entertainment world but only moves behind a phalanx of bodyguards.

Thinking about Gable's strength, I'm reminded of what Charlotte Greenwood said to me one day. She is a devout Christian Scientist, the wife of our Practitioner, and a great lady of stage and screen. One day we were discussing inner values, and she said, "Always remember, Emma [her pet name for me]—your strength is in your simplicity." That was Gable's strength. It is the simplicity and directness in an actor that people respond to, and once the actor loses it and takes on airs, the public seems to sense it right away. How many of the stars I've known are illuminated by this simplicity. Paul Newman is. Certainly Spencer Tracy was. Gary Cooper. Dustin Hoffman. Rock Hudson. Jimmy Garner. Jack Lemmon. Just to mention a few of the men. Oh, and Jimmy Stewart—most certainly Stewart.

In 1958 and 1959 I made a couple of pictures that did not do well at the box office. *Tunnel of Love* with Richard Widmark, and *It Happened to Jane* with Jack Lemmon. The former had a poor script that I didn't want to do but Marty had already signed me for; the latter, which Marty also contracted for, should have done all right, it was pert and funny, but whether it was the insipid title or something else, it just didn't make it. However, I'm grateful to the film, for Jack and I became friends and we saw each other socially over the ensuing years. Jack is a disarming and charming man, and a gut actor with a natural sense of comedy—very challenging to work with.

JACK LEMMON

I thought *It Happened to Jane* was a good, funny movie that didn't do well because of that terrible title. I felt that Doris and I had very good chemistry together, and I regret that we never made another film.

Doris is a joy to work with. She was never a minute late, always good-humored, and always solicitous of the people around her. They were her family and she cared about them, not for appearance's sake, but she *cared*. In her performance, Doris has an unerring instinct as to her moves, motives, and impact. Once she performs a scene, she locks it in, and no matter how many takes are required, she gives the same matched performance. In my book, this is the most difficult part of movie acting. I came to Hollywood from the Broadway stage, and my first part

192

was opposite Judy Holliday. My Broadway training did not prepare me for picking up scenes in the middle, which is necessary for changing camera angles. Every time we had a different take, I had to start the scene all over from the beginning. Judy was very understanding helpful, and so was the director, George Cukor. Doris has this ability to the nth degree—she's a director's delight.

She also has impeccable comedic timing, which is the quality I most admire in a performer. To play with her is elevating. She makes you want to give all you've got to a scene, to rise to her level. I also feel that Doris has an enticing sexual quality that is there but subliminal. She doesn't lay it out there, like a Marilyn Monroe, but it's there nevertheless —the difference between a nude and a woman in seductive clothing.

I think Doris would be a tremendous stage performer and it's a pity she's never tried it. She's a presence; she radiates charisma. I am sure that if she came onstage in a live performance, the audience would look at no one else. That's a superstar, that's the measure. I think all of us should go on the stage occasionally, for the stage hardens the muscle of acting.

Doris is a method actress even though she never went to the Actors Studio or studied Stanislavsky. Hers is an intuitive method. All good acting is method—remembering from your own experience, that thing in your past that can induce the emotion you are striving for in your acting. In my case, one of my key acting remembrances is the loss of my dog. As a boy, I had a little mutt whom I was more attached to than anything else in my life. One summer my parents sent me to camp for the first time, and all the time there I was homesick for my dog. I wanted my dog more than anyone or anything else in my life. When I came home, I rushed in the house to find my dog only to discover that my parents had given him away and told me nothing about it. I didn't cry. I didn't rage. I went to my room, locked myself in, and from the emotions I felt that day, still sharply etched in my memory, I can act the desire to kill, to hate, and various other kindred emotions.

Another thing about Doris that I discovered in making *It Happened to Jane* with her is her healthy self-confidence. To lose confidence or even to suffer the wobbles is just about the worst fate that can befall an actor. You must believe in yourself, in what you are doing, or else the audience won't believe in your performance. Reminds me of the first sneak preview we held for *Some Like It Hot*. There was a very bad audience reaction. A lot of walkouts. Badmouthing by the audience afterward. The lobby was full of wise guys from the studio, the ad agency, etc., all with advice for Billy Wilder, the director. Scenes to reshoot, to add, to cut. I asked Billy what he was going to do. "Why, nothing," he said. "This is a very funny movie and I believe in it just as it is. Maybe this is the wrong neighborhood in which to have shown it. At any rate, I don't panic over one preview. It's a hell of a movie." He held the next preview in Westwood, where the audience stood up and cheered.

That's the kind of confidence Doris has. It has to do with her instincts and her taste. A few years ago, I indulged a secret ambition of a lifetime and made an album. I sang songs, played the banjo, and, in general, had a musical ball. But when it was finished, I didn't know how to judge what I had done. I took the record over to Doris's house to get her advice. She listened to each band as if the recording were her own,

193

and made very sharp, helpful suggestions about a lot of technical things such as the balance between my voice and the backup music. Confidence. Doris oozes it, and it helps explain why everything she does is so damn good.

~~~~~~

Marty became terribly concerned over the box-office failures of *Tunnel of Love* and *It Happened to Jane*. I had dropped out of the top ten, which meant nothing to me but everything to Marty, primarily because it would have an effect on my earnings. I pointed out to Marty that if he hadn't hustled me into doing these films, if he had waited, I might have found good scripts that would have produced better results.

But actually, as I look back, there was more to it than that. I had been making films for a dozen years by then, primarily films of nostalgia, costume musicals, films depicting wholesome families. There had been a few notable exceptions, of course, but there is no gainsaying the fact that a "Doris Day movie" had come to mean a very specific kind of sunny, nostalgic, sexless, wholesome film. It had not happened by design (I think that the minute a performer tries to tailor-make a film for a supposed audience he is in a lot of trouble) but the Doris Day movie was nevertheless entrenched in the public's mind. America had undergone great change in the Fifties, the Korean War being one of the main influences, but the Doris Day movie remained a stable commodity.

It was against this background, then, that I read a script submitted to me by a producer named Ross Hunter. It was a very funny screenplay, written by Stanley Shapiro, that I particularly liked because the humor came from situation and characterization rather than from jokes; very sophisticated comedy, high chic, the leading lady an interior decorator, an "in" lady very much tuned into the current New York scene. The plot, for 1959, was quite sexy, and even involved a climactic scene in which the leading man grabbed me from bed and carried me, in my pajamas, down an elevator, through lobby, and out onto the street. Clearly, not the kind of part I had ever played before.

I told Ross Hunter that although I dearly loved the idea of playing an interior decorator, since that has always been what I'd much rather be than an actress, I was not sure that I was right to depict this rather sexy, beautifully dressed, sophisticated New York career lady. Ross Hunter is a very persuasive man. Not only did he convince me that I was God's gift to this part, but he also persuaded Rock Hudson, who had never performed in a comedy (his latest role had been in *Giant*), to play opposite me. Marty enrolled himself as co-producer and tried to get Ross to call the picture *The Way the Wind Blows,* which happened to be the title of a song Marty was about to publish, but in the end Ross stayed with the original title, *Pillow Talk.*

I had never met Rock Hudson before, but the very first day on the set I discovered we had a performing rapport that was remarkable. We played our scenes together as if we had once lived them. Every day on the set was a picnic—sometimes too much of a picnic, in that we took turns at breaking each other up. Rock was sexy in the part, but not lascivious; bemused, but not overbearing; tough, but not rough.

And I? Well, if I say it myself, I just soared. After all those early years of suffering at the hands of those Warner Brothers embalmers who posed as makeup men, now I was made up and my hair done as I had always hoped it would be done. Two things about Ross Hunter were immediately apparent—he was a man of taste and a big spender. He hired Jean Louis to create my wardrobe, and I adored everything he made for me. For the first time I was wearing clothes in a picture that I felt accentuated my body and enhanced the part I was playing. I had always felt that I was too contemporary-looking for all those period films I had made. My whole attitude is contemporary even though I have a fondness for those lovely, long-ago days before high-rises, modern cars, machine-made bread, freeways, and the rest of such "progress." In *Pillow Talk,* the contemporary in me finally caught up with a contemporary film and I really had a ball.

There was one other element that added to the effectiveness of the film—the casting of Tony Randall in the second male lead. Tony, Rock, and I were made for each other and it was hard to tell sometimes where life left off and make-believe began. We were destined to make two more pictures together, *Lover Come Back* and *Send Me No Flowers,* which did not quite equal the success of *Pillow Talk* but which did very well indeed.

I was surprised at being nominated for an Academy Award for my performance in *Pillow Talk,* and even more surprised to find that by the end of that year I had shot up to number one at the box office. For the next several years, besides the films with Rock and Tony, I did pictures in the *Pillow Talk* vein with James Garner (*Thrill of It All* and *Move Over Darling*) and Cary Grant (*A Touch of Mink*).

I had the same kinship with Jimmy that I had with Rock—truly a blessing to have had two such talented, amusing, darling men to work with, men with whom I have had enduring friendships. I really love Rock and Jimmy.

~~~~~~

JAMES GARNER

I think Doris is a very sexy lady who doesn't know how sexy she is. That's an integral part of her charm. The guys who look at her on the screen and think she's the girl next door would love to ravage her but they wouldn't dare admit it, they're not going to mess up that vanilla ice cream cone, no way—but in the dark recesses of their minds, they want her. Beautiful Doris with that fantastic body, all sweetness and charm up front, and that turns people on, and I don't think she could have had the success she's had if she didn't have this sexy whirlpool frothing around underneath her All-American-girl exterior.

I remember the first time I saw her on screen. I was just a regular moviegoer then, hadn't turned to acting yet, and here was this new girl, Doris Day, on a train with Dennis Morgan and Jack Carson, singing a song, and I looked at her and said to myself, "Oh, God, ain't that beautiful, and listen to that voice!" Then I went into one of those quick fantasies involved with how sexy she was, but I yanked myself out of it in a hurry because she was on a high level where, God, you wouldn't dare mention it to her, you wouldn't want to make a pass because you might spoil the whole thing and get her upset. But, poor Doris, that's one of the crosses she's got to bear—this business of men who are turned on by her but back away because of her image. I'm sure that's why she's without a fellow today. Men are afraid to make a move at her.

It's a damn shame, because in Doris one of God's great natural resources is going to waste. I've had to play love scenes with a lot of screen ladies (sometimes with ladies I don't particularly like, and believe me, that's a difficult assignment), but of all the women I've had to be intimate with on the screen, I'd rate two as sexiest by far—Doris and Julie Andrews, both of them notorious girls next door. Playing a love scene with either of them is duck soup because they communicate something sexy which means I also let myself go somewhat and that really makes a love scene work. You just can't do that with someone you don't like or who's a lump unless you're a hell of an actor and I'm not that good an actor.

The cliché thing to say about a movie love scene is that it's just a mechanical thing—you sit in front of the camera and kiss the girl and the whistle blows and you go home and never give it another thought. Well, that's useful propaganda for the wives at home ("Now, honey, how could there be anything going on between us when there's one hundred grips and electricians and cameramen all around us?") but the fact of the matter is that with Doris, one hundred grips or not, there *was* always something there and I must admit that if I had not been married I would have tried to carry forward, after hours, where we left off on the sound stage.

196

One other thing about acting with Doris—she was the Fred Astaire of comedy. You know the way Astaire used to change partners—Ginger Rogers, Rita Hayworth, Cyd Charisse—but the dancing was always uniformly spectacular because Astaire just did his thing and anybody who danced with him was swept up by it. Well, same thing about Doris. Whether it was Rock Hudson or Rod Taylor or me or whoever—we all looked good because we were dancing with Clara Bixby. I used to come to the set with a preconceived notion of how I was going to play a particular scene, but when I saw what Doris was doing in the scene, her tempo, her feel for the scene, 99.9 percent of the time I'd toss my preconception away and play it her way. Making a movie with Doris was a piece of cake—a sexy ride on her coattails all the way.

~~~~~~

For five years I stayed in the number-one position, which was gratifying in the sense that you like to know you are doing well at your job; but basically I really object to the numbers psychology. I was no better or worse an actress than when I was number nine or number twenty, and I knew only too well that if you play the numbers game and become obsessed with it, as so many in Hollywood are, sooner or later you have to face the depressing fact that if you are number one the only place you can go is down.

Of course, when you are number one the film pundits have a field day analyzing why you are number one. In my case, the consensus seemed to be: first, that I had had the good luck to have had this script turn up just when my career needed a lift; and second, that I had become a new kind of sex symbol—the woman men wanted to go to bed with, but not until they married her. Sexy put pure.

As for luck, as I've said I think there's no such thing. Good or bad. I would hate to think that my life is a life of chance. That what you are, what you do, your dreams and drives are all subject to a roll of the dice. No, no one will ever convince me of that. In my view, we are all subject to a predestined order of things which has been arranged under the auspices of some overall force, call it God or whatever you will. It is not luck that one seed grows into a purple flower and another, identical seed grows up to be a yellow flower, nor is it luck that Doris Kappelhoff of Cincinnati grows up to be a sex symbol on the silver screen.

One thing I was careful about in those films was to avoid vulgarity, which I truly despise. I liked those scripts about the man-woman game as long as they were done with style and wit and imagination. In my vocabulary, vulgarity begins when imagination suc-

197

cumbs to the explicit. There was a scene in *Lover Come Back* in which Rock Hudson and I wake up in bed together in a motel, I in pajama tops, he in the bottoms. We have both been put under the spell of intoxicating wafers we had eaten. I felt the scene had a vulgar tone to it as it was originally written. In the reworking of it, it was established that we had visited a justice of the peace, in our cooky-intoxicated condition, and even though, in the film, Rock is the last man in the world I want to wake up with in a motel bed, and I run out on him, at least we had the blessings of a justice of the peace upon us. That is the film that has that wonderful scene at the end, in which Rock learns I am about to have the baby, rushes to the hospital just as I am being carted into the delivery room, and marries me in a cart-side ceremony.

ROCK HUDSON

In 1944 I was an ordinary seaman shipping out of San Francisco Bay on a troopship to an unknown destination. It was evening, and as we passed under the Golden Gate Bridge its lights went on, and the voice of Doris Day began singing "Sentimental Journey" over the loudspeakers. Well, that was the saddest bunch of sailors you ever saw. She had the whole ship in tears. Including me.

Fifteen years later, Doris and I worked together for the first time in *Pillow Talk* and, by way of contrast, it was a laugher all the way. But before we got under way, I had some apprehensions. I had never played comedy before, and here I was, thrown together with one of Hollywood's most accomplished comediennes. Before we started, I went to the director, Michael Gordon, and told him that I had this slight problem of never having played comedy. He thought for a moment. "I'll tell you, Rock," he said, "comedy is the most serious tragedy in the world. Play it that way and you can't go wrong. If you ever think of yourself as funny, you haven't got a chance." Best acting advice I ever got.

But the best acting lesson came from Doris. Her sense of timing, her instincts—I just kept my eyes open and copied her. Tony Randall has another style of comedy, totally different, a deliberate delivery, holding back—very funny but the kind of timing that would never work for me. Doris, though, was an Actors Studio all by herself. When she cried, she cried funny, which is something I couldn't even try to explain; and when she laughed, her laughter came boiling up from her kneecaps. Halfway through the picture we had fallen into a style of playing together, an easy rapport, an instinctive give-and-take, that put our stamp on *Pillow Talk* as well as on the next film we made, *Lover Come Back.*

I don't really know what makes a movie team. Gable and Lombard, Tracy and Hepburn. I recently saw an old flick starring Joan Crawford and Spencer Tracy in a "team" picture, and that was a glaring example of what didn't work. Absolutely no chemistry between them. But when

198

Tracy teamed with Hepburn, it worked like a charm. I'd say, first of all, the two people have to truly like each other, as Doris and I did, for that shines through, the sparkle, the twinkle in the eye as the two people look at each other. Then, too, both parties have to be strong personalities—very important to comedy so that there's a tug-of-war over who's going to put it over on the other, who's going to get the last word, a fencing match between two adroit opponents of the opposite sex who in the end are going to fall in bed together. God knows Doris is a strong personality—I used to call her Miss Adamant of 1959. But the great thing that Doris does in a film is the way she plays hurt when she realizes that she's been had—she is genuinely hurt and the audience's heart goes out to her. She's not a revengeful woman, and when she plays hurt over what the man has done to her, she wins hands down.

But I have a confession to make about the long, climactic sequence in *Pillow Talk* where I sweep Doris out of bed and carry her through the lobby and down the street. I hate to admit this, but Doris is a tall, well-built girl and I just couldn't tote her around for as long and as far as required, so they built a special shelf for me with two hooks on it and she sat on the shelf and all I did was hold her legs and shoulders. I could have managed if only one take had been involved, but we went on end-lessly, primarily because there was a bit actor who played a cop on the street, and as we passed him Doris's line was "Officer, arrest this man," and the cop was supposed to say to me, "How you doing, Brad?" but that stupid actor kept calling me Rock. So back to our marks we went for another take and another and another. I'll bet we did that scene twenty times. That's why the shelf for Doris to sit on.

Marty Melcher was around quite a lot, and primarily what he did was to tease Doris unmercifully. A relentless tease, but amusing, a man very protective of Doris. One weekend they invited me to their beach house and Marty spent a lot of time telling me how wealthy he had made Doris with his oil wells and bond deals. He said he'd like to do the same thing for me, if I turned my capital over to him. I had heard, though, that he was a crook, so I begged off.

〰〰〰〰〰〰〰〰〰〰〰〰〰〰〰〰〰〰〰〰〰〰〰〰〰〰〰〰〰〰

I was offered the part of Mrs. Robinson in *The Graduate* but I could not see myself rolling around in the sheets with a young man half my age whom I'd seduced. I realized it was an effective part (Annie Bancroft was nominated for an Academy Award for it) but it offended my sense of values. Of course, in the years since then, ex-plicit sex has become commonplace on the screen—so commonplace that it is considered novel when a film appears without a few naked bodies thrashing about. Now I really don't put anybody else down for doing such scenes. To each his own. Many actors enjoy doing these turns, and obviously many people enjoy watching them. I don't, either doing or watching. I can't picture myself in bed with a man, all the crew around us, doing that which I consider so exciting and

199

exalting when it is very personal and private. I am really appalled by some of the public exhibitions on the screen by good actors and actresses who certainly have the talent to convey the impact of what they are doing without showing us to the last detail of pubic hair and rosy nipple how they are doing it.

〰〰〰〰〰〰〰〰〰〰〰〰〰〰〰〰〰〰〰〰〰〰〰

ROSS HUNTER

When I produced *Pillow Talk,* I had a hell of a time getting it done, and then I had a hell of a time getting anyone to book it. For Doris, it was an enormous departure from the kind of films she'd been doing for a dozen years. A sophisticated sex comedy. Doris hadn't a clue as to her potential as a sex image and no one realized that under all those dirndls lurked one of the wildest asses in Hollywood.

I came right out and told her. "You are *sexy,* Doris, and it's about time you dealt with it."

"Oh, Ross, cut it out, I'm just the old-fashioned, peanut-butter girl next door, and you know it."

"Now, listen, if you allow me to get Jean Louis to do your clothes, I mean a really sensational wardrobe that will show off that wild fanny of yours, and get some wonderful makeup on you, and chic you up and get a great hairdo that *lifts* you, why, every secretary and every house-wife will say, 'Look at that—look what Doris has done to herself. Maybe I can do the same thing.'"

I felt that it was essential for Doris to change her image if she was going to survive as a top star. She had been the girl next door for too many years, with her freckles and blousy dresses, nondescript hairdo, down-to-earth personality, but what had happened in her decade of star-dom was that moviegoing women had become more sophisticated and had invaded Doris's world, so now it was necessary for Doris to step up a few rungs to lead them into a much more sophisticated and sexier play-ground. The barometer of all this was to be found in Doris's box office, which had suddenly fallen off.

Once Doris decided to make the movie, she characteristically threw herself into it. And so did Rock Hudson, who also began with misgivings about making this kind of picture. But the real convincing was needed after the picture was made.

No one wanted to book it. It was a period when everybody was doing war pictures, Westerns, or never-never spectaculars. The big movie chains all sadly told me, after seeing the picture, that sophisticated comedies like *Pillow Talk* went out with William Powell. They also said that Doris and Rock were things of the past who had been overtaken by the newer stars. Well, my theory is that there's no such thing as a dated actor, and I knew very well that the performances in that picture were as up-to-the-minute as anything then being shown on the screen. In fact, *ahead* of the minute.

Finally, after weeks and weeks of turndowns everywhere, I induced Sol Schwartz, who owned the Palace Theatre on Broadway, to book the picture for a two-week run. That's all it needed. The public found it was starved for romantic comedy and all those theater owners who had turned me down now had to close their deals on *my* terms. It was a bonanza for Doris and me—critically, and in the bank, where bonanzas count the most.

~~~~~~

All the films I made after *Pillow Talk* were comedies, with one exception—a psychological drama called *Midnight Lace*. I was surprised that Ross Hunter, who had introduced me to the *Pillow Talk* sex-comedy world, would bring me such a heavily dramatic script. The part I was to play was that of an American wife in London, married to a wealthy Britisher, played by Rex Harrison, who was terrorized by some unknown person who was trying to kill her. After the emotional beating inflicted on me by *Julie,* I had resolved not to do this kind of searing part again, but the script was so well-written and Marty, who was to be coproducer, was again so insistent that I consented.

I should have known better; the effect on me of playing the part was even more shattering than in *Julie.* When I study a script I develop a mental image of the woman I am playing. I study that woman from every possible angle, inside and out. By the time we are ready to start filming, that woman is very real to me, and I know just what she will do, so that actually I become that woman to the best of my ability. But the woman I am playing isn't like *me* at all. She's what I think *she* is. That's why I never went to see rushes during the filming of any picture I ever made. That's because I might look at that woman up there on the screen and not like her. I might look at some of the terror scenes in *Midnight Lace* and see how awful I looked. My mouth crooked, my hair mussed, my eyes swollen, my dress a shambles—I just might march into the director's office and ask him to reshoot the scene, or perhaps the next time I played a similar scene in the movie I would be consciously trying to keep myself from doing those things that made the rushes I had seen so effective. That woman on the screen was supposed to look like that, but I don't like *myself* looking that way, and subconsciously I might have been tempted to make that screen woman look pretty instead of real.

In *Midnight Lace,* to create the fear which the character I played had to project, I recreated the fear in myself which I had once felt in my own life. I relived it. It was painful and upsetting to dredge up ugly experiences that I had paid a suffering price to forget. In the

201

film it was my husband, Rex Harrison, who was the one who was trying to kill me, so to convey the terror of my reaction I re-created the ghostly abuses of Al Jorden. In one scene in which I had to become hysterical, I imposed on myself that moment when I was pregnant and ill, and Al Jorden burst into the room, dragged me from the bed, and hurled me against the wall. I wasn't *acting* hysterical, I *was* hysterical, so that at the end of that scene I collapsed in a real faint. Everyone was terribly alarmed. The director, David Miller, suspended further production. I was carried to my dressing room. Marty and Ross Hunter hurried to my side. My pretend life and my real life had fused. I just can't walk away from a scene and shed my emotions.

Ross closed down further production and asked Marty to keep me at home for a few days until I completely recovered. Ross was genuinely concerned about my health. So was Myrna Loy, who played my aunt. As I remember, Rex helped me out to the car. A darling, witty man, Rex, whose light sense of humor helped keep my sanity balance throughout the rough part of the picture.

That evening, after I had had a light dinner in bed, Marty propped himself up beside me with a book of Christian Science hymns. He started to sing my favorite ones, in that low, off-key voice of his. The lovely, inspirational words were balm to my ears. The tension inside me began to peel away. After a while I fell asleep and I didn't wake once in the night. The next morning I felt refreshed and decided I could carry on. But I told Marty, "I think for the sake of my physical well-being, I should never get involved with any more films like this. The next time I might not recover so easily." Marty agreed.

My clothes for *Midnight Lace* were every bit as stunning as they had been for *Pillow Talk*. In this case, the couturière was Irene, darling Irene, who was one of my dearest friends. And one of the most talented designers in Hollywood. Irene was a very classic designer, not of a French look, but of an elegant American look. Irene's choice of fabrics, the attention to detail, the buttons, beading, use of chiffon—what a super gown she created! She also did imaginative and exciting things with fur which suited me terribly well—of course, that was back in the days when "fur" had not yet become a dirty word. Today, with my awareness of what fur trapping has done to the animal population of the world, if I see a woman wearing a fur coat I have to restrain myself from stripping the coat off her back.

Irene designed the clothes for several of my pictures so I got to know her very well. She was a nervous woman, introverted, quite unhappy, and at times she drank more than was good for her. She had an unhappy marriage to a man who lived out of the state and only occasionally came to visit her. One time, toward the end of a long evening, when she had been drinking quite a bit, she confided in me that the love of her life was Gary Cooper. Irene was a very attractive woman, a lovely face, and when she talked about Cooper her face glowed. She said he was the only man she had ever truly loved. There was such a poignancy in the way she said it. It really broke my heart.

After that, she several times confided in me about Cooper. I got the impression that she had never mentioned him to anyone before me, and she was so happy to declare her love for him. Thinking about it now, I cannot honestly say whether Irene's love was one-sided or whether she and Cooper had actually had or were having an affair. But the way she loved him touched jealousy in me, for I had never loved a man with that much intensity.

The last picture we worked on together was *Lover Come Back*. Irene had just shown me her completed sketches for my clothes. She was drinking more than usual. Cooper had died of cancer, quite unexpectedly, a month or so before. I was at the studio, getting my hair done, when the radio carried the announcement. Irene had taken a room at the Knickerbocker Hotel under an assumed name and had jumped out the window. I was terribly shaken by her death. I can't honestly say how much of Cooper she actually saw while she was here, but the way she loved him, I could certainly understand why she had followed him.

Fourteen

O F all the people I performed with, I got to know Cary Grant least of all. He is a completely private person, totally reserved, and there is no way into him. Our relationship on *A Touch of Mink* was amicable but devoid of give-and-take. For somebody who is as open and right out there as I am, it was hard at first to adjust to Cary's inwardness. Not that he wasn't friendly and polite—he certainly was. But distant. Very distant.*

But very professional—maybe the most professional, exacting actor I ever worked with. In the scenes we played, he concerned himself with every little detail: clothes, sets, production values, the works. Cary even got involved in helping to choose the kind of mink I was slated to wear in the film. There was one scene in *A Touch of Mink* that took place in a town-house library. On the morning we were scheduled to shoot this scene, Cary arrived with boxes of things which he had brought from the library in his own house, and outfitted the movie set with them. Not only did it make the set much more attractive, but when Cary played the scene his own belongings obviously made him feel right at home, and it gave his performance that peculiarly natural, suave quality that is a hallmark of his pictures.

There was one moment during the picture when a little conflict arose between Cary and me. In setting up for our first close-up, it developed that we both preferred to be photographed from the right profile. I prefer the right side of my face because it is more open and less cheeky than the left. Almost all movie performers have such preferences. Of course, both actors in a scene cannot be photographed

---

* The only other actor whom I know quite well but don't *know* at all is Kirk Douglas. He is a smiling, charming man who seems to have an interior that belies his exterior. He shows very little of himself.

from the same profile, but our awkward impasse was quickly dispelled by Cary's graciously forgoing his preference.

If you look closely at your own face, you will discover differences between your right and left profile. Virtually no one has a perfectly matched face. In my own case, when I was younger I had a very fat face that seemed to be less cheeky on the right side. But I no longer care which side is photographed because when I was in my thirties, my face began to change. The fat cheekiness of my face gave way to more contour, more definition of my cheekbones and the valleys between my nose and cheeks. But back when I was convinced that my right side was better for close-ups, some directors didn't agree with me. When we made *Love Me Or Leave Me,* the director, Charles Vidor, preferred my left profile for close-ups. All through the picture I kept saying, "Charles, you're making a mistake, I'm better on the right," but he stayed with my cheeky left and, considering the way the picture turned out, I really can't say that he was wrong. However, there have been some actors and actresses who have *never* shown one side of their face. Claudette Colbert, for example—God really wasted half a face on Claudette.

Much more important than which profile is used is how that profile is photographed. For this reason performers have always had favorite cameramen. I particularly liked the work of Willfred Klein and Leon Shamroy. In critical close-ups, the slightest imbalance of the camera can cause distortions. If the camera is a trifle too high it will shorten your face; if too low, the underside of your features will be prominent. And lighting is very critical. By adroit use of lights the cameraman can minimize such defects as puffiness under the eyes, a weak chin, and crow's-feet. Grace Kelly was never shot straight on because she has a very square jaw, which was softened by the camera angle and lighting.

But some Hollywood faces seem to have been made for cameras. Judy Garland had such a face—right, left, up, down, it didn't matter. Judy and the camera were always harmonious.

I loved Judy. We were good friends, and where we mostly saw each other, of all places, was aboard the transcontinental Super Chief. Judy shared my aversion to flying and it so happened that just about every time Marty and I went cross-country, Judy and her husband, Sid Luft, were aboard. Occasionally Judy and I would check with each other and arrange our trips so we'd be aboard at the same time.

Sid Luft's relationship with Judy was about the same as Marty's and mine. Sid was Judy's manager and became involved in her pictures to the extent that Marty was involved in mine—but I never felt that Judy had as much confidence in Sid as I did in Marty. Perhaps that was attributable to Judy's nature. She was a terribly confused, unhappy woman who drank excessively, and Sid's job was more to keep Judy functioning and out of harm's way than to work on her career. Judy would often stay in her compartment while Sid, Marty, and I were in the observation dome or lounge. At some point, Sid would say he'd better check on Judy; sometimes he didn't return, other times she would return with him. My heart really went out to her. She was one of the funniest, wittiest ladies I have ever known, a marvelous conversationalist who would set me laughing until I actually doubled over. I adored being around her. Unhappy as she was, there was something straight on about Judy that I truly admired. I love that in people—that openness and directness that make me feel I can trust them. The ones who are just exactly what they are—that thrills me. And Judy was precisely that. I can't overemphasize the appeal of a person like that, especially in a place like Hollywood that is so shot through with phonies and pretenders.

Perhaps Judy drank so much to keep herself loose enough to stay here as long as she did. She was the most tightly wound person I ever knew, and drink may have kept her from snapping. I am a very wound-up person myself, so I have great empathy with anyone like Judy. We had many things in common, especially the fact that we both started in show business at an early age and really never had any other life than that. There was a scared little girl in Judy, afraid to come out. Maybe it was the childhood she never had. She kept so much of herself locked up, but what she did let out was beautiful.

I have previously mentioned the change in my relations with Marty, but now the marriage actually started to unravel. I loved him, I continued to love him until the day he died, but I was no longer in love with him. For me, being *in* love is an essential ingredient of marriage.

The confrontation about our marriage occurred the day Marty, in a fit of anger, struck Terry. Marty had a quick temper, and I suspect he had hit Terry before, but this was the first and only time he had struck Terry in front of me. It provoked one of my rare outbursts of anger, for I deeply feel that no one has the right to hit another living thing, human or animal. Being a nonviolent person, I almost never raise my voice, but that day I really screamed at Marty. I told him that

I had had enough brutality in my first marriage to last me a lifetime, and that I didn't want to go on living with him. "What right have you to hit Terry? Who do you think you are that you think you can inflict yourself on another human being like that? I don't want to be around a man who has to use his fists because his mind can't cope with his problems."

It was a propitious time to break up. Marty was about to go on the road with a play he was producing, *The Perfect Setup*. Marty had given it to me to read; I had hated it and begged him not to do it. It was old-hat and boring, nothing to commend it. But Marty had not listened to me, and now the play was ready to go on tour prior to its Broadway opening. I don't suggest that I am infallible, about plays or anything else, but this was so palpably a stinker that I felt Marty should have given some credence to the intensity of my reaction to it. Of course, Marty had an intense desire to achieve something on his own, something that was unrelated to me (just as the Gimp in *Love Me or Leave Me* had tried to open a nightclub to prove himself) and I appreciated what such an achievement might mean to Marty, but *The Perfect Setup* had failure built into it. At any rate, since Marty was leaving for the tour, I asked him to move out altogether. Too many things had gone wrong with our marriage, and this altercation with Terry had simply triggered the inevitable.

One of the things that had gone wrong was that in many ways Marty had changed from being a husband to trying to be a father figure. He was becoming more and more rigid and dictatorial, trying to make me into a child. He was *telling* me to do things, rather than discussing them with me. And when I showed any resistance, he'd have a temper tantrum. He never hit me, he knew better than that, but there were times when his anger became so uncontrollable, his face wild with rage, that he would smash his fist repeatedly against a wall. I didn't want this ugliness in my life. I felt I had earned the right to have a peaceful and harmonious home life. I worked hard, with very little respite, and I did not want to have to put up with anger and turmoil.

There were other things. Our sex life had deteriorated. In the beginning it was fine but in recent years it had become meaningless. I could just feel it going. I still loved him in a way—that never stopped—but I love quite a lot of people, and if I was to be truthful with myself I knew that with Marty it was no longer the kind of love that embraced sex. Good sex requires that each person be aware of

207

the other, a mutually shared experience, but Marty had lost that ability and desire to create the kind of flow that is so vital to making love; his patience had become very limited and he was satisfied simply to gratify himself. But I'm not one of those women who can be a fixture. I simply can't. I can't fake it. I know that a lot of women do. Many women have confided things to me about their sex lives with their husbands. How they fake a reaction to their husbands when they approach them for their once-a-week Saturday-night sex act. Some of them can barely stand the thought of having to face those Saturday nights. They pretend sleepiness, headaches, whatever; they much prefer those pretenses, they say, to pretending orgasms. Well, that's not for me. I have never faked a reaction to anything and I wasn't about to begin with sex.

It was to be a trial separation, but the day after Marty left (he moved into the Sunset Towers) I knew that, for me, it was permanent. His departure gave me a sense of freedom; I realized I had been rather smothered by him and the sense of being on my own released a certain tension which I had had for a long time. In the years I had been married to Marty, I felt I had grown as a person—in my work, in my religious convictions, in knowing myself, in asking questions and seeking answers. There comes a time when a marriage must be terminated. Nothing is forever. It isn't so much a matter of getting tired of someone as it is a question of whether a relation has sustained itself, whether it's growing, moving *toward* something. The past is fine for a scrapbook, a photo album, but the memory of how things were contributes nothing to how they are or will be.

I think it's a terrible handicap when husband and wife are involved in the same profession. When we first married, I thought, How nice that we can work together, but I came to realize how much better it would be if my husband had a career of his own and we could talk about his work as well as mine, and have a circle of his acquaintances, instead of being confined to the narrowness of my movie work and movie people. I came to realize too that I really wanted my husband to be the star of the family. A strong man. All the things that Marty and I had to deal with should have been left to an agent and kept out of the home.

The old saw about familiarity breeding contempt is certainly true about the weaknesses and shortcomings that are uncovered in marriage. I had become contemptuous of Marty's uncontrolled anger, his insistence on keeping me constantly at work, his treatment of

Terry, his dependence on my career, and even his attitude toward Christian Science. He was an avid convert who always had C. S. books around him, and unfailingly did his daily lesson before going to work. He involved himself with the Malibu church and was one of the ushers on Sunday morning. But then, despite all these manifestations of his devoutness, he would sleep through the service. That irritated me. I'd nudge him awake. "Now look, Marty," I used to say to him, "if I intended to sleep through the service I wouldn't go. But by God if I go to a service then I make sure I hear every word. I'm going to get something out of it or I don't go. Now, why do you go? Why don't you stay home and sleep? You're bored. You're obviously bored. You lose track of what the readers are saying and then you fall asleep."

"You're right, I do lose track . . ."

"That's because you don't concentrate, and then when you lose track you get bored."

"Yes, that's what happens. I force myself to go on Sunday because it's right that I go."

"No, no, it's wrong that you go if that's why you go. You should go because of what you get from going, not because it's a duty."

"I like to be there. That's enough for me."

This rigid adherence to the doctrines of a religion that he didn't really understand or try to understand would eventually have dire consequences for Marty. At the time, all it did was to make me a little contemptuous of him, because his attitude toward Christian Science was uncomfortably near the old, too familiar attitude fostered by the Roman Catholic church which I had long ago rejected.

After Marty's departure I got to thinking about how difficult it is for both partners to be happy in a marriage. If I had to do it again, I would never marry a man without first having lived with him. As I said before, if I had lived with Al Jorden, I'm sure I would have never married him, and since one is much more careful in an affair it's quite likely I wouldn't have had a child with him. I had had an affair with George Weidler but if I had actually *lived* with him, I don't think we would have gotten married. I don't know about Marty. There were so many things between us that were good, they might still have won out in the balance. But the point is, I would have much more clearly known the nature of the man I was marrying. If I had a young daughter who came to me with plans to marry a young man with whom she was in love, I would strongly urge her first to have an affair with him. I think it is downright sad for a young woman, barely out of her teens

209

(and sometimes in her teens), to turn off her life, so to speak, because she has fallen in love. For there are no two ways about it, when young marrieds have a baby, the woman must give up a good part of those years that should have been devoted to her own growth, enrichment, and education. I'm not saying for a minute that a baby is not an enriching and rewarding experience—what I'm saying is that it has so much more meaning when it comes somewhat later on, after the young woman has had a fair chance to enjoy the freedom of her very young years.

Marty and I had one of the shortest separations on record. After a few weeks on the road, *The Perfect Setup*, somewhat less than perfect, opened on Broadway and lasted one night. A short time later, Marty phoned and asked if he could see me.

He was pale and subdued. I attributed his appearance to the dismal failure of his play. I was wrong.

"I had to see you," he said, "because I've just had a long conference with Rosenthal about us."

"Meaning what?"

"Well, I explained about how we were separated and how you wanted to get started on a divorce."

"I don't want Rosenthal for my lawyer."

"All right, but that isn't what's involved here. What's involved is that there's no way we can part company."

"What are you talking about?"

"All our investments, Doris. All our capital is tied up in joint ventures that require loans and reinvestments. Rosenthal showed me that it is impossible to divide up the kinds of things we own, like oil wells. And we don't own them outright. It's very complicated. All I can tell you, I can *assure* you, if we split up we will lose everything." Marty became quite agitated and there were tears in his eyes. "All your hard work, Do-Do, and you'd wind up with hardly anything. I can't do that to you. Isn't there *some* way we can stay together? We do get along, in many ways. And I promise to . . . well, try to, you know, make it work. . . ."

I got up and walked out to the patio, trying to assimilate what Marty had told me. I would check Rosenthal's dire pronouncement with financial people I knew, but I had a feeling that if we were stretched out as far as Marty indicated, that we would indeed be ruined if we got divorced. I was very moved by the pathetic figure of Marty still sitting in the living room, trying to choke back his tears. As I have said, in many ways I still loved Marty and I certainly did not want anyone I loved to suffer. I walked around the swimming pool and thought about all this before going back to talk to Marty.

"I'll tell you, Marty. You can come back and we can save our investments but there are some things we've got to talk about and clear up. We've never talked about how it is between us but now we've got to if you come back to live here. I'm talking about our sex life. I've reached the point, Marty, where I can't have sex with you anymore. I don't have anyone else; it's just that I don't feel anything for you in that way any longer. I like you in a lot of other ways, but I'm not the type that pretends, you know that. You know I'm honest about how I feel and I've got to be honest about this."

Marty looked at me as if he didn't understand. I expected him to say something but he just looked at me.

"You say we have to stay together for financial reasons," I said. "All right, but then it has to be on my terms. From now on, what you do is your own business. I don't want to know about it and I hope you'll be discreet."

"And you?" Marty finally managed to say.

"If I'm not really in love I just don't think about it. I'm not interested in sex just for sex. Back when it was good between us, I loved it. Well, that's gone. But I'm not looking for anything. You don't have to worry about me. You've got me working so damn hard there's not time for it anyway."

The newspapers headlined our reconciliation, and when Marty returned he brought me a diamond ring, a large four- or five-carat solitaire. It had a flaw in it big enough to see with the naked eye. But flaw or no flaw, I'm not a big diamond lady. I like antique jewelry, but big rocks leave me as cold as they are. When I see Liz Taylor with those Harry Winston boulders hanging from her neck I get nauseated. Not figuratively, but *nauseated*. All I can think of are how many dog shelters those diamonds could buy.

~~~~~~

ALMA (KAPPELHOFF) DAY

The day Doris and Marty moved into the new house on Crescent Drive, I was standing in the living room with Marty when Terry came into the room. "When are you going to get your own place?" Marty asked him. "Do you plan to camp on us for the rest of your life?"

211

"Don't worry," Terry said, "I'm leaving."

"Yeah, but when? I can't stand the sight of you around here anymore."

"But, Marty," I said, "give the boy a chance—you just moved in here today."

"It's all right, Nana," Terry said. "I'm getting out."

"Yeah, but *when?*" Marty demanded.

"Tomorrow," Terry said. "That soon enough?"

And he did. Oh, that broke my heart, the way Marty treated Terry. He'd been good to him in the beginning, and then, as Terry began to grow up, Marty turned on him. I remember once, when Terry was twelve or so, he was singing and Marty told him to shut up, and then he grabbed Terry's arm and twisted it up and I thought he had broken it. Just because Terry hadn't stopped singing fast enough to suit Marty.

~~~~~~

TERRY MELCHER

Marty had made it clear that my choice was to spend four years at Principia College or not to go to college. Since I didn't want to be a Practitioner I quit and went to work for Columbia Records. If my mother was upset by my not going to college, she never expressed it to me.

I moved out of their house, and within a year or two I was doing okay at Columbia with the albums I was producing. One of my groups, The Byrds, was a big hit, and for a kid of twenty-two I had a highly respectable income. Occasionally, I'd go to have dinner with my mother and Marty. On one of these evenings, while we were at the table and Marty was carving a roast, I made some comment that he didn't like, and without looking up, he said, "Get the hell out of this house." Well, I was now independent and self-sufficient and I felt the time had come to put an end to all this shit I had been enduring all my life, so I stood up and said, "This time you're going to have to throw me out." Marty stood 6 feet, 3 inches, weighed around 230, which was a lot too much for me when I was fourteen; but now I felt I could handle myself. Besides, I'd seen anger in Marty but never a sign that he had the guts to do combat. My mother gasped and started to cry. Any kind of violence is surreal to her and she was really shook by young Terry finally asserting himself. Marty stopped cutting the meat and just sat there with his mouth open, looking at me, not believing this turn of events, but not about to challenge me. Instead of seeing my tail disappear through the door at his command, as it had been doing for fourteen years, he was seeing the end of his reign as the Bully of Crescent Drive. Through her tears my mother smoothed things over and we finished that dinner, but Marty never took me on again.

I guess Marty was bitter because he couldn't achieve a thing in life on his own, literally couldn't make a quarter without Doris. The things he tried on his own were all disasters. I think he probably hated her for that. Other men could have been married to her and enjoyed their relationship for what it was, but Marty wasn't that sane, or that sophisticated, or that compassionate; he wasn't educated and he didn't want to learn anything. He knew no more about movie producing at the end of his life than he had known when he first met Doris. He misused the power he got from controlling Doris and made a whole slew of enemies, virtually everybody in the business. I think the whole drive with money, with Rosenthal, with ripping off his business associates and Doris's friends was because he felt cornered into having to do something really spectacular; being a man of no talent, he had turned to money as a means of accomplishment, and I think what he was trying to amass was not ten or twenty million, but two hundred million.

I think my mother enjoyed her relationship with Marty, because he appeared to be solid, conservative, very concerned about her welfare, moral in a kind of Elmer Gantryish way. She liked his sense of humor—he did have a very black funniness that made her laugh. But my mother never played up the star role, she never gave people any shit, she never made people grovel; she got along with everyone she worked with, and I never saw her pull rank on anyone, or yell at any one of the little people around her. She has a very old-fashioned work ethic—"they're paying me and I have to do my best."

Marty, though, really liked to bust people, humiliate them in front of their co-workers, show what a big shot he was by loudly nailing some poor little bastard for some insignificant mistake he made.

When I moved out of their house, my only ambition was to make it big enough so that in no circumstances would I ever have to go back. Living with Marty was like growing up in a Beverly Hills ghetto. A few years later, when I was about twenty-four and making around $250,000 a year, and I was living with a beautiful young movie star, Candy Bergen, and we had a nice big beautiful house, with a houseman in a coat, a couple of fancy cars, a pool, two or three acres, Marty and my mother came to a big Christmas party I gave. I had several groups that I had at Columbia performing at the party and my mother was thrilled, she had a great time and she was delighted that I had put together such a marvelous life for myself. During the party I walked out to the pool with Marty, where there was a great view of the city spread out below us. "What do you think, Dad," I said, "doing okay, huh?"

"It makes me sick," he said, with a kind of snarl to his voice. "A snotty kid to fall into something like this."

He just couldn't stand it that I had gone out on my own and made it. I pitied his jealousy.

But I did remain loyal to his music-publishing company. All the songs that I wrote or on which I owned copyrights I published through his company. They made a lot of money for his firm, a half-million or so. But one day when I was in his office, which was just about the only place I saw him after I moved out, we got into an argument about something, and he said, "Why don't you take your fucking copyrights and get the hell out of here?" I said that was fine with me. Marty called the accountant and told him to make out a check for every penny that the firm owed to me. The accountant came in with a check for $345,000 which Marty thrust at me, telling me again to get the hell out.

I took the check and tore it up into as many little pieces as I could. "This is for all the time you've given me, and for all the years I boarded with you." I threw the pieces in his face and left. That was the turning point. From that time on, he didn't treat me like a kid anymore. I guess he figured that if I could throw a check for $345,000 in his face, I was a man.

The arrangement with Marty worked out better than I had expected. It was a strange relationship, in that despite the ground rules, we enjoyed each other's company. We adored going to the Dodger games, where we sat in a special section next to the visitors' bench, where many of our friends—Cary Grant, Dyan Cannon, David Janssen, Milton Berle, Nat "King" Cole, to name a few—also had boxes. For a couple of seasons we also went to most of the Laker basketball games. We had great times at our beach house, where we had long Sunday brunches with friends like Ernie and Edie Kovacs, Jack Lemmon and his wife, Shirley MacLaine, Richard Quine, Danny and Rosie Thomas, Tony Randall and his wife, Ross Hunter, Gower and Marge Champion, Gordon and Sheila MacRae, Jean and Dino Martin, and Warren Cowen, who was then married to Barbara Rush.

For five years our arrangement worked perfectly all right for Marty and me. If Marty had "outside interests," as the Victorians used to say, he kept them discreetly to himself and I was never aware of them. As for me, as I predicted, my body followed my heart, and since I wasn't in love with anyone, I had no interest in sex. When I am in love, I want to make love with that man all the time. As it was, I gave my all to my work—God knows there was enough of it. Life was mostly up at 5:30 A.M., work till six, bed by nine. Some life.

But in the press, my sex life was something else again. I was Lady Bountiful of the Sheets. Some of the best fiction of the Sixties was written about my amorous adventures with an assortment of lovers who could have only been chosen by a berserk random sampler.

My most consistently reported affair was with Maury Wills, the Dodger shortstop, who at that time had captured everyone's fancy with his base stealing. What seemed to have caught the gossip columnists' fancy was the fact that Wills and his wife were reported to be getting a divorce at just about the same time Marty moved out of our house. Since I had been going to most of the Dodger games, and of course, Marty and I knew many of the ballplayers, it was easy to stir all that together and come up with the conclusion that Maury Wills and I were having an affair. The only times I had seen Maury were at the games, at an occasional function given by the team's owner, Walter O'Malley, and at parties given by Barbara Rush and Warren Cowen, who were great fans. I never once saw Maury when Marty wasn't present and we certainly never saw each other alone anywhere. I don't know if some Dodger publicity man helped stir up those rumors, which persisted for a long time.

After Marty and I stopped going to the Dodger games (baseball seemed to be getting slower and slower and frankly we got bored) and transferred our interest to basketball, the columnists transferred my affair from Maury Wills to the Lakers' star forward, Elgin Baylor. Marty and I had become friendly with the owner of the Lakers who invited us to several parties where we met the players and their wives. That was the extent of my acquaintance with Baylor, but not in the press.

My most recently reported fling is the zaniest of all. My son, Terry, phoned me recently from New York, where he had gone on business.

"Hey, Mom," he said, "guess who you're having a hot love affair with."

"Am I having a hot love affair?"

"You sure are! And wait till you hear who it is."

"Who?"

"Sly."

"Sly who?"

"Sly—you remember Sly, Sly and the Family Stone. He came by my house that day."

Terry produces albums for RCA, and musician friends often drop by his house. I was visiting him recently when in came a young black man who was dressed in one of the most bizarre costumes I ever saw. That was Sly. He told me that "Que Sera" had always been a favorite song of his, and that he wanted to do an offbeat version of it in his new album. He proceeded to sit down at the piano and sing it for me as he planned to record it. The whole visit lasted maybe fifteen minutes. I never saw him again. Terry read me some of the reportage about Sly and me from an assortment of magazines and newspapers and I had to marvel again at the inventiveness of the press.

Of course, it occurred to me that one basis for these rumors could well have been the fact that my father married a black woman. Like father, like daughter. Mind you, I have no feeling about white or black—I believe I could just as easily fall in love with a black man as I could with a white man; my problem is, I don't fall in love easily.

But my media affairs were by no means limited to black men. At one time or another I was reported to be sexing around with Jerry West, Pancho Gonzales, Glen Campbell, Frank Sinatra, and, would you believe it?—Jimmy Hoffa! Variety was certainly the spice of my life.

The Jerry West rumor started because we talked on the sidewalk one day when I was on my bicycle and Jerry was taking some things to the cleaners. The Gonzales rumor came out of the fact that he would occasionally hit the ball with me at the Los Angeles Tennis Club, and on two or three occasions Marty and I had dinner with Pancho and his wife. At the time of the Glen Campbell rumors, extensively reported, I had never even met him and knew him only as a voice on his records. But there were heavy items about us everywhere. Big picture of Glen, next to big picture of me. Imagine my shock and surprise when, at the height of these press accounts, I was sitting at a table at the CBS Affiliates Dinner when Glen Campbell came up to me with his wife and introduced himself. I nearly panicked.

"My wife wanted to meet you because she's such a fan of yours," Glen said. And that's all there was to it. Not one word about all the silly items in the press. I wondered what the people at the dinner who saw us talking were thinking.

I hadn't laid eyes on Sinatra in years, only once after we finished *Young at Heart*. Yet my housekeeper had picked up a magazine at Ralph's Supermarket that depicted my torrid romance with Frank, which at that very moment was being hotly pursued in Frank's place in Palm Springs. Of course, I had never set foot in Frank's house. As for Jimmy Hoffa, who was then president of the Teamsters union, I haven't the remotest idea how that rumor originated. I wouldn't know Hoffa if I fell over him. Someone suggested that it might have come out of the fact that one of the mortgages on that atrocious Palo Alto Cabana was held by the Teamsters' Union pension fund. That's a helluva basis for a romance, isn't it?

By pouring cold water on all these rumored romances, I don't want to give the impression that I was completely celibate. There was a time, when I was doing my television show, that I did have an exciting and fulfilling affair that lasted over a year—I'll go into that later. It was a beautifully kept secret that the press never got wind of.

I must confess that there were times over the course of those five "arranged" years with Marty when every once in a while I did have a crush on a leading man in one of my pictures. In the course of the many weeks it took to make a picture, there was sometimes an intensity and intimacy that developed that I responded to. There were times in the playing of romantic scenes, which often had to be shot over and over again, when my leading man would clearly react to me and I to him. Had we both been free, it's possible that something would

216

have come of it, but since we weren't, our "affairs" were as make-believe as the film we were making.

SAM WEISS

As for being a Christian Scientist, believe me, Marty was only interested in making himself look good in Doris's eyes. He had no feelings about any religion but he took on Christian Science the way he did to prove that he could be an even more devout C. S. than Doris was. He had to prove himself *some* way, and if you don't have talent this is one of the ways you can do it. So he became a fanatic, but the hell of it is, in trying to prove what a devout C. S. he was, he killed himself.

There was a time that I was in the hospital for a gall bladder-ulcer operation when I got a call from Marty. "Listen, Doris and I just heard about your operation, Sam. Cancel it. We're on our way to the hospital with the Christian Science books. We're going to take you home and read these books to you."

"Now, Marty," I said, "it's now four p.m.—the operation is tomorrow morning and I don't want to go home and read books." He called again a little while later but I was already a little groggy from some pills they had given me. Marty harangued me on the phone but I was too groggy to follow what he was saying.

A few days later Doris called to question me about how I was feeling, how the operation went, all that. She said her doctor had found a lump in her breast which they wanted to perform a biopsy on, but she had her doubts—and Melcher was urging her against it. She obviously had phoned me for reassurance. I urged her to go, which she eventually did.

But when it was necessary for Melcher to go to the hospital, he wouldn't give in. He'd show her that he was a better Christian Scientist than she was. I really think that's what his death was all about.

There was a time when Melcher used me as a beard to help cover up some of his affairs. Mostly it took the form of asking me to have dinner with him. The first couple of times it happened, I was surprised to find that he came to dinner with some broad he had met, usually in Europe. After that I got wise. When he'd call I'd ask if he was going to be alone. I didn't want to get involved in a thing like this that might have wound up hurting Doris. He would beg me to come along. He told me that Doris had become frozen up on him, didn't respond to him anymore. Frankly, feeling about Marty as I did, I was very happy to hear that, although I figured it was probably the old malarkey you hear from most married men who are cheating.

Those rumors about Doris's affairs, like the one she was supposed to be having with Maury Wills, were all hogwash. I introduced Doris to the Dodger games. I was there whenever she was. She was no more having an affair with Wills than I was. It just happened that he was the most exciting player on the team and it made good copy to involve him with the most glamorous star at the games. Reminds me of a movie star of many years ago, Lupe Velez, who was a boxing fan, went to all the fights—the papers at that time were full of reports of an affair she was having with a black prizefighter who was an exciting contender. There wasn't a word of truth in it.

Marty made several trips to Europe by himself, and it's my theory that some of the money that disappeared from Doris's bank account wound up in Geneva or Zurich in a numbered account. Marty loved money for the sake of money. He was a loner who didn't have a friend or a real interest beyond making money. I thought he might take an interest in Terry when he first adopted him, but the way he treated that boy as he was growing up—well, all I can say is it made me despise him. The things he said to Terry in my presence, the brutality of it. Terry would come in the room, excited about something as boys get, and he'd start to say, "Hey, Dad, let me show you—" and Marty would say, "Get out of here, you little shit. I can't stand the sight of you." There were times I thought about talking to Doris but I knew that Marty would deny my accusation and I'd have a family quarrel on my hands. But how I hated him for what he did to Terry. Then when Terry got old enough to get out of the house and go to work, he was very successful and made good money producing albums; and that made Marty very jealous of him and he hated him all the more.

Marty once tried to get me to see Rosenthal about investing my money with him. He told me how much he was making for people like Kirk Douglas. But I figured the less I saw of Marty Melcher the better, so I didn't go. Smartest thing I ever did.

JAMES GARNER

I liked Doris so much that I couldn't like Marty Melcher because I knew what he was doing to her. I think everybody in the business knew but nobody had the nerve to tell Doris.

Marty was a hustler, a shallow, insecure hustler who always ripped off fifty thousand dollars on every one of Doris's films as the price for making the deal. You want to make a film with Doris? Okay, fifty G's for Melcher and you list him as executive producer or whatever, but you never see him from start to finish of the picture. When he did visit the set, I'd edge away from him. You don't get too close to a guy like that, just good morning, no conversation, and keep your hand on your wallet.

Naturally, he was always talking about his big deals. What he said in the steam room to Zanuck or what Jack Warner offered him over lunch. When we were making *Move Over, Darling,* he was bragging a lot about money he had just borrowed from the Teamsters to finance some big hotel or other. A wheeler-dealer businessman, but of course we all knew where his clout came from and without Doris he couldn't have driven a truck for the Teamsters.

I never knew anyone who liked Melcher.

Fifteen

‚‚

IN the early Sixties, the comedies I made with Rock Hudson and James Garner, plus a big MGM musical, *Jumbo,* produced an era of high earnings and, for five consecutive years, a continuance of my number-one rating at the box office. But later in the Sixties, Marty began to bring me scripts which I disliked and wanted to turn down; but to my growing consternation, I was forced to accept them because he had already signed me to contracts to do them.

These movies were *Do Not Disturb, Caprice, Ballad of Josie,* and *Where Were You When the Lights Went Out?* There were good actors like Rod Taylor, Richard Harris, and Peter Graves cast in them, but these poor men were the pearls before the swine of these scripts. I particularly recall the day Marty, wth his usual nonselective enthusiasm, handed me the script for *Caprice.* That evening, when Marty returned from the tennis club, we had a discussion that went something like this:

"Marty, I read the script—all I can say is, thank God I don't have to make movies like that anymore."

"What are you talking about?"

"You can't be serious—that's a terrible script."

"You're wrong, Doris, *wrong,* and you'll realize it when you see how it turns out. Now, I'll tell you who we've got—Richard Harris and—"

"Wait a minute, Marty! Whoa, hold it! What are you trying to tell me?"

"Well, that you have to make the picture."

"You mean without asking me . . . ?"

"You were so busy on *Glass Bottom Boat* that I had to—"

"I wasn't *that* busy!"

219

"Doris, we've made a deal and there's no sense getting all steamed up about it."

That did it. I blew my stack. *"You* made a deal—you and Rosenthal, that it? Well, you and Rosenthal don't have to get in front of the camera and try to make something out of terrible stuff like this! I know that you and your friends are only interested in making money, but I'm interested in something more. I don't give a damn about money. I never see any of it and I don't have the time to use any of it even if I knew what to do with it—which I don't. When are you going to stop chasing money for the sake of money?"

"That's not fair. I'm doing it for your sake and you know it. How many superstars out here wind up with nothing because they didn't handle their money right when they were making it big? Well, I'm trying that for you—us. You keep putting Rosenthal down, but he's a genius and what he's doing for you, you should write him a thank-you note every day."

"What he's doing for me is getting me into a lot of terrible movies and putting me into hotels and oil wells and all kinds of things I know nothing about."

"Then why raise such a fuss about them?"

"Because I don't trust Rosenthal, that's why."

"Do you trust me?"

"Yes, of course I do."

"So when I tell you that Rosenthal has made some of the most brilliant investments for you, that they are paying off like you can't believe—"

"Then why do you keep pouring my money into them? All these rotten scripts, one right on top of the other—"

"That's the nature of this kind of investment. You keep pyramiding your capital—"

"I'd like to pyramid a couple of good movies."

"This is a good movie, believe me."

"This . . . this thing, *Caprice?*"

"It's a lot better than you think."

"If *Caprice* is your idea of a good script, God help my investments."

The movies went from bad to worse, and I quickly tumbled off the box-office perch. *Ballad of Josie* was nothing more than a second-rate television western that required me to get up at four-

Jumbo was a romp for Doris, who did most of her own equestrian and aerial acrobatics.

In *The Thrill of It All*, James Garner took over where Rock Hudson left off.

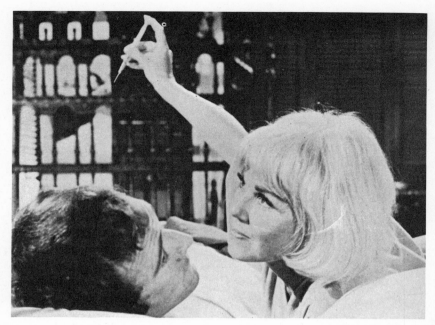

Caprice needed more than a hypodermic, here being administered to Richard Harris, to make it work.

With son Terry and husband Marty who shared the name Melcher but that's all.

The Ballad of Josie, replete with fright wig, was one of many projects Marty Melcher forced Doris into.

Doris's television series was started by Melcher against Doris's expressed disinterest, but in its second year Doris turned the series around and made it work.

With her guest star, John Denver, in Doris's 1975 television special, "Doris Day Today."

Doris's real loves—her garden and her dogs. The one here is Biggest, pride of the pack. (Photo: H. Benson)

thirty every morning.* My memory of *Where Were You When the Lights Went Out?* which was an alleged comedy about the New York City power blackout, is little more than a blur because I spent most of the time in traction. During rehearsals for the film, we ran through a scene in which I was half-drunk, half-sedated, and had to be moved from place to place in a living room; I had to play the scene completely limp, a dead weight. During the rehearsal, Patrick O'Neal picked me up in the wrong way and I suffered a severely pinched nerve in my back that affected my neck, arm, and hand. The pain was excruciating and constant, but there was not much the doctors could do for me. I had suffered a similarly painful accident during the shooting of *Move Over, Darling*, when Jimmy Garner, a man of heft and muscle, picked me up under his arm a little too enthusiastically and cracked a couple of my ribs. I made that movie mummified with adhesive tape, which made it difficult to breathe and painful to laugh.

The first specialist Marty brought in said that I should remain immobile for four months. Marty quickly got rid of him. Finally, by shopping around, Marty found a doctor who said I could go ahead with the movie (which had already been delayed for several weeks) as long as I stayed in traction when not actually on the set. So that's how we made the picture. Poor Clara would lie in traction in her dressing room until a setup was ready for her, then she'd be helped onto the set, the scene would be shot, and back to traction she'd go. It was a great comfort to know, however, that the oil wells were gushing, the hotels overbooked, and the cattle all in foal.

Which brings me to *With Six You Get Egg Roll*, the last movie I made. Finally, it seemed to me, Marty had come up with a pleasant, funny family film and I urged him to produce it himself, something he hadn't done since *Julie*, the first movie I had made, twenty movies ago, after leaving Warner Brothers.

One day my makeup man said to me, "I've been noticing how thin Marty is getting—is he dieting?"

"No," I said, "he isn't dieting and I don't know why on earth he's getting so thin."

---

* It was a terrible movie but there were compensations: the camaraderie of cast members Peter Graves, George Kennedy, David Hartman, Andy Devine, and Bill Tallman; the sun rising behind the purple hills, igniting the world; the sheep dogs and the herders working the herds of Australian sheep; cattle and horses moving across the distant range. All in all, a moving, spiritual experience.

That afternoon I mentioned to Marty that everyone was beginning to notice how thin he was. He said yes, he was losing weight but it was nothing to worry about. I suggested that he go to a doctor for a checkup.

"Why? I feel fine," he said, rather testily. "Just don't bother me—I'm fine."

A few nights later, I was working on location when Terry dropped by, just to hang around the set for a while. He asked where Marty was. I told him that he had gone to my trailer to take a nap. Terry looked surprised—it was so unlike Marty to take a nap at any time.

We went back to my trailer and found Marty there on the couch, asleep. He woke and complained that he was cold. Very cold. It was a bit nippy out but the dressing room was well heated. I distinctly recall my reaction at that moment in the trailer—a little bit frightened. Terry suggested that maybe Marty was getting the flu, and I was relieved to think that that was probably all that was wrong.

The day the picture ended, Marty picked me up at the studio and complained on the way home that he seemed to be getting a bad cold and felt wobbly. When we got home, he undressed and went to bed. In all the years I had been married to Marty, he had never taken to a sickbed. I tried to get him to talk about how he felt, but he would only say that he had the flu, that he certainly didn't need a doctor, and that it was just a matter of putting Christian Science to work.

For three months Marty stayed in bed. He developed chronic diarrhea; nothing stayed in his stomach; the color slowly drained away from his face until he finally turned gray. I tried every which way to get a doctor in the house. I even asked my friend and personal physician, Dr. Robert DeMangus, to come to the house, but Marty got terribly agitated about seeing him and I had to turn Dr. DeMangus away.

Marty constantly studied his *Science and Health* and desperately wanted to see Martin Broones, but all this time he was on a lecture tour. Marty talked to him on the phone virtually every day, and I overheard Mr. Broones telling Marty which page and which lines to concentrate on.

There were nights when I would go into the little study and sit on the telephone until I reached Mr. Broones, wherever he was, and urged him to come to see Marty. I told him, "Something is happening to Marty, something terrible—I just know it. He's gray, he never eats, and he can hardly walk to the bathroom. And at night, when I lie in bed with him, his heart is pounding, *thump, thump, thump,* so loud and heavy it shakes the bed and I can feel every thump as it reverberates through the mattress." (Although we had been using separate beds, when Marty took sick he had asked me to sleep in his bed.)

Mr. Broones said he certainly wanted to get back to see Marty, but his lecture commitments were such that he just couldn't work in such a long trip.

Marty would allow no one to be in the house except my mother and our housekeeper, Katie. Some nights I would sit in the little darkened study by myself and cry all night long. I was so weak from worry, from not being able to eat, from the frustration of watching Marty slip away from life without letting me help him, I didn't have the strength in my arms to comb my hair. I never slept. The night was an agony of sleepless worry. I thought he had cancer and I feared that every day that passed might be worsening his condition. I turned to Mary Baker Eddy for help, but found none. All I knew was the black taste of despair.

All through Marty's illness, I stayed in the house night and day, with the exception of an occasional bicycle ride in the afternoon for a half-hour or so. Once when I was returning to the house after having biked over to Beverly Drive to meet a friend for a cup of coffee, I was shocked to see Marty in his robe and slippers, sitting on the curb across the street from our house. I got off my bike and walked over to him.

"Where have you been?" he asked. "You've been gone so long."

"Why, Marty, it's only been a half-hour at most."

"I get so—nervous when you're not around," he said.

He was a child impatiently waiting for Mama to return. The father figure had come full circle. I helped him get up and assisted him across the street and into the house. He could hardly walk.

Terry was the only outside person that Marty saw, and then infrequently. Terry too tried to persuade Marty to get medical help, but Terry got no further than I had. Finally, on one of Terry's visits, he brought Dick Dorso into the room without asking Marty's permission. Dick had been Marty's partner in the Century Artists Agency, and he was a man whom Marty respected and liked. It was Dick who finally forced Marty into letting a doctor examine him—

and even then the only doctor that Marty would accept was a man he used to play tennis with.

This doctor, whose name I don't recall, came right over and spent a half-hour alone with Marty. When he emerged from the bedroom he told me he was calling in a heart specialist. I was amazed. "Didn't you know that Marty has an enlarged heart?" the doctor asked. Of course, I didn't. He said it was a condition Marty had had for a long time.

The specialist came and ordered Marty into a hospital immediately. The doctor explained to me that Marty was suffering from an inflammation of the heart muscles. I felt a sense of relief that it wasn't the cancer I had feared. "That can be treated, can't it?" I asked.

"Two months ago, quite effectively—now, well, we have a much more difficult job on our hands."

Marty refused to go in an ambulance, so we drove him to Mount Sinai. He went in his pajamas and bathrobe. It was a long, slow process getting him from the house to the car. On the way to the hospital, I remember feeling absolutely elated by the discovery that Marty didn't have cancer.

I spent every day and night at the hospital, from eight in the morning until midnight. Marty didn't talk much; he was completely listless, an air of resignation or defeat about him, but he liked for me to be there in his room with him.

Just about the only thing in which Marty showed any interest was the crossword puzzle, a lifelong passion. One afternoon, while we were doing one of the puzzles in a crossword book I had brought him, a particularly lavish display of flowers arrived. The nurse handed me the card.

"They're from *your* friend, Jerry Rosenthal," I said.

The nurse started to arrange the flowers in a vase. Marty put down his crossword pencil and stared out the window. Then he turned and looked at me, and his eyes were different than I had ever seen them before.

"Please take those flowers out of here," Marty said to the nurse. She hesitated. "And keep them out of here," Marty said.

I went over and sat down on the floor in front of the chair in which Marty was sitting. I put my arms on his legs and looked up at him. "Marty, when you get out of here, we have to have a talk about Rosenthal," I said. "The time has come, don't you think?"

He took one of my hands in his and nodded his head affirmatively.

He turned his head and looked out of the window, then for quite some time kept my hand firmly pressed between his. After a while he said, "We have to go away and really have a good time." He continued to look out the hospital window. "These last few months, I kept thinking about you and how you've worked so hard. When we have gone away, it's always to do with your working. Now you've got to go away to have fun."

"But work for me is fun. If I hadn't enjoyed it, I wouldn't have done it. I don't regret working."

"I know. But you haven't had the fun you should have had."

"Well, when you get well and get out of here, before we take a vacation or do anything, Rosenthal is the first thing on the agenda, okay?"

Marty looked at me in agreement, squeezed my hand, then released it. "I think I'll get in bed," he said. "Here, do you want to finish the puzzle?"

I took the puzzle from him and helped him into bed. He was so thin I could feel the bone through the flesh on his arm. I pulled the covers over him and he dropped off to sleep almost immediately. I pulled down the shade and left the room.

In the corridor I glanced at the crossword puzzle he had been working on. The letters weren't in the right squares, so that none of the words in the puzzle made any sense. It was a shock. My God, I thought, something terrible is happening. Marty was always so neat and efficient about his crossword puzzles.

Early the following morning I received a call from the hospital, asking me to come as soon as I could. They told me that Marty had awakened around four in the morning and had asked to sit in a chair. A short time later he had fallen from the chair, and he was now in a deep coma. I looked at the clock—ten to seven. I phoned Terry, who said he would come right away to pick me up. While I was waiting for Terry, I phoned Marty's brother, Jack, who lived in San Francisco, and told him to go right to the hospital.

At the hospital, the doctor told me that Marty's heart condition was tied in with a cerebral condition, and that they were now into emergency procedures which included a tracheotomy. Numb with despair, I went to the little waiting room down the corridor while Terry went downstairs to await Jack's arrival. I was thankful that no one else was in the waiting room. I sat down and stared at the wall, not really able to comprehend what was happening. I caught sight of myself in the mirror on the wall and was amazed to discover that I was wearing a bright-red jacket. I couldn't imagine why I had put on a red jacket at a time like this.

When Jack arrived, he and Terry immediately went into Marty's room. The doctor had asked me not to go in, until he gave permission. Terry and Jack stayed in the room for only a few minutes. They told me not to go in. They said that Marty was all open with tubes, that he was in a deep coma, and that the room was busy with medical personnel. The doctor had asked Terry to take me home, and had promised to send for me as soon as it was the right time for me to come. I was rather reluctant to leave, but both Terry and Jack insisted.

Four o'clock the following morning, the phone rang. Marty was dead. I could not bring myself to tell anyone. Not just then. I walked out on the patio that adjoins my bedroom, the night air heavy with the scent of flowers in their hanging baskets. Marty. Marty gone. I hadn't lost a husband, because he hadn't been that in the past few years, but I had lost a man I had loved for seventeen years. He had done everything for me. And with me. Made every decision. Had total control of everything I had. At this moment of his death, in my aloneness, he was my father, and I was a ten-year-old child. And I loved him very much.

I said it aloud out there on the patio: "Oh, I loved him, I loved him."

I recalled a talk we had one evening when we went for a walk along the beach in front of our Malibu house. "Isn't it funny and strange," Marty said to me, "this relationship we have? The way we love each other without there being anything physical between us. And yet, that's supposed to be so important."

"Maybe it isn't so important," I had said. "Who's to say? Maybe what we have is stronger. I don't know." We walked along for a while, our arms around each other's waist. Then I said something that came straight from my heart. "I just have a lovely feeling, Marty, that I would like to grow old with you."

He loved that.

And I meant it. I truly did. And now that possibility was gone.

Sixteen

THERE was no funeral. No family gathering. Nothing. Marty was cremated without ceremony of any kind. That's the way he wanted it. I knew this, not from his instructions about his own death, which he had not anticipated, but from his remarks about funerals of departed friends, none of which we ever attended. I shared Marty's antipathy to funerals. I think grief is a very private matter, and that the public nature of a funeral is barbaric.

Marty's death was the one thing that happened in my life that I really handled badly. I had lived closely with Marty for seventeen years; he had done everything for me; and we were together much more than the average couple. As a consequence, his abrupt departure left a terrible void in the conduct of my life. The earth had opened and he had fallen through and I was totally alone. Those first weeks, secluded in the house, I was once again the ten-year-old hiding behind the curtains in the Cincinnati house, watching my father disappear down the driveway.

I couldn't talk to anybody on the phone. Close friends would call to express sympathy, but my tears never stopped and communication was impossible. I couldn't see anyone, either. I saw a few very close friends who came to the house, but that's all I could manage. I had lost the center of my being. I could not even turn to Christian Science, which had always been my support, for C. S. does not embrace death (hence there is nothing to grieve); God is love and God's love should replace your grief. It didn't work that way for me—when I am filled with grieving tears, I shed them. That's the way I was, and am. I do what I must do, what my honest feelings command me to do. I wasn't going to put on an act for anybody, for Christian Science or anyone else. It was during this period that I turned from Christian Science as my religion. I still devoutly believed in much of what Mrs. Eddy preached, and I would always make her revelations a part of my life, but I no longer wanted to be a member of a formal church; I did not want to call myself anything. I wanted to have my own personal religion, one suited precisely to my own spiritual emotions. I don't honestly know how much this judgment was affected by Marty's too stubborn adherence to Christian Science at a time when he should have been seeing a doctor. I don't know if perhaps I felt some kind of subconscious guilt for having brought Christian Science into Marty's life. I just don't know. It was a long period of scrambled emotions for me, and anything was possible.

The year following Marty's death I bitterly rejected the whole concept of there being a God. I could not explain to myself why, if there were a compassionate God, he should have taken Marty from me. I stopped thinking about religion. I stopped reading those books which had always given me strength. In my grief I rejected what they taught. All that had sustained me before was as dead as Marty.

But my feelings about Marty began to be assaulted by a series of revelations that occurred soon after his death. The first of these revelations happened when I forced myself to open the door of his room and go inside. I was very moved by the impact of his familiar belongings, but when I went into his dressing room I received a severe jolt from what I found on top of a bureau—two completed television scripts for a "Doris Day Show"!

Marty had often discussed television with me—I had been approached many times to do a series—but I had always said I wasn't interested, that I'd much rather stick with movies. Marty, though, felt that films were running toward explicit sex and that television was a much better medium for my kind of movie. He also felt that the whole theater concept of entertainment was finished.

But I had been quite emphatic about how I felt. "The whole nature of television is wrong for me," I had said. "The constant pressure of having to shoot an entire script in a few days is not for me. Under no circumstances do I want to do television."

Now here, on top of his dresser, were two shooting scripts for what looked like a series that was all ready to go. But perhaps the series was not as far along as it looked. I asked Terry to investigate for me. But whether I was committed or not, that Marty had gone this far in the face of my emphatic opposition came as a shock.

I received a much greater shock a few days later. It was Terry,

228

poor Terry, who had to bring me most of these shocking disclosures. It was on the evening when Terry had said that he was going to come by the house around dinnertime. Terry had been appointed administrator of the estate, and he had said he would drop in after an afternoon appointment which he had scheduled with Rosenthal on some estate matters. But Terry didn't show up. I was somewhat concerned because Terry usually called when he was not coming. I finally gave up on him and went to bed.

It was quite late when my mother came into my room to tell me that Terry had arrived with Dick Dorso and they were in the den waiting to see me. "I think something's wrong," my mother said. I put on my robe and went into the den and sat down in a chair facing the two of them. Terry came over to me and hugged me, just held me for the longest time. He didn't say a word. Just held me and held me and I started to cry.

Finally, he sat down directly in front of me and talked to me in a low voice. "After I saw Rosenthal this afternoon, I phoned Dick and asked him if he'd drive around with me for a while. That's what we've been doing, for hours now—just driving around."

"Why?" I asked.

"So I could screw up my courage to the point where I could come in this house and tell you what I've got to tell you. I was discussing with Dick whether maybe I should put it off—God knows you've been through more than enough for now—but we finally decided I have to tell you because there are things we've got to act on right away."

"What can be so terrible?"

"The day after Dad died, a check arrived for sixty thousand dollars. One of your film checks which came to me as executor of the estate. Rosenthal called and said, 'Son, endorse it and send it right over to me. I have to have it right away.' I said, 'I don't know what I'm signing, Mr. Rosenthal. That's my mother's check for sixty thousand dollars and I have to know where it's going.' Rosenthal said, 'Now, son, don't you trust me? Haven't I been around long enough for you to trust me? You know that I handled all financial affairs for your father.' I said, 'I'm sorry, Mr. Rosenthal, but since I'm the executor, I'll have to find out things for myself.' "

Terry looked down at his hands for a few moments before he went on. "Mom, these past four days, I've had a showdown with Rosenthal, and the bad news is—God, I wish I didn't have to tell

229

you—but the fact is, you don't have anything. Not a penny. The hotels are bankrupt, all the oil wells are dry, and there aren't any cattle. Nothing, Mom, and what's even worse, you have a lot of debts—like around four hundred and fifty thousand dollars. Most of it is taxes. They have to be paid. You may have to sell this house."

I had stopped crying. I don't shed tears over money things. "But where has it all gone?"

"It will take a lot of digging to find that out. Right now I've got to concentrate on getting rid of Rosenthal, and then to get someone to take the whole thing apart to find out what really happened."

"Twenty years of hard work—all those films," Dick Dorso said, shaking his head, "and nothing to show for it. Christ!"

Only one thing seemed important to me at that moment. "Do you think—was Marty in on this with Rosenthal? I mean, did Marty know it was all gone—or was Rosenthal just using him?"

"I don't know, Mom."

I was finding it difficult to assimilate this additional tragedy. I had not slept for too many nights, and I did not have enough energy to mount a reaction. "I've got to know," I said. "More than anything, I've got to know about Marty."

"Well," Terry said, "it won't be easy. I went to Dad's office this morning, and there was nothing there—all the file cabinets were empty. His desk was cleaned out."

"What? When did he find time to do that?"

"He didn't. It just so happened that Don Genson was looking out of his office window on the morning after Dad died, when he saw a Bekins moving van pull up. The Bekins men carried a steady stream of cardboard packing boxes out of the office. Of course, that entrance also serves Rosenthal's offices but you can bet that that's what happened to Dad's files."

"What does Rosenthal say?"

"He claims it was a shipment that had nothing to do with Dad's office. But we have no proof . . . so . . . just as we have no proof about the will."

"What about the will?"

"There isn't any. We've opened the safety-deposit box, looked all through the office—no will."

"But Marty was frantic about people having wills. The way he used to lecture Aunt Marie and Blanche Shand and God knows who about having a will. No way Marty didn't have a will. Did you ask Rosenthal if he ever drew one up for Marty?"

"Sure. Says he didn't. Most likely went the way of those files."

"We've got to pay those debts, Terry. I've never owed anyone in my life and I'm not going to start now. If we have to sell the house, then sell it."

"But you've got to live somewhere—"

"Sure, but not in an expensive house when I'm in debt. I'll rent a place somewhere."

"Everything that could be borrowed against has been used. Rosenthal and Dad even borrowed against your record contract."

"You mean albums I haven't even done yet?"

"Yes, they've already taken the money for them. And the money's all spent."

TERRY MELCHER

I never imagined for a second that Marty was going to die. Not even after they took him to the hospital. He swam a hundred laps every morning and a hundred laps every night, he had been a health-food addict twenty years before it became fashionable, he didn't smoke or drink, lived by the Christian Science book, and with his perpetual tan he looked like he'd be around for a hundred years. I figured certainly he'd outlast me with my cigarettes and vodka and hell-raising life.

So when he did die, it really didn't register with me, so sure I had been that he would never die as long as I was alive. His death wasn't believable, I wasn't prepared for it—not that it was a great personal loss, you know, it wasn't going to ruin my Christmas, but I had figured he wouldn't *allow* himself to die until he had at least a hundred million stashed under the sod someplace.

I hurried to my mother's house the minute I was told that Marty was dead. I took her hands in mine and she looked at me with an expression on her face that said, What do I do? I found myself saying, "I'll take care of it, Mother," but I didn't have much of an idea of what it was that I'd be taking care of. Little did I know what I had let myself in for.

As executor of the estate, I had a meeting with Rosenthal, whom I'd known as Uncle Jerry since I was seven. I felt good about having Rosenthal in the picture because he had been involved in everything for so long and he would help me a lot. But about ten days after my meeting with Rosenthal, there was another meeting, this one at CBS with Mike Dann and about twenty other people in his department, Ted Ashley, who was my mother's agent at the time, Rosenthal, myself, and the two producers of the television show, Dick Dorso and Bob Sweeney. The purpose of the meeting was to get started on the series for the fall. The producers had been complaining to Dann that they were unable to commission scripts or build sets because Rosenthal refused to give them any of the preproduction money which CBS had advanced.

Dann gave a little pep talk about how great the "Doris Day Show" was going to be and how it would have at least a five-year run. Then he turned to Rosenthal and asked him just what he had done with the half-million dollars that CBS had advanced for the show. Rosenthal said, "I don't have to tell you. Look at the contract. I don't have to account for it."

Dann tried to be pleasant about it, but he persisted in wanting to know where the money had gone, but Rosenthal, in effect, was telling him to go fuck himself. Finally, Dann blew his stack. He threw some papers off the desk, picked up the briefcases on the conference table, and hurled them against the wall; and knocking over some chairs as he left, he hurled a thunderbolt of profanity at Rosenthal, who appeared unruffled by the outburst and rather self-satisfied.

After Rosenthal left, I had a talk with Dorso, whom I always respected as a very straight guy. He put it right on the line for me. "Be careful, Terry," he said. "Rosenthal's not to be trusted."

That was rather unthinkable to me, since I had been weaned on the notion that Rosenthal and Marty were synonymous, and although I figured Marty as rather fucked up, I always rated him as honest; because how else was he able to live up to all those lofty Christian Science goals? I went to see Rosenthal. "Jerry," I said, "I legally represent my mother and I want it straight from you—where is that half-million dollars?"

"You ask too many questions," he said. "Go home, Junior, and let me take care of this. Don't worry. I'm running things, just leave everything to me. Now go on home."

"That's your answer?"

"That's it. When I need you I'll send for you."

"Well, Jer, I'll tell you how it is—you're fired. I've hired a new set of attorneys who will be in touch with you. In the meantime, all power of attorney is canceled and you are to freeze everything just as it is."

It's a brutal thing to say, but just about the best thing Marty did for my mother was to die when he did. At the rate Marty and Rosenthal were going, and the direction they were headed, in another year I don't think my mother could ever have recovered. They would have wiped out all her future television earnings, her house, everything, and put her in hock for years to come. Rosenthal had it all figured out, every rathole protected, but he hadn't figured on Marty's death. Considering what was to happen to Rosenthal over the next five years, it was as if Marty had reached a hand out of the grave and stabbed his old buddy.

I had to get away from the house. A coldness had settled into my bones, cold despair, and I felt desperately that I had to go where there was heat. I rented a house in Palm Springs and drove there with my mother, my brother-in-law, Jack, and my dear friend Barbara Lamston. It was a lovely house, on the grounds of the golf course, with a broad, sweeping view of the desert and the mountains.

Before I had left, Terry had brought me the doleful news that Marty had indeed signed my name to a contract for a television series, and that he had received a large advance, ostensibly for preproduction costs, which had long since been spent by Rosenthal. To make matters worse, I had to start work in six weeks.

When I first arrived in Palm Springs, I was a vegetable. I could do little more than sit in a chair and stare at the desert and the distant mountains. I swam a little, but mostly I sat zombielike in the sun, grateful that I could feel the desert heat warming my insides. But regeneration, I found, was a long, arduous process. I tried not to think about Marty. Soon after his death I had locked his closet and refused to discuss anything about his effects. But, unbeknownst to me, my mother had gone into Marty's room and given Jack a few items of light clothing because Jack was unprepared for this visit to Palm Springs. I was sitting on the edge of the pool the morning Jack walked out wearing something Marty had purchased rather recently. I had seen Marty in it and I recognized it immediately, but the shock of seeing Jack, without warning, in those clothes of Marty's completely threw me. Poor Jack. He certainly got those clothes off in a hurry. "Give them away to somebody else," he said to my mother. "Not me."

I was taking sleeping pills but every night I cried myself to sleep. And during the day I began doing peculiar things. One hot afternoon, when we were all sitting around the pool, I went into the house, took a shower, put on a dress and all that, and went back out to the pool. It must have been 110 degrees.

My mother said, "Doris, why are you all dressed up? Are you going somewhere?"

I had no idea why I had gone in and put on all those clothes. "No," I said, "I'm not going anywhere." And I walked into the pool with all my clothes on and had a swim.

There was another afternoon when I had gone for a walk with Barbara on the golf course. There were two men on the course playing golf, and one of them said, "Doris, is that you?"

I turned my back on them but they came up closer and one of them was an old friend, David Janssen. I had been crying and I didn't want to see anyone. David was terribly embarrassed; the way I acted, he felt I didn't want to talk to him. "I just wanted to tell you how sorry I am about Marty," he said. "I'm sorry I intruded on you." I just cried and walked away. I tried to say, "That's okay, David," but I don't think he heard me.

I began to swim a little more each day, and I was eventually able to keep some food down. I knew I only had a few weeks to get myself in good enough shape to begin the television series to which I had been committed. Of course, there was no possibility that I could get myself in a good mental state in so short a time, but I hoped that physically I would have regenerated myself to the point where I could get to the set each day. At the end of a month I was swimming twenty laps and taking long, vigorous walks. But mentally I had made very little progress.

I had spent long hours thinking about death, death itself, reassuring myself that there is no such thing as death. The Bible tells us that life is eternal. The eye of God is in the individual, so the individual will always exist as long as God exists. It has been said that the body is like an automobile—it's yours, but it isn't you. Who are *you*? You could be cut up every which way but surgeons could never isolate who you are—nothing exists in your body that could be identified as you. That being so, I cannot accept death as a final act. The you who you really are lives on. This concept of death gave me some comfort, but more often my bitter thoughts about God negated His existence. And if I doubted there was a God, then of course eternal life through God was not possible. For all of that year, I turned away from religion—and from God. I could not believe. I could no longer be optimistic. There were so many nights when I went to bed wishing never to wake up.

Who was Marty Melcher? That was the question that constantly thrust itself at me. How could I have lived with a man for seventeen years and not know who he was? I kept hearing his voice: "We have oil wells that are gushing so much that we don't know how to handle them." "Do you know how long it would take me to explain this contract to you? I'm your husband—don't you trust me?" "Now, how can you ask those things about Jerry Rosenthal? He's your friend and my friend and the best damn lawyer in L.A. Do you know how much money he's made for his clients? Well, he's doing the same for you. It's hard to tell how much we actually have, that's how it's pyramiding."

Marty was certainly a fool, to have been duped to this degree by a man who had mismanaged my life's earnings, twenty million or so, to the point of wipe-out. I could try to understand Marty's being a fool. He was a fool to tie up with Rosenthal, a fool not to see through him. But was he devious? Was he in league with Rosenthal? Did he knowingly plunder and siphon off and manipulate what I had placed in his care with trust? Did Marty know there was no oil in many of those wells? That the hotels were a disaster? That the cattle ranches had no cattle? Was he duped by Rosenthal's fake reports or was Marty a part of Rosenthal's operation, taking advantage of my trust in him with lies and connivances? Who was this man

234

I had lived with all those years—fool or thief or both? The answer would have to come from those who knew him and saw him with some perspective. From people who never really expressed themselves about Marty until after his death. The more I thought about it, the more it seemed to me that Marty had suffered a peculiar death—death by resignation—which could have been caused by guilt over what he discovered had been done to me, or anguish when he knew that what he had been doing was about to be found out.

GORDON MacRAE

I was one of the original clients of Century Artists—the Andrews Sisters, Jack Smith, Doris, and me. The agency consisted of Dick Dorso, Al Levy, Marty Melcher, and a kid who worked in the mail room named David Susskind. Melcher is the one who came to me and talked me into letting him handle my investments. He said he was working with a lawyer named Jerome Rosenthal who was making a fortune for Doris in oil wells and bonds and he said, "Listen, Gordon, you put your faith and trust in me and you're going to be a rich man."

If you're a busy actor—and I was very busy at the time, making movies (five of them with Doris) under contract at Warner Brothers—you don't have time to pay much attention to your business affairs. It's the nature of the business that you trust someone to represent you. So I trusted Marty. My wife and I used to go over to his house on Sundays, when he was married to Patty Andrews, to play volleyball, and he seemed like a pretty straight guy. Kind of melancholy fellow, with a basset-hound look, but he had a sense of humor—talked a lot, very alive.

Marty read off a list of Rosenthal clients, people like Kirk Douglas and Ross Hunter and, if I'm not mistaken, Eisenhower, and he explained to me how Rosenthal was a genius who had found a wonderful loophole in the tax laws that was making a fortune for his clients. It had to do with buying federal land-grant bonds through the Gibralter Finance Company, but not putting up actual cash for them, just on paper, and then deducting from your income tax the amount of interest involved. Over the course of eight years I was able to deduct $480,000 from my tax.

At one point Marty called me and said that if I heard any rumors about Kirk Douglas not to believe them. Shortly afterward Kirk called me and warned me that I was being taken, as he had been, but I followed Marty's advice and didn't follow Kirk's warning, which was to drop Melcher and Rosenthal as fast as I could.

Eventually the IRS caught up with me, and all the other Melcher-Rosenthal clients, and disallowed all those deductions on the grounds that no risk had been involved since we hadn't actually paid for the bonds. Which meant that I had to somehow amass $480,000 in cash, which, of course, I didn't have, to pay the government for those illegal deductions that Rosenthal had taken. Doris was hit for even more. For me, it meant that a lifetime of savings was wiped out. It took me years of hard work to pay the government.

To this day, I don't know what to say about Melcher. He did tell me

235

that the oil wells he had put me in were gushing profitably when in fact they were bone-dry—but how do I know if he was in cahoots with Rosenthal, or if he was simply repeating what Rosenthal had told him? Most people I know think he was on the take. But I have no proof of it. But one thing for sure, he brought all of us a lot of misery.

DICK DORSO

In my opinion, Marty was not dishonest, just hungry for money so that he could prove that he could make it on his own. Unfortunately, he fell under the spell of that lawyer Jerry Rosenthal, who did about as much damage to members of the Hollywood community as anyone who ever came along. I knew many of Rosenthal's victims. Once he started his operation, the victim couldn't get out, caught up in the spiral of ever-increasing demands for money on threat of losing what he had already invested. That's what happened to Marty.

Six months before Marty died, I had a long session with him during which I pleaded with him to get out of his involvement with Rosenthal. Marty kept saying he couldn't, that he'd be ruined. I pointed out that others, like Kirk Douglas, had incurred huge Rosenthal losses but were glad that they got out when they did. "Don't you see that every day your situation with Rosenthal gets worse?"

"But what if those oil wells start producing? We could get it all back in no time."

"Marty, Marty, it's all a hoax—why can't you realize that? Rosenthal's wells have about as much chance of producing oil as I have."

"But, Christ, how would I explain it to Doris?"

"Marty, you just have to face it—it's better to be ruined than to be destroyed."

It wasn't long after that conversation that Marty took sick. I phoned him a couple of times, but he didn't want to see me or anyone else. Finally, Terry asked me to help him induce Marty to see a doctor. I was shocked to see how Marty had deteriorated in just a few months. I insisted that either he call a doctor or Terry and I would pick him up and bodily cart him off to the hospital. This went on for about an hour. Finally, when Marty saw I meant business, he called a doctor friend of his with whom he played tennis.

In my opinion, Marty wanted to die. The deliberate neglect of this illness, which the doctors said could have been cured if he had been treated earlier, was in my view Marty's way of committing suicide. Marty fully knew by then what Rosenthal had done to him. He knew he was wiped out. The will to live had gone out of him. He simply could not face Doris and tell her that he had lost all of her money—the sacred-cow money that was all-important to him. That's why Marty wanted to die. I know there are those who think that Marty was in league with Rosenthal, and that he had squirreled away several millions of Doris's money in numbered Swiss accounts, but I'm not one of them. Marty simply took the coward's way out.

WARREN COWEN

I handled Doris's publicity for virtually her entire career, but beyond our business relations, my wife and I were close friends of Doris and her husband. I think Doris and Marty had a mutual feeling of love and affection; they shared interests and had fun together, and Marty took very good care of her. We saw each other socially at least once a week, and I think I got to know Marty as well as anyone.

In my book, Marty was a very direct person, warm, outgoing, with a marvelous sense of humor. He was one of the cleanest men I knew, in the sense that he didn't gamble, drink, or play around. He wasn't interested in clothes or prestige automobiles or any such trappings. But he was an inveterate dreamer, and his dream of empire is what did him in. There was a time that the four of us went to a hotel in San Diego, the Hotel Del Coronado, a very fancy resort hotel, a jewel of a hotel, and we weren't there ten minutes when Marty had worked up a full head of enthusiasm for buying the hotel and going into the hotel business. That's how he got involved in all kinds of rich deals, many of them stupid, involving oil wells, and cattle, and hotels, and so many other things that he knew nothing about. The more he pursued his dream of a financial empire, the deeper he got. His loyalty to Rosenthal could be looked upon as admirable or venal, depending on one's point of view, but the fact was that Marty wouldn't desert Rosenthal even in the face of that expensive Price-Waterhouse report that was an explicit warning that he was in over his head.

Marty always envied the big executives who ruled the Hollywood consortiums. He sorely wanted to prove himself their equal. I went with him when he arranged a meeting with MCA, which at that time was Doris's agent. Marty met with Lew Wasserman, the multimillionaire MCA head whom Marty particularly envied, and Wasserman's staff in the MCA conference room. Marty berated them for not doing a good enough job for Doris; he got angry; yelled at them, said they were lousy agents, just out for the buck, banged the table, threw his weight around something awful. Lew Wasserman just sat there, watching Marty's performance, not showing any emotion. When Marty had gotten everything off his chest, Wasserman rose, announced that the meeting was adjourned, and walked out. Marty admired that kind of executive cool, but, pathetically, didn't have the makeup for it.

Marty's greatest failing was that he was forever changing his mind, hardly the trait of a big executive. Like the time he wanted me to get someone to write Doris's life story. He was on the phone every day about it. I got a free-lance writer and set it all up, but when I took the completed project to Marty he told me it was a bad idea and he wasn't interested. It was as if I had originated the idea.

He was the same way about his religious convictions. One day he would tell me he wanted to be a Practitioner, another day he would say it was the last thing he wanted to do. During the time I knew him, he must have changed his mind about being a Practitioner at least ten times.

Contrary to what Terry thinks, Marty cared about him very much. Marty called me one summer to say that Terry wanted to work for me. He knew that I didn't have a job opening for a thirteen-year-old, but he asked me to arrange a job for Terry for which he, Marty, would pay the salary. However, he didn't want Terry to know about the arrangement and even asked me to have an interview with Terry before giving him the job.

I liked Marty. I considered him a friend. I think he was honest, but foolish; if I considered foolishness a terminal defect, I wouldn't have a friend in Hollywood.

LES BROWN

Marty Melcher was an awful man, pushy, grating on the nerves, crass, money-hungry. He lived off Patty Andrews; then, when Doris came along and looked like a better ticket, he glommed onto her. We used to call him Farty Belcher.

ROSS HUNTER

I produced three Doris Day movies—*Pillow Talk, Midnight Lace,* and *The Thrill of It All*—and Marty Melcher injected himself into each of the deals by demanding a fifty-thousand-dollar fee and coproducer status. I knew that Marty just wanted to put his name on the pictures and didn't intend to work on them, but I really didn't mind since I don't have the kind of ego that has to have solo credit. I don't think any one man produces a movie, anyway; it's a conglomerate effort, so what's one more name?

Unfortunately, the price of association with Melcher was a lot steeper than the fifty thousand he got. Like so many others who got involved with Melcher, I wound up in the clutches of Jerome Rosenthal; but the way I look at it, I'm a grown man who can make his own decisions, and if I went in the wrong direction because of Melcher, it's my own damn fault. I can't believe that Marty intended for me to get wiped out (that's exactly what did happen, I was indeed stripped of almost all my money). I think it was a *condition* he got into rather than an intent to do me in. I think, basically, Marty was driven by a desire to prove himself on his own, and making big money was about the only way he could do it. It's very, very difficult to be the husband of a big movie star—I have several friends who are in that position and I only know one or two who handle themselves well. So to overcome being Mr. Doris Day, Marty tried to become a self-made millionaire. He got in with the wrong man. He was forced to rip off his friends and business associates. He even wound up ruining his wife financially. But you know something? I do think that Marty loved Doris. I believe it with all my heart. I don't think he meant her any harm.

Seventeen

〰〰〰〰〰〰〰〰〰〰〰〰〰〰〰〰〰〰〰〰〰〰〰〰〰〰〰〰〰〰〰〰〰

IT was bad enough that I had been forced into television against my will, but what made it doubly repulsive was the nature of the setting that had been chosen for my weekly series. A farm. A widow with a couple of little kids living on a farm. With Grandpa, naturally. Whatever reputation I had made in films, it certainly wasn't bucolic. A farm would make it rather difficult to portray those characteristics of chic and sophistication that were so identified with the screen ladies I had portrayed. An Yves St. Laurent dirndl for milking the cows wouldn't quite do it. In my wildest nightmares I would never have done scripts like those handed to me.

But I was too enervated that first year really to care. I looked upon my ability to get from my bed to the set and back to my bed again as an end in itself and something of a miracle. Unfortunately, my condition made many of the shows very expensive, because instead of doing them in the regular four days, it often took me six or seven. I should have worked on the scripts but I couldn't. I didn't have the energy or the desire. I simply didn't care. When there had been such deep sorrow and upset in my life, how important was a script? My resignation to mediocrity was strange, since by nature I am a perfectionist and I am normally concerned about every aspect of a role I am performing. But I would sometimes stop right in the middle of shooting a supposedly happy or funny scene and burst out crying. I'd have to leave the set and go up to my dressing room. More often than I like to remember, I gave way to hysterics and couldn't work anymore that day. I felt terrible, falling apart like that, letting down the whole company, but I had no way to control it. For that entire season, I was prey to my erratic emotions. I had lost three things: my husband, my life's savings, and my freedom—for television was much more rigid and confining than Warner Brothers ever was.

I didn't realize it at the time but the necessity of having to go to work on the CBS television series was a godsend. No matter how difficult it was to crank myself up every day, it was infinitely better than sitting in a dark room staring at the four walls, which was my inclination. The best therapy in the world is the camera. Quiet on the set! Speed! Action! Commands that defy withdrawal. When that camera turned, I *had* to come out of myself however low I was, and in the process I promoted my own healing.

One hot afternoon in August, 1969, the summer after Marty died, I was swimming in my pool when a bulletin came over the radio. A bizarre, multiple cult murder had occurred at the home of the Polish movie director Roman Polanski. He was away, but one of the victims was his beautiful actress wife, Sharon Tate, in her eighth month of pregnancy. The bulletin gave the address of the house: 10050 Cielo Drive.

I stopped swimming. "That address," I said to my mother, who was sitting poolside, "that's where Terry used to lived."

"Are you sure?"

"Yes, of course. My God, all those people were murdered in his house."

Thus began one of the most frightening periods of my life— fright for Terry rather than myself, for those were the Manson murders; and later on, when Manson and his followers were identified, it was believed that Manson had sent his killers to that house looking for Terry.

Since Marty's death, Terry had been having as bad a time as I. Marty's death had hit him in a variety of ways that are best left to Terry to explain. As administrator he was saddled with the responsibility of investigating my financial plight and of trying to find some way for me to function without going into bankruptcy. He was with lawyers day and night. Depositions were the order of the day—long, arduous, exhausting inquiries that attempted to get some clues as to just what Rosenthal had done with the millions Marty had given him. As a result of all this legal activity, Terry had to give up his own career in music. He also had to find new lawyers and accountants and work with them in an attempt to reconstitute my affairs. And Terry also had the problem of his own finances. As a producer

240

of albums since he was twenty-one, Terry had made a considerable amount of money, all of which Marty had induced him to turn over to Rosenthal. Of course, Terry's money had gone the way of mine and he was now as broke as I was.

Besides all that, Terry was executive producer of my new television series. He tried to supervise it but he simply did not have any time to give to it, which was an additionally frustrating thing for him.

Now came the Manson-murder involvement on top of all this. Terry had moved out of the house on Cielo Drive the previous December. My house on the beach was unoccupied. I simply couldn't go there after Marty died (I tried to go there once with my aunt but left in tears after twenty minutes) and Terry feared that the house would be prey to vandals, which is what happened to many unoccupied houses along that stretch of Malibu. So with reluctance Terry gave up the house on Cielo Drive, where he had been living with Candice Bergen, and they moved into my beach house to protect it.

Of course, I had been to the Cielo Drive house many times. It was a charming little French farmhouse that had been built by the French actress Michele Morgan. It was not at all a big estate as the press made it out to be. It was an intimate house with two bedrooms, a big stone fireplace in the rustic living room, and a loft that was reached by ladder. There was a well outside the front door, with an old oaken bucket, and cats were everywhere. Terry loved that little house and I was sorry to see him give it up for the beach. I tried to talk him out of it but he said that he had discussed it with Candy and they both felt that the beach house had to be protected.

Now, eight months later, five young people lay brutally murdered in and around that house, and the irony of it was that Terry was no longer living at the beach. In his efforts to raise money to pay off my debts, Terry had recently sold the beach house and rented a little place off Sunset Boulevard. He had also, after several lovely years together, come to a parting of the ways with Candy. This too was a result of the aftermath of Marty's death, for Terry told me that he still loved Candy, and she loved him, but the pressures of his life were such that he felt he was cracking up and that it would be better for him to be alone. Terry felt that Candy was someone to look after, to care for, and Terry said he was no longer able to do that. It seemed that life for both of us had become just one casualty after another.

Of course, when news of the Cielo Drive killings first broke, the

241

killers' identities were unknown; it was not until November, three months later, that the full impact of Terry's involvement with the murders became evident. The way I learned of it was when Terry came by one evening and led me into the den for a "closed" talk. He looked terrible, simply terrible.

Two detectives had come to see him that day, he told me, to report that a young girl named Susan Atkins, who was in jail on another matter, had confided to a cell mate details about the Cielo Drive murders which identified the killers. According to this girl, Susan, who identified herself as one of these killers, the mastermind behind these murders was a man named Charles Manson, and the culprits were all members of his nomadic "family."

"You know Charles Manson, don't you?" the detectives had asked Terry.

"Yes, I've met him a couple of times."

"Well, we hate to tell you this," the detectives had said, "but from what Susan Atkins says we have good reason to believe that when they went to the Cielo Drive house that night, they were looking for you."

"You mean, they had come to kill *me?*"

"Yes, and when they didn't find you, they simply went ahead and butchered everyone they did find."

"But why would they want to kill me? I've never done anything to Manson, or any of these people. I treated Manson very well."

"Who knows? When you're dealing with crazies you can't look for logical explanations."

I knew enough, from the details of these killings which I had read in the newspapers, to realize what a dangerous predicament Terry was in. People who could commit a massacre as hideous and bizarre as this one were capable of any mad brutality. This was certainly the most revolting crime that had occurred in my lifetime. The victims had been mutilated, beaten, and stabbed repeatedly, even after death. The police had found Sharon Tate's body in front of a couch in the living room, on which an American flag had been draped, bathed in the blood from her stab wounds; she had been stabbed sixteen times in her chest and back; and there was a white nylon rope looped twice around her neck, one end of the rope going up to a ceiling beam, the other end trailing across the floor to the body of a man who was lying in a pool of blood. This end of the rope was also looped twice around his neck. This man was

Jay Sebring, a prominent Hollywood hairdresser; he had been stabbed repeatedly and shot at close range.

There were two bloody corpses on the lawn outside the house, one a man in his thirties, his face and head severely beaten, his legs and body covered with stab wounds. This man, whose name was Voytek Frykowsky, had been shot twice, hit on the head and face a dozen times with a heavy instrument, and stabbed over fifty times.

The other corpse on the lawn was Abigail Folger, a coffee heiress, who had been living with Voytek. According to the papers, she had been stabbed twenty-eight times. The police also found the corpse of a young man named Steven Parent, who was in the driveway at the wheel of his automobile, a victim of bullet wounds.

The blood of the victims had been used to smear the word "PIG" on the front door, and to smear other words, like "DEATH TO PIGS," on the walls of the house.

I repeat these gruesome details, which all of us read at the time, in order to point up the terror and revulsion that Terry felt as a result of the detectives' visit. Terror that these savages might be looking for him, and perhaps me; revulsion in that he felt he was somehow responsible for these innocent people being murdered. But his immediate concern, that evening he came to see me, was with our safety.

"Now I don't want you to get alarmed," Terry had said, "but the detectives think—and this is just pure precaution—that we ought to have a couple of guards around us until this whole thing is finished and over."

"Why? I don't understand."

"Well, you can imagine what kind of people would commit mass murder like this. Absolute crazies. So if they came for me once, they may still want me. And you, as my mother—if what they want is some kind of notoriety—well, who knows?"

"My God, Terry—you mean the detectives think they may try to kill both of us?"

"No—like, look, it's just for protection. For all we know they may never give me another thought." There was absolutely no conviction in his voice. Terry was frightened, for me as well as himself. I thought, Oh, God, what he has been through since his stepfather died, and now this! He's only a kid in his twenties. How will he bear it? And for that matter, how will I?

Terry said that although the detectives had recommended protection, they unfortunately could not furnish police bodyguards because we were not technically linked to crimes. That meant we would have to furnish our own bodyguards, which is what Terry did. From that day until the end of the trial, a period of over a year, Terry had a private bodyguard at all times, and I had a guard who patrolled my house around the clock. Even after Manson and the four followers of his who actually did the killing were taken into custody, the other members of Manson's fiercely devoted family continued to pose an ever-present threat. They tried to kill a prosecution witness by lacing her food with a lethal dose of LSD. Another witness who had identified Manson as the mastermind of the murders mysteriously disappeared and was never found. Still another witness was found dead under circumstances that left the cause of death in doubt. One of the defense lawyers, Ronald Hughes, who had incurred Manson's displeasure suddenly disappeared during the course of the trial. His battered corpse was eventually found wedged beneath some rocks in a camping area north of Los Angeles. There was even an almost-successful attempt by a band of Manson's women to steal a large supply of guns to be used to hijack a passenger jet whose passengers were to be bartered in exchange for Manson's release. After their arrest, one of the girls told the police that their plan had been to kill one passenger every hour until Manson was set free.

The black shadow of these people hung over our lives for more than a year. I think it's best that Terry himself describe his encounters with Manson and his followers, and what happened after the murders and during the trial.

<hr />

TERRY MELCHER

In the summer of 1968, a few months after Marty's death, I met Charles Manson. I had hired a friend of mine, Gregg Jakobson, to scout potential recording talent for me, and one of the people he wanted me to hear was this fellow Manson, who lived in a commune on a deserted movie ranch way out in the Valley.

When Jakobson and I arrived at the ranch, Manson was sitting in a chair in front of a defunct saloon on a simulated Western street, sound asleep. Gregg woke him and he led us along a path to where there was a rope hanging from a tree. That rope swung us across a gulley to a low place where there were about forty people, sitting in a circle around a campfire site. Of these, five or six were men, and all the rest were girls. There were tents pitched all around. Several of the girls were holding babies. Gregg had urged me to come because he thought the setup was

244

interesting on a kind of cultural level as well as musical, and that it might make a television special. "You won't believe these people," he had said. "They live like an Indian tribe, in tents, and they really live off the land and eat roots, bark off the trees, and leaves, and they collect throw-outs from the supermarkets, you know, garbage, and make it into food, and it's a real subculture kind of phenomenon."

They had all been awaiting my arrival and they were obviously well organized. They rolled some cigarettes, using weeds as filler, and I don't mean pot, I mean *weeds*. (I'm sure they smoked pot and anything else when they could get it.) A couple of the girls had some rhythm instruments—tambourines, pieces of wood, whatever, and they backed up Manson as he started to play his guitar. Acoustic guitar. It was soft, peaceful music, all those voices in back of Manson, and they all smiled a lot while they sang. In between numbers I asked Manson about their lifestyle, and he said it was easy to slip beneath the awareness of the culture, of society, so you could exist in a place where you didn't have to pay taxes to the society or work for income in any way, and it was possible to exist on the vegetables and fruit that the supermarkets threw away every day.

Manson was very anxious that I hear all his songs. My arrival was a big event in their lives because I was on the board of the Monterey Pop Foundation; I had been one of the producers of the original Monterey Festival that had made stars out of a lot of unknown people like Jimi Hendrix, Otis Redding, Janis Joplin, and The Who. So in Manson's eyes I was a talent discoverer with a big track record and he was very anxious to impress me.

Unfortunately, the music was below-average nothing, and as far as I was concerned, Manson was like every other starving, hippie songwriter who was then jamming Sunset Boulevard, a hundred thousand every day, who looked, dressed, talked, and sang exactly like Charles Manson, sang about the same topics of peace and revolution, about the themes that were in the Beatles albums. They all wore the same Levis, boots, and shirts, the same scruffy beards, Manson included, and there wasn't anything about him that gave any indication of the Manson who was going to shock the nation a year later.

After an hour or so, the audition ended and I said the usual noncommittal things—sounded pretty good, nice blend of voices, did he belong to any guilds or unions. (He didn't, of course.) When Manson pressured me about how I liked his music, I suddenly remembered a friend of mine who had an interest in Indian tribal music and who had a specially equipped truck for recording it. I said I'd like to return with my friend in about a week. I was fascinated with the communal aspect of Manson's tribe and I did think that something might work out for television along those lines. (In 1968 the commune was a new concept and nobody knew much about how they actually functioned.)

It occurred to me that the girls were very happy, very content. Their talk had a religious tone to it, a lot of *Jesus* and *brother* and *sister* and *Lord,* and many of the songs had religious overtones. Of course, I didn't find out until after the murders that all those followers were convinced that Manson was Jesus reincarnate and that's what was being acted out that day. I don't recall how the subject of money came up, but before I left I gave Manson fifty dollars, which was all the cash I had on me. I guess the sight of all those little babies, dependent on supermarket garbage, really got to me.

I went back to the ranch about ten days later with my friend Michael Deasy, who, in addition to owning the recording van I mentioned, was one of the best, highest-priced guitarists of his day. I didn't stay very long, but Deasy went back several times by himself and recorded a lot of their stuff. (I later heard from Deasy's wife that on his last visit he took some LSD with Manson that sent Deasy completely off his rocker, a horrendous trip that took Deasy a year to recover from.) But that second time when I was at the ranch was just as peaceful as my first visit, except for a brief flurry as I was leaving. Manson was walking me to my car when a big guy dressed up like Cat Ballou—black hat and jeans and black gun in a black holster—came careening out of the saloon front, quite drunk, pulled his gun on us, and ordered us to freeze in our tracks. Later on someone told me he was a Hollywood stunt man who got like this when he was loaded. At any rate, there he stood, weaving slightly, the gun pointed right at us. Manson started talking to him in a low steady voice, meanwhile the guy telling Manson to stay put, but Manson kept right on walking, talking all the while; and when he got to the guy he walloped him in the stomach. As the guy doubled up and fell to the ground, Manson took his gun and tossed it away. The guy was twice Manson's size.

"Who was that?" I asked Manson as I got in my car.

"Oh, just a guy who takes care of the horses here and gets drunk a lot," Manson said.

I said good-bye and drove off, and that's the last time I saw Manson, until two years later, in court, when I testified for the prosecution.

About a year after that last visit to the ranch, two detectives came to my door one evening and asked me if I knew anyone who wanted to kill me. I said no, I didn't.

"You're familiar with those murders that were committed in the house on Cielo Drive where you used to live?"

"Sure." For the past two months that's all anyone talked about. I hadn't been in the house since I moved out, but I had presumed that the murders had had something to do with the weird films Polanski had made, and the equally weird people who were hanging around that house. I knew they had been making a lot of homemade sadomasochistic-porno movies there with quite a few recognizable Hollywood faces in them. The reason I knew was that I had gone out with a girl named Michelle Phillips, one of the Mamas and the Papas, whose ex-husband, John Phillips, was the leader of the group. Michelle told me she and John had had dinner one night, to discuss maybe getting back together and afterward he had taken her up to visit the Polanskis in my old house. Michelle said that when they arrived there, everyone in the house was busy filming an orgy and that Sharon Tate was part of it. This was just one of the stories I had heard about what went on in my former house.

"Well," the detective said, "we've got a girl in custody who's spilling the whole thing. You know a guy named Manson? And a group that used to hang out with him at the Spahn Ranch? Well, the night they killed all those people—they came there looking for you. This girl says Manson wanted you to record him but you didn't and he was mad at you. We've picked up some of Manson's people, but there's still a lot of them running around loose. So we've come here to warn you that you'd better get yourself some bodyguards with guns—and for your mother. You're dealing with some genuine crazies here and there's no telling what they might do."

From then on the cops were at me all the time. Mostly to show me pictures that they wanted me to try to identify. They must have had mug shots of every hippie in Hollywood. And because I was Doris Day's son, the newspapers and magazines really went to town on my alleged involvement in the killings. There was one account I read that said I was the backer for the revolutionary predatory army that Manson had been assembling, and that the only reason I wasn't prosecuted was that CBS had put pressure on the government because they thought it would hurt the ratings of my mother's television show.

There were other accounts of how I was into dope with Manson, and we had had a falling out over that. Several times I was grilled by the police about some of the babies in the Manson camp. The cops said that five or six of the Manson girls claimed that Manson had set me up with them and that I was the father of their babies. I finally got so fed up with the cops over these sex inquiries that I got out the pictures of the most recent ladies in my life, real beauties, all of them, and I said, "Listen, when I've got beauties like these to get in bed with, why would I want to screw any of Manson's clap-ridden, unwashed dogs?" That logic seemed to reach the thinking level of the cops and they stopped pursuing me about my fatherhood.

Not all the rumors were about me. There was one persistent one to the effect that Jay Sebring had lured some of Manson's girls into one of the sado-porno movies they were making and had whipped them and beat them up for the camera, and that that's why Sebring and all the others had been killed.

While all this was going on, I was suffering from a monumental guilt feeling that I was the one who was responsible for all those killings, since it was I they had been looking for. While all the Manson fracas was going on, I was also (1) meeting with lawyers every day in my battle with Rosenthal, (2) trying to help my mother with her television show, (3) trying to do my own recording work, and (4) trying to deal with the glut of guilts Marty had left me as his legacy when he went to that big numbered account in the sky. He had made me feel guilty for having made money ("It's too easy for you, you made it too fast"), guilty because I hadn't starved, guilty because I had talent, guilty because I had survived him. It was all too much. Just too much.

One day I simply cracked under the load. I went to a psychiatrist two hours a day and unloaded on him. "They were looking for me—why couldn't they have found *me?* How much easier it would have been, just knocking *me* off instead of all those people—and that unborn baby."

"I don't know what to tell you," the psychiatrist said, after several sessions, "except that you're going to be crazy for a while. Try to get through it." He gave me some tranquilizers.

And so I was crazy for a while.

I cut off everything. I got someone to answer the phone and to cook and I shut out the world. For two years. I pressed the down button and went all the way to the bottom. Russian vodka and those tranquilizers. Plenty of time to think, and the more I thought, the blacker everything got. I began to put the blame on my mother, to resent her—a real buildup of hostility. I was the one spending all my time with lawyers and court-rooms but I didn't marry that son of a bitch Marty, yet I was having to deal with Rosenthal because my mother said, "This is Marty—he's your dad."

And it was my ass in the Manson escapade because my mother was who she is. All the notoriety I was getting, the darling of the *National Enquirer,* not because I really had anything to do with the case but because I was the son of a superstar. So for a long stretch there I was really resenting the hell out of her, resenting her because she brought Marty into my life, but at the same time trying to protect her from the real truth of what he was about.

But I have to mention again that the one thing I did have to thank Marty for was my ambition. I had wanted to get away from him so badly that I had the kind of ambition that a ghetto kid has to escape the ghetto. It doesn't matter where you get your ass kicked, Versailles or a six-floor walk-up, the motivation is the same. I worked seven days a week and really produced a prodigious number of records and albums, with rock-and-roll groups as well as with people like Pat Boone and Wayne Newton. I coauthored songs with Bobby Darin and I produced my mother's last hit album.

What I was striving to be was a person with my own identity, not somebody's son, and I had substantially achieved that; but Marty's death and the Manson murders had turned me into a movie star's son again. I was bitter about that. It really griped my ass to have to deal with the CBS network executives. I was twenty-six, so compared to them I was a kid, but I wasn't used to being treated like a kid in my own business, where I had been earning around $250,000 a year, probably six times what any of those CBS hotshots were making. Yet they were treating me like a necessary evil—"Well, we have to deal with this kid because his mother is Doris Day." Right back where I started from.

I also resented the role I had assigned myself with my mother. I had worked hard on turning her mind around and getting her interested in her television show. But as she responded to this and began to look happier, I got to thinking, goddamn it, she's going along fine now, whereas all I do is sit in lawyers' offices and in court for three months and it's only the beginning. Then when the Manson thing broke on top of that—well, I was really feeling used and abused. Kind of a flybed feeling for almost everything in my life. My resentment grew. Sure, my mother's rolling along with her television show now, lots of dogs and daisies, not having any trouble, but goddamn it, because of those hotels I just spent three weeks in Dallas in a courthouse without any air conditioning.

And to top it all off, I broke up with Candy simply because I was determined to be miserable and lonely. I just didn't want anybody around trying to cheer me up. I had gone with her since I was nineteen, and the years with her had been very good. I have nothing but glowing things to say about Candy. Giving her up like that, when I still loved her, was more depressing than anything else.

But what I brooded about most was Marty, trying to square the reality of finding out the truth about him with the image I had lived with. For a few weeks after his death I went to this office every day to wind up the business. There were phone calls from ladies in town who wondered what they were going to do about their rent. Of course I knew that Marty had an interest in outside ladies. Occasionally I'd find dollies in his office when I stopped in to see him about some music business. But it was still a shock to find that he was keeping a few of them around town. Marty, the sanctimonious usher. There was also a time when he was around Angie Dickinson quite a lot, and another time when Raquel Welch was a cocktail waitress at one of the hotels where he'd disappear; I had put those things out of my mind at the time, but now they all washed back and mounted up. I don't know how much my mother knew about all that. We never discussed it. It really wasn't all that important. What was important was discovering his hypocrisy, his lack of values, understanding his shallow rigidity. He was the kind of parent who is proud to see his kid make it if the kid makes it exactly as he outlines it—if the kid doesn't, then no matter what success the kid has, it's much worse than failure.

As far as the Manson thing was concerned, I found out at one point that Manson knew I had moved to the Malibu beach house. That he had, in fact, stolen a telescope from the deck of the Malibu house, presumably to let me know he knew my whereabouts. But then why didn't he knock on the door, if he wanted to get in touch with me? None of it made much sense. Susan Atkins, one of the murderers, had told her attorney on tape, "The reason Charlie picked that house was to instill fear into Terry Melcher because Terry had given us his word on a few things and never came through with them." I have no idea to what she was referring. I made no representations to them about anything. But facts and logic don't mean much when you're dealing with minds like these.

A prosecutor in the District Attorney's office who interviewed most of the members of Manson's family stated in an interview, "There was a kid from Texas living at the ranch at the same time, and one day after he'd been there about a month, Manson said to him, 'That Melcher, he thinks he's pretty hot shit, but he isn't worth a damn. I can kill him just like that. In fact, it would be better if you did it. I'll give you five thousand dollars and a three-wheel motorcycle and you leave the ranch right after you do it. Will you do it?' And the kid says, 'Let me think about it.'

"A couple of days later Manson says, 'Have you thought about it?' The kid says, 'Are you serious?' He says, 'Yes, I'm serious.' The kid says, 'All right, I'll do it.' Manson says, 'Fine, meet me at such and such a time.'

"Well, this kid, his mind wasn't blown or anything, so he knew the kind of trouble he was in. He immediately called his mother. He says, 'Mom, wire me money, I'm coming home.' He knew that he was up to his ears in something he just couldn't get out of."

It didn't mean much, as far as retaliation was concerned, that Manson and four of his followers, who slaughtered Sharon Tate and others, were in jail. Manson had a legion of devoted henchmen who were at large. And they were totally capable of carrying out their leader's wishes wherever he was. During the trial, one of the defense attorneys, Ronald Hughes, who had fallen out of favor with Manson, confided to friends that he was in mortal fear of Manson. He mysteriously disappeared during the trial—turned up as a corpse.

An important prosecution witness, Barbara Hoyt, was told that if she testified at the trial both she and her parents would be killed. Subsequently, she was lured to Hawaii by a couple of Manson's flower girls,

249

who fed her a lethal dose of LSD (ten tabs of acid—one tab is the limit for a far-out trip) in a hamburger. She luckily survived because of very fast and efficient hospital action.

I cite all this to explain why I hired round-the-clock bodyguards for my mother and myself.

At the trial I was not cross-examined; Manson's attorney said that Manson had no ill feelings toward me. But what did that mean? Manson and his people killed for love as well as other things. And the fact that Manson was sentenced to life imprisonment also didn't do much to promote my peace of mind, for according to California law he will be eligible for parole in 1978.

So I stayed in my house and avoided everyone. In a sense, I had given up on myself. My heart was full of bitterness and fear, and it looked like it was going to permanently stay that way.

There's no doubt that what happened to Terry was much harder on me than Marty's death and all those shocking postmortem revelations. Terry collapsed under the weight of all the problems that had been imposed on him, and in an act of self-preservation he shut himself off from everything and everyone. The Manson business had induced a terror in him that he couldn't handle. Terry was scheduled to be a witness for the prosecution, and from November, 1969, when the detectives had first informed him that he was the intended victim, until the end of the Manson trial and sentencing, in April of 1971, Terry lived in rather constant terror of what the Manson family might do to him.

He withdrew to his house, where he was under guard, and stopped seeing almost everyone. I myself rarely saw him and I couldn't get him on the phone. He became a recluse, and his refuge was alcohol and pills. He couldn't face anything. Couldn't face daylight. Couldn't face getting up in the morning.

I was desolate about Terry, but there was no way to reach out to him. In fact, he had developed a quiet hostility toward me. On those few occasions when I did get him on the phone, his conversation was often incoherent. What made it even worse was that I had no one to talk to about Terry. My mother and my aunt were living with me, but to have discussed Terry's condition with them would have unduly worried them. I would sometimes walk circles in my bedroom, and weep out of frustration. I never felt lonelier than I did then, and the feeling of being a rather helpless twelve-year-old persisted.

One afternoon I went to see Terry with my lawyer to discuss

certain problems that had come up. It was frightening. Terry couldn't understand what we were saying. His speech was slurred and incoherent. He wore dark glasses and sat in a corner, sipping vodka. He lived alone except for an elderly handyman who came in daily to do chores. I tried so desperately to reach Terry that afternoon. I suggested he come live with my mother and me, but he didn't react to anything. He could have been a mute.

Terry never phoned me or his grandmother, whom he adored. I tried to kindle some response in him by telling him how much I needed him on my television series, which wasn't going well. He was executive producer, I pointed out, and the program desperately needed leadership. He couldn't have been less interested. He was completely out of it, completely withdrawn.

There was one occasion when his secretary, who came in for a few hours every day, phoned to say that Terry would like me to come to dinner; he was having a few friends in. I was elated. It was the first time he had invited me to his Benedict Canyon house. It sounded as if he was beginning to come out of himself. I had been telling myself that if I were patient and just reassured him of my love for him, sooner or later he would emerge from his black despair and be his old self.

The door to his house was open when I arrived. Several of Terry's young friends were already there. But I could tell from the subdued atmosphere that the change I had hoped for had not materialized. Terry was worse than I had ever seen him. He didn't know what he was doing or saying. I tried to talk to him but he made no sense. He couldn't stand properly. Life didn't make any sense to him, so *he* wasn't making any sense. Nothing made any sense. I could understand that. But it broke my heart to see him like that. I tried to talk to him about seeing a psychiatrist but he was beyond communication. I only stayed a short while. I don't think he knew if I was at dinner or not.

Sometime later, Terry rented a little house in Idyllwild, which is a small mountain community on the way to Palm Springs. This remote hideaway intensified his withdrawal. He never invited me there.

There were a few occasions during this period when Terry unexpectedly showed up during my television shooting. He was all wound up, talked a blue streak, full of energy. Whatever he was on was having that kind of effect on him. His eyes were too bright, his gestures exaggerated. Whenever I saw him, he was either very high or very low—depending on the kind of pills he was taking, I suppose. I tried to discuss these pills with him, but to no avail.

Through it all though, I had an underlying conviction that something would happen to turn it all around. I felt that Terry was in the hands of God, and that He would eventually cause something to happen that would make Terry face the other way. Until then I would cry over him and worry about him and try, every way I could, to let him know how much I loved him.

I had hoped for a turning point in Terry's life, some God-given intervention that would set him back on his course, but I had not anticipated the kind of brutal intervention that actually occurred.

The call came at night from the Hemet Valley Hospital. Terry was in intensive care. Details on the phone were sketchy. A motorcycle accident. His legs were shattered. He was in critical condition.

The Hemet Valley Hospital is located a short distance from Idyllwild, where Terry was living at the time of the accident. The hospital is just off the main road to Palm Springs, about a two-hour drive from Los Angeles. It is a small hospital and there was but one orthopedic surgeon on the staff, Dr. Howard Lieberman, who fortunately happened to be in the hospital when Terry was brought in.

Terry was heavily sedated when I got to the hospital. Despite the sedation he was experiencing intense pain. There was little I could do but wait outside the intensive-care room. I was told that Terry had gone for a ride on his motorcycle, a high-powered bike that he hadn't ridden for two years. Going down the mountain, he had negotiated a turn badly, turning the wheel instead of leaning, and had rammed head-on into a car occupied by a minister and his wife. The impact had catapulted Terry high into the air; he had landed on his feet, shattering both legs, as glass shatters, and inflicting other injuries.

The day following the accident, Terry developed a high, persistent fever and a deep infection. But that was not the worst of it. Embolisms had also developed, dangerous blood clots that put his life in jeopardy. The doctors put me on notice that quite possibly both legs might have to be amputated. Twice, over the course of those first five days, as the medical team carefully monitored the embolisms, I was warned that Terry might not get through the night. Those long vigils through the endless nights brought me closer to

Terry than I had ever been before. And closer to God. I would sit in a chair outside the intensive-care room and close my eyes and think. I can't pray to a God to make him well, because there is no duality, no God outside of Terry. God is the eye of his being and my being, and whatever is supposed to be will be, and I will accept that, whatever it is. Just as I have accepted Marty's death. There is but one power, and if that lovely son of mine is supposed to *live,* then nothing on this earth can take him. Not an embolism. Not the infection. Nothing. I don't care what they tell me—that the blood clot is moving to the heart, whatever—it doesn't matter a damn. I don't care how black it looks. I can only say, "All right, God, he's Yours. I trust in You."

That was my thinking, but underneath everything I feared the worst. The events of the preceding weeks had conditioned me to expect disaster.

The only light during those dark days was the presence of Dr. Lieberman, whose personality and extreme competence gave me some measure of hope. Dr. Lieberman had had a great deal of experience with leg injuries, especially those inflicted by the motorcycle. The highway that passed Hemet was a flyway for young people motorcycling to Palm Springs, and hardly a day passed that young motorcycle victims were not carried into the hospital. Some were dead by the time they arrived, beautiful teen-agers whose parents, overcome with grief, came to the hospital to claim them. It was one of the terrible realities that were commonplace during the long period of time I visited Terry. As a parent, as an observer of the motorcycle's butchery, I wish it were in my power to destroy all of them. I think it is one area in which there should be absolutely no permissiveness. The first time the subject of getting a motorcycle is brought up, the parent should issue an absolute no and stick with it. The motorcycle is death on wheels, and it is certainly stupid to try to be lenient with death.

I went into the intensive-care room as often as they would let me. Terry's legs were in splints and elevated. There was a network of tubes feeding into him. I'd sit close beside the bed and Terry would take my hand and hold it tightly, neither of us saying anything, our joined hands giving us a closeness we had never had before. Sometimes Terry would fall asleep without relaxing his grip on my hand, and I'd look at him and think, It's going to be all right. He won't die, and they won't amputate, and someday he will walk out of here.

I tried to believe, and at times like that I really did feel that Terry was going to make it. But at night, when he was behind the closed door and I was alone in the bare, forbidding waiting room, I often lost my confidence.

It took two weeks to dissolve the embolisms and contain the infections that had threatened his legs. With those two afflictions eliminated, Dr. Lieberman moved Terry to a private room and went to work on his shattered legs. The intense pain continued unabated but now it was possible to deal with the bone breakage that was causing the pain. It was the most bizarre treatment imaginable, and in the beginning I had little confidence that Dr. Lieberman's method could conceivably work.

The bones of both of Terry's legs were in as many pieces as a difficult jigsaw puzzle. Thirty-seven fractures. Dr. Lieberman's method was to reconstruct those bones and align the broken pieces without performing surgery. To accomplish this, he would sit Terry on the side of the bed, with his legs dangling down, and pull on them. Obviously, this caused excruciating pain. After a series of tugs and pulls, Dr. Lieberman would wheel Terry into X ray and study the bone alignment; then he would sit him on the bed again, and pull and yank the legs some more to correct whatever he had seen in the X rays.

Slowly but surely over the ensuing weeks, using only this process, the bone fragments began to fall into place. Finally, under a general anesthetic, Dr. Lieberman prepared Terry's legs for plaster casts, but at no time during this long process was surgery involved. Just pulling and observing.

Shortly after Terry was removed from intensive care, he was visited by the chief of mental therapy, Dr. Charles Head, to see if there was anything he could do for Terry. Terry told him no, that he really had it all together and it would be better for the doctor to spend his time with the people who really needed him.

"Well, that's really rare," Dr. Head said, "flat on your back, both legs smashed up, a long hospitalization and recuperation staring you in the face, and you feel really on top of everything?"

"Yes, I'm okay, no problems."

"That's great, but if you ever feel like talking, just call me."

A few days later, at three o'clock in the morning, Terry called Dr. Head. I wasn't at the hospital that day—I usually stayed for three or four days in Hemet at the Ramona Inn, and the other days of the

254

week back in Beverly Hills. Dr. Head dressed and drove to the hospital; Terry had fallen apart. His brave front had deserted him and he desperately needed someone to talk to. That's how Charles Head, a really remarkable man, came into our lives. I say "our" because I too began to see Dr. Head professionally, and until recently I had an appointment with him on the day when he made his weekly visit to his office in Los Angeles. Both Terry and I, in our relationship to each other and in our ability to handle the problems that have beset us during the past five years, have benefited enormously from having this professional help. Friends help, religion helps, but a psychologist with his trained perspective uniquely augments whatever else you've got going for you. Or haven't got going for you.

What Chuck Head did for Terry and me was to free us toward each other as we had never been before. By the time Terry was ready to leave the hospital, we had completely overcome the strain that had developed between us after Marty's death. It had taken the horror of that motorcycle accident to achieve this, to rescue Terry from the pit of booze and pills into which he had fallen. As a result of the accident, he had *needed* me for the first time, and I had eagerly responded to that need. As I said previously, out of such disasters in my life there has always emerged a new positive force, something attained, something learned, albeit at a stiff price. Terry's accident was an awful ordeal but the relationship that Terry and I have now, which dates from that accident, is rare and fulfilling and surely one of the most sustaining parts of my life.

During the weeks that I kept vigil over Terry, my religious feelings, which had deserted me after Marty's death, began to return. But they were changed. I no longer felt a rapport with the Christian Science church as such. My enthusiasm for Mrs. Eddy's writings was just as great but I wanted to be free from the tight, organized demands of the church itself. I came to resent the guilt feelings I got when I missed a church meeting. And I disliked the social nature of the meetings. What it comes down to, I guess, is that I don't like organized religion. It's fine for some people, but I gradually realized that what I want is a religion of my own practiced in my own church.

One of the new forces which came into my religious thinking was Joel Goldsmith, whose background was Christian Science but who had evolved his own religious philosophy in a series of powerful books. One of these books in particular, *The Thunder of Silence*, has had an enormous influence on my way of thinking. That and an earlier book, *The Infinite Way*. During very tough times, passages from those two books have sustained and uplifted me. Sometimes when I wake in the night, sleepless and disturbed, I put one of Joel Goldsmith's lectures on my tape machine and I find marvelous solace in what he says and how he says it.

In essence, what Goldsmith and Mary Baker Eddy are both telling us is that our body is the temple of the living God. We place our body at God's disposal to use as He chooses. Thus our body becomes an instrument for God, with the "I" as the center of our being. But we have to be willing to make some sort of a beginning. And that is done by knowing that there is no good or evil in the body. The body as such has no qualities of its own; it merely expresses that which is imposed upon it. There is no age or youth in the body. No strength or weakness in it. The body is an instrument for the "I." The God within us. Which is the creative and maintaining principle of our being.

Instead of praying up to God, Joel Goldsmith says, we should instead be so silent within ourselves that we can hear the still small voice. That is when God manifests and expresses Himself—as the still small voice within us. The thunder of silence, the silence of my own room in the absolute quiet of the night, no thoughts of evil or good, listening, listening for the still small voice within me. That is the essence of my metaphysical belief. That is my religion.

In addition to Joel Goldsmith, I have found metaphysical sustenance in the writings and preachings of Kathryn Kuhlman, a truly remarkable, Christlike woman. Her book, *I Believe in Miracles,* has been a source of inspiration to me, as have her appearances on television. Seeing her in person at her shrine, as I have a few times, has intensified my feelings about her and what she preaches. She takes no credit for the many healings that occur during her appearances. I was in the audience the day a man who had not walked since 1945 suddenly rose from his wheelchair and limped onto the stage. He was sobbing uncontrollably. He had been coming to her meetings for many months but on this day this miracle had occurred. "I had nothing to do with it," Kathryn Kuhlman told the audience. "Nothing. There's only one power. That power helped you, and I have only spread His word."

I know that many people put down Kathryn Kuhlman and do mocking imitations of her, but I respect her and I think that God has given her something special. When my dear friend Billy De Wolfe became grievously ill, I took him to see Mrs. Kuhlman in hopes that the healing power expressed through her would touch Billy. It didn't, and Billy died soon after that visit, but that has not lessened my respect for her and belief in her. There is no system to miracles, but they sustain hope and that is what's important.

In my dark hours, hope was best sustained for me by keeping my eye on the target Mrs. Eddy had set for me—you are what you think. And the more you are free of addiction—liquor, cigarettes, drugs, coffee, overeating—the more control you have over your thinking. And the more control you have over your thinking, the less your anxiety. I think it was Jesus who said, "Be anxious for nothing."

Marty and I were both very heavy smokers when we decided to follow Mrs. Eddy's advice and stop smoking. We turned it off just like that. As Mrs. Eddy says, no addiction is really a part of you. You don't assimilate it. Therefore you don't give it up—it leaves you. "Whatever is offensive," she says, "removes itself—as long as you *think* properly."

The fat woman who says, "I tried but I can't," doesn't want to get thin.

The smoker who says, "I wish I could cut it out like you have," doesn't *want* to give up smoking.

I *wanted* to control myself, my own destiny, and when those positive thoughts became dominant, Mrs. Eddy's formula worked like magic—the offensive things in me removed themselves.

But it's not necessary to deal in absolutes as I did in the beginning, when I went so far as not to offer alcohol to guests in my house. Now I drink moderately, but drinking is entirely incidental and meaningless in my life. I don't smoke because it gives me no pleasure to smoke; and besides, the risks of smoking offset everything else. In short, my metaphysical beliefs control my thinking, and what I am is indeed what I think—and vice versa.

When Terry finally got out of the hospital, six months later, six months in that 12- by 12-foot white-walled room, I fixed up my guesthouse for him. Confined as he was, first to a wheelchair and then to a walker, I made the guesthouse, which is on the far side of my patio, as easy for him to live in as possible. When I had to be at the studio, either my mother or my housekeeper was on hand to take care of Terry. Ironically, this long period of convalescence was the first time that Nana, Terry, and I had lived together amicably as a family under the same roof. It took four months, casts on both legs, for

Terry's legs to mend and grow strong, but it was also a time during which our family ties also grew strong. Terry and I established a real mother-son relationship. Although he was thirty years old, it was the first time I had really taken care of him.

The day Terry left to go to live in his own place again, I was happy to see him strong enough to be on his own, but sad to see him leave the guesthouse. I had watched my son fight his way through a terrible ordeal, with courage, intelligence, and a loving heart, and I was proud of him. I didn't tell him that, of course, because that would have embarrassed him, but when he left we had a farewell drink, and although he was only moving ten minutes away, I wept a few tears. I'm sure that told him everything.

Eighteen

$\approx\approx\approx\approx\approx\approx\approx\approx\approx\approx\approx\approx\approx\approx\approx\approx\approx\approx$

BY the end of my first year in television I came to realize that if the program was to continue successfully, it was up to me to take over the "Doris Day Show" and turn it around. I had always left production and management to Marty and others, but now I would have to acquaint myself with every aspect of the show and make my own decisions.

I hired new producers and new scriptwriters and worked out a new locale and concept for the show. It was removed from the farm and relocated in San Francisco. It was a comedy series but I emphasized that I didn't like joke comedy that relied on funny dialogue; I much prefer situation comedy, like *Pillow Talk.* I worked with the writers, set designers, costume designers, makeup, music—there wasn't an aspect of the show that I didn't get into. For the first time in my career I saw all the daily rushes and even involved myself in editing.

The new San Francisco locale enabled us to move from the dreary, depressing Golden West Studio in Hollywood, where the farm had been located, to CBS Studio City, which I loved. I had three dressing rooms, which were redecorated and remodeled to my specifications.

The preparation and shooting of the series were arduous and demanding but the people around me, cast and crew, were friendly and amusing, and the show itself was considerably improved. Personally, I felt a good resurgence of energy and spirit. I even started doing things to my house, mostly those things that Marty had always nixed because they were too expensive. In Marty's home-furnishing book, almost anything that cost more than twenty-five dollars was too expensive.

What little time I had to myself I spent out in the patio under the huge sycamore tree that I loved so. I heard it said that it was the biggest and oldest sycamore in Beverly Hills. That tree had a mystic quality for me. I feel about trees as I do about dogs. For me, trees have a spirit and an inner force that I can identify with. That great old sycamore was a symbol of protection and wisdom and God's force on earth. I just loved sitting under it and watching the sky through its maze of branches.

The other ways I relaxed were on my bicycle and swimming. One of the reasons I like living where I do in Beverly Hills is that I can bike everywhere I want to go. The bike has been a part of my life for as long as I can remember. It's marvelous exercise and it also allows me to explore. I know all the unusual trees in my neighborhood, every backyard that has a dog, flower beds of distinction. My bike is an extension of my body, a part of myself. Every time I go for a ride, it's an adventure—and when I return home after an hour of pedaling, my body has had a workout from head to toe.

The specifics of how I feel about the care and decoration of the body are dealt with in an Appendix at the back of this book, but as for my basic philosophy, I think that every woman must project—in her makeup, her wardrobe, her hair style, her perfume, in every respect of her looks—her own true self. You cannot successfully impose on your personality and your body the looks of someone who is not you. Of course, we all go through our periods of imitation—there was a time way back in Cincinnati when I was trying to look like Ginger Rogers—but nine times out of ten the person you're imitating is nothing like you so that your looks are phony, in the sense that they have nothing to do with who *you* are.

I get a lot of mail from women who ask me where they can get a certain dress they have seen me wear in a movie or on television. I always warn them that what may be right for me and look good on me may not suit them at all. I feel that way about style changes. Some new styles may suit me, some may not, and when they don't, I don't wear them just to be stylish. I will only wear that which looks right for me, and I don't give a hoot whether *Vogue* approves. I loved the midi, worn with boots, and I have continued to wear it.

There is only one other generalization that I can make. I think women are divided into two types: outdoorsy and indoorsy. I am an outdoorsy type and every aspect of how I look takes that into account. It's not difficult for a woman to determine to which category she belongs. What *is* difficult is when a woman tries to pass from her natural category into the category that she'd like to be in but isn't suited to. Don't do it. It almost never works. You seldom fool the men and you *never* fool other women.

Nineteen

ANYONE who knows anything about me knows how involved I am with dogs. Dogs are as important to me as people. The dogs I live with are just as much my family as are my mother and son. During the bleak, difficult years since Marty's death, my canine family has been a source of joy and strength to me. I have found that when you are deeply troubled, there are things you get from the silent, devoted companionship of a dog that you get from no other source.

In a way I never got over what happened to Tiny, the little black and tan, who, when I was on crutches, was hit by a car and died in my arms. It was totally my fault for walking him without a leash, and I've had a lingering sense of guilt about his death all my life. How important Tiny was to me during that lonely, interminable stretch when I was waiting for my leg to mend, and how tragic a death he suffered! I learned my lesson—no dog should ever be allowed to run free; to this day, if I see a dog in the street, I will hop out of my car, stop traffic, and try to lure the poor little thing into my car so that I can take him home (if he has a collar with identification) or turn him over to the volunteer group I'm associated with, Actors and Others for Animals, which will try to locate his owner or, failing that, find a home for him.

My passion for and understanding of dogs are really directly attributable to two remarkable books which I read as a girl—*Letters to Strongheart* and *Kinship with All Life*, both written by a man named J. Allen Boone. I'm sure they are still to be found in most public libraries. The books are primarily about a German shepherd named Strongheart, who was a big movie star long before Rin-Tin-Tin came on the scene. Boone lived alone with Strongheart for a long period of time, during which Boone, intrigued with the unusual and uncanny powers of the dog, began to experiment with ways and means of communicating with him, but not using the ordinary master-dog method of communication.

In *Kinship with All Life,* Boone taught me the difference between training a dog and educating one. Trained dogs, Boone points out, are relatively easy to turn out. All that's needed is a certain amount of bluff and bluster, and things that can be used for threatening and rewarding purposes. Educating a dog, though, demands keen intelligence, integrity, imagination, and a gentle touch—mentally, vocally, and physically.

Conventional training is mostly concerned with the physical. The trainer assumes that he is dealing with a dumb animal who has to be dominated so that he will be completely subservient to him, obeying his every command and focusing idolatrous attention on his master at all times. But *educating* a dog requires just the reverse of all that. Full emphasis is placed on the mental rather than on the physical. The dog owner must treat the dog as an intelligent fellow being whose capacity for development and expression he does not limit in any direction. He tries to help the dog make use of his thinking faculties.

Boone found ways to communicate with Strongheart during the long silences they shared, and it was those revelations that had such a profound effect on me. Boone relates how he freed himself of prejudices and purified his thinking to the point at which Strongheart was truly able to share precious dog wisdom with Boone, "wonderful secrets having to do with the great dog art of living abundantly and happily in the present tense regardless of circumstances." Boone found that after establishing a strong rapport with Strongheart, he was able to establish a mental two-way bridge between them, over which it was possible for Boone's thoughts freely to cross into Strongheart's thinking areas and for the dog's thoughts just as freely to cross over into his.

I realize that, summarized like this, Boone's account seems rather irrational, but I can assure you that with the details and documentation in the book it is all very rational indeed. In fact, it is this attitude toward communicating that I brought to my relations with my own dogs, with extraordinary results. I do indeed communicate with my dogs but not in the usual dog owner's manner of talking down to them in a way that smacks of baby talk.

What I have learned is that dogs are here on earth to teach us. They have taught me how to be serenely patient, and they have taught me about love—fundamental love, such as Jesus taught. No matter how abusive or inconsiderate its owner has been, a dog will turn his other cheek and continue to love him. And loyalty—I have never found in a human being loyalty that is comparable to a dog's loyalty. And yet people buy a dog as they buy a plant, and they treat him like a plant after they get him. They buy him from pet shops and back-yard breeders without checking on the dog's condition. They breed the dog because they think it would be cute to have puppies. They haven't the slightest interest in or concept of the spiritual qualities of the dogs they buy.

My dogs are completely tuned in on my moves and moods. When I start to put on my bathing suit, they immediately rush around and get their pool toys. When I start to get ready to go for a bike ride, they go off to their quiet corners and settle down, for they know I never take them with me when I'm on my bicycle. When they are in the car with me and I'm going over a familiar route—for instance, to and from the studio when I'm working—if I deviate so much as one block from the regular route they will react nervously and anxiously until I get back on familiar roads. When I wake depressed and not wanting to communicate, they keep their distance. When I wake feel-ing good, they are on the bed saying good morning. They too have their moods of depression, of joy, of feeling antagonistic, and I respect their moods as much as they respect mine. If I cry, they all nestle around me and lick my tears and give me their paws and try to cheer me up. And when they grieve, their suffering is very deep.

I put music on for my dogs, and they enjoy listening to it. When I am going somewhere on a trip, I tell them just where I am going and what I am going to do and when I will be back. But often I can tell them things without saying a word. That is the kind of communication I learned from J. Allen Boone, and I can tell you that if you establish a relationship with your dog that permits this kind of thought flow between you, such communication is not at all difficult. One of my dogs, a malamute named Bambi, actually talks to me in inflections that closely resemble human speech.

Mr. Boone says, "Had someone come upon the dog and me sitting quietly shoulder to shoulder in some picturesque outdoor lo-cation, and had our observer been told in all seriousness that we were exchanging stimulating points of view with each other through the medium of silent talk, he would probably have found it exceedingly difficult to believe. But such would have been the truth. Had he cared to become one of us, had he been sufficiently flexible and receptive for such an experience, he could have joined in with us and shared in the simple universal language we were using, that language which moves without the need for sound from heart to heart."

From heart to heart. That is precisely how my dogs and I communicate. And that is how my dogs communicate with each other. I think it is wrong for anyone to own a single dog, thereby denying him the pleasure and fulfillment of having a dog friend to talk to. I feel strongly that no animal should be deprived of one of his own kind for companionship. But I also feel that all dog owners should have their animals spayed and neutered. The world's dog population has long since passed the explosion point. We have a serious food shortage and it relates to dogs as well as to humans. The old shibboleth that every female dog "deserves" to have one litter is nonsense. Spayed females who have never had a litter are just as happy and often healthier than females who have given birth a time or two. Backyard breeding in order to earn money is one of the worst offenses. Pet stores that sell puppies should be outlawed. If you knew as much as our organization knows about the health of many of these pet-store puppies, I'm sure you would readily agree. I realize, of course, that there must be some breeding to sustain a reasonable dog population, but even the reputable breeders have to take their sights off the almighty buck and look at the overall picture.

There are so many homeless, deserving dog waifs in pounds and shelters around the country that it is a crime that people who want nice companions for their children pass them up because they are so obsessed with having a pedigreed dog. I always say to such people, "Are you purebred?" That startles them. "What's *your* mixture?" Well, they say, I'm Scottish and English and some German. . . . "Oh, ho, wait a minute," I say, "you're *some* mixed breed—why must your dog be such a thoroughbred? I can assure you, that won't make him a better dog." I know. From my own experience.

My dogs were all strays, rejects, most of whom would have been put to sleep if I had not rescued them. My oldest dog, Myra Muffin, is a brown poodle, mostly, who was found wandering alone without identification by a roadside in Las Vegas. She had three sons, Red, Bo-Bo, and Charlie—but this was ten or eleven years ago, before I had learned the facts about the dog population. Bambi is the malamute-shepherd mix I mentioned whom I found running in the rain as I left CBS Studio City one day. She was in a run-down condition and had terrible mange which I treated for a long time. She is now absolutely gorgeous.

I found Rudy, a dachshund, limping along in the Valley. One of his eyes was badly infected. I went from house to house all up and down the street but the dachsi didn't belong to anyone, so I took him home and treated his foot and his eye. I gave him a good German name, Rudy. Schatzie is another dachshund, a refugee from the house Terry had in the mountains. El Tigre de Sassafrass is a little gray poodle who was brought to me by my set decorator. Tigre had been badly neglected by his owner, was completely neurotic, and spent most of his time under the bed. He is super cool now and spends most of his time *in* the bed.

Bubbles is a black schnoodle (mix of schnauzer and poodle) who was left at the poodle parlor by someone who never called for her. The owner of the parlor begged me to take her to avert having her put to sleep. Daisy June, a collie who is den mother of the group, came from the Holiday Humane shelter.* Bucky, a spaniel mix, was found roaming around Studio City. Big Tiger, or just plain Biggest, is a poodle mix who was brought to me by a former housekeeper who found him in a vacated house.

Obviously, I could not continue befriending every stray orphan who came my way. So I have turned my compassion and energy toward the Actors and Others for Animals organization. But personnel and finances limit the scope of what we can do. We raised substantial amounts at our annual bazaar and other fund-raising events, but all of it goes out as fast as it comes in, for emergencies, spaying and neutering, and housing strays and unwanted animals. Scarcely a day passes that someone does not call about or come by with some poor little creature who needs care and attention and a place to live. They break my heart. They really do. So beautiful, and vulnerable, and alone. Totally dependent upon a human being, who, if he takes the orphan to his heart, will become just as dependent on the dog for those unique qualities that only a dog can bring into your life.

I have previously mentioned the magnificent sycamore tree in my backyard. It soared ninety feet into the air and its limbs were the size of ordinary tree trunks. It towered over the roof of my house and

---

* Holiday Humane is a simply marvelous place in North Hollywood with which Actors and Others is now affiliated. It's an orphanage with a clinic on the premises, and every dog is spayed or neutered on admission. It is a prototype of the kind of shelter, like Bide-A-Wee in New York, that we'd like to see established in cities all over the country.

was as wide as the house itself. It was truly a tree of majesty and splendor. One of my great pleasures, after coming home from a hectic day at the television studio, was to have a swim and then lie under that sycamore tree with my dogs all beside me—love above and all around.

I took very good care of the tree, having it regularly pruned and inspected by the tree men, and its huge branches wired to lessen strain. It was a tree, I felt, that was destined to be the rock of ages. But then, one afternoon about two years ago, as I lay under the tree watching the clouds through the leaves, I became aware that a few pieces of bark were falling from the trunk. I called the tree men, who came to inspect it but assured me that the tree was sound and that the pieces of falling bark were meaningless.

That night around three in the morning, the dogs who were sleeping in my bedroom became restless and woke me. It was a very hot, humid night. I got out of bed and went to the screen door that gives onto the patio. The sycamore tree was located just outside that door, its main branches extending over the roof of my bedroom and the entire house. I opened the door to let the dogs out, intending to take a walk around the pool with them. But curiously, they did not leave the bedroom but stood at the door looking up at me. They were utterly quiet, and I remember thinking, as I stood there, how silent the night was. Just then, however, the silence was slightly broken by a little cracking sound, and then, after a moment, by another. Then I heard a small piece of bark fall from the trunk of the tree. The dogs didn't budge. Invariably, when I opened that door they would go bounding into the yard, especially if I was going to walk with them. But they just stood there, mute, looking up at me.

Something about the night, the eerie silence, the strange behavior of the dogs, and the little squeaks of the sycamore's wood, made me step back into the room and close the screen door. Just as I did, at the precise moment that the screen door slid shut, there was a great, thunderous screeching sound and the huge tree fell with a roar of wrenching cascading wood—but miraculously it fell away from the house, toward the open area of the yard, the deadly branches completely avoiding the roof above my bedroom. If the tree had fallen the other way, there is no doubt it would have crashed through the roof and killed all of us. And if the dogs and I had stepped out of the door that night—I shudder to think.

The fallen tree completely filled the yard. It took a week to have it cut up and carted away. The tree men marveled at the miraculous way the tree had fallen.

I sorely miss the tree, and grieve for it as I grieve for friends who have died. I often think about that night. I think about that moment when those dogs of mine stood there at the screen door and communicated something to me that kept me from leaving that room. Overall, I'm convinced, it was an act of God, and I think that God had chosen to speak to me through my dogs, who are looked after by Him as well as I am.

Twenty

During the fourth year of my television show, I fell in love—completely, unexpectedly in love. For four years I had been so immersed in the traumas of Marty's death and of Terry's near-death, and in the demands of turning out my weekly television shows, that I had forgotten that the love part of me even existed. That's why it was such a shock when it happened—and how fast it happened!

It all began when, by chance, I ran into an actor I knew from having once worked on a film with him. He had a supporting role in that film, so we hadn't had many scenes together. He lived in the East but I had occasionally bumped into him when he was in Hollywood for a picture. There had been nothing at all between us; we were acquaintances, not even friends.

On this occasion, when we met, he had come to Hollywood to make a movie-of-the-week for television. He invited me to dinner, and before the evening was over I had fallen head over heels in love with him. Who can explain it? I had been so uneager to see him that when I came home from the studio that day I had wanted to cancel our date, but I didn't know where to reach him. Then, a few hours later, the earth was trembling under my chair at the restaurant.

I don't have much insight into why I fall in love or even what love is. I only know that a curious, mysterious reaction sets off inside me, like some mechanism that is tripped and starts to function with no way to turn it off. I do know that when it happens, it totally consumes me. I want to be with that person every minute of every day. I want to sleep with him and eat with him and talk with him and breathe the air he breathes. My eyes are blinded to his faults. He is letter-perfect. He has weaknesses but I only see his strengths. I am engulfed with a physical desire for him, but that is just one of three things which must work for me if I am to be completely in love. The other two are spiritual rapport and absolute honesty.

Of course, love has to be built on a physical bedrock—I had a relationship with Marty without physical love and I could never go through anything like that again. I also need a spiritual oneness with the man I love so that we can share that along with what we share physically. And I want honesty because I've been with men who weren't honest with me and I know how badly that can hurt and tear up a relationship. I want the kind of honesty where the man can say, "Look, I think it's ended. I don't love you anymore and I think we should part." Regardless of how I might suffer because of that, I would part from that man with respect and admiration.

This man I fell in love with was totally different from the men I had known before him. He wasn't a father figure, as Marty had been, a guardian telling me what to do and when to do it and what not to do. He was as interested in metaphysics as I was and we had a wonderful time talking and exploring each other's minds. I'm not one who likes to talk about show business or indulge in current gossip. I find that boring and worthless. What I enjoy is talking about the metaphysics of life and how to cope with the problems that assail us as individuals and as a people.

Our affair lasted for over a year, for, as luck would have it, the movie he made became a television series on which he had a regular weekly part. So during the day we were both busy at our respective studios and every night we shared the sweet excitement of being together. He was married to a woman he no longer loved but to whom he stayed married for the sake of his three children. I didn't care whether he was married or not. I have no qualms about the other person's marital life. He was an adult, a forceful man, and if he had honest feelings for me, that's all I asked of him. Sometimes he wanted to talk about his marriage, and we discussed whatever he wanted to discuss, the talk on a few occasions revolving around his indecision about leaving his wife. I didn't try to exert any pressure about that, for having had three marriages that turned out as badly as mine did, I was in no way thinking about getting married again. I don't know what I would have said if he had left his wife and proposed to me. Thank God I never had to make that decision.

By that I mean he neither left his wife nor proposed to me. It was a perfectly marvelous year for me. It was a time in my life when I badly needed to be uplifted, and uplift me it did. When we met, he was feeling depressed and very unhappy about his marriage, and I brought as much into his life as he brought into mine. We really helped each other enormously.

I was amused to discover that during the course of the year we were having our affair, the gossip columns and movie magazines were all regaling their readers with accounts of how I was into a heavy relationship with the producer of my television show, Don Genson. I never denied the rumors or discussed them, thereby keeping alive a perfect cover for the affair I was really having. That's the way it's always been about my rumored affairs.

Of course, my real affair had to be kept clandestine but I didn't mind. Being out on the town has never appealed to me, and as far as I'm concerned, if you have an intimate thing going, there's nothing more intimate than being alone with the man of your intimacy. There was one evening, though, when he decided he wanted to take me out to dinner. In Beverly Hills yet. I said it was a rather risky thing on his part since, in public, I'm not what you might call an unrecognizable character. (I once went to a Broadway musical wearing a black wig and other disguises, certain that I was going to enjoy an unrecognized evening in the theater, but as I went down the aisle to my seat, the usherette said, "Doris Day! What are you doing in that silly wig?" and that was the end of that.) But he took me to a marvelously cozy restaurant he had found up in Laurel Canyon, dimly lighted, our table in an alcove, excellent food and wine. I didn't see a soul I knew or anyone who knew me, and even the waiter and maître d' showed no signs of recognition. Which shows you that there are special protective angels for lovers.

When the season was over and his series wasn't renewed, he went back East and I never saw him again. We had had a little disagreement before he left but that really had no effect on our parting. I realized after he left that I did not love him in an enduring way, but that he had brought something important into my life at a time when I sorely needed it. But as it turned out, he was a man who passed through my life without leaving a trace of himself.

271

Twenty-One

ON March 4, 1974, after five long years of investigation and preparation (not to mention enormous legal fees), we finally brought Jerome Rosenthal to trial in the Superior Court of California. It was a trial destined to last for one hundred days, with twelve attorneys participating, at a cost of $250,000. It was my great good fortune to have an extraordinary lawyer representing me, Robert Winslow, a soft-spoken, gentle man who was as dedicated to nailing Rosenthal as Terry and I were. Bob Winslow did virtually nothing else for five years than stalk Rosenthal. Bob's health broke down at one point during the trial under the pressure of the work, but he gamely fought his way back on his feet and resumed the battle.

At stake in the trial was the possible recovery of some of my money that had been dissipated by Rosenthal in his oil and hotel ventures. I was told he had no visible assets, but there were six malpractice insurance companies involved and there was the possibility of recovering several millions of dollars from them.

But in all honesty, I was as much interested in the justice of bringing Rosenthal to his knees as I was in the money itself. And Terry's hatred of Rosenthal (I had never seen any sign of hate in Terry before) had risen to the point at which he was positively obsessed by nailing Rosenthal to the jailhouse door.

And there was something else. I was still baffled and deeply troubled by Marty's role in all this. I had never stopped wondering if he had been a villain or a dupe. It was my hope that the trial might throw some light on exactly what happened between Marty and Rosenthal. Terry had received a phone call from Kirk Douglas, who said that many years ago he had phoned Marty to tell him that he, Kirk, had fired Rosenthal as his lawyer because he had discovered that Rosenthal was squandering his investments in questionable deals that smacked of double-dealing. At that time Kirk and his wife, Anne, were good friends of ours whom we saw all the time. Marty never told me about that call, but I do remember that just about that time Marty came to me and said, "I don't think we should see Anne and Kirk anymore. Kirk's done something—well, let's just say he's no friend of yours. Take my word for it. I'd rather not talk about it." As a result we didn't see them anymore. Of course, Marty never told me about Kirk's warning, but if Marty had listened to Kirk and fired Rosenthal, most of my money would have been saved. Why didn't he? Why had Marty reacted as he did?

〰〰〰〰〰〰〰〰〰〰〰〰〰〰〰〰〰〰〰〰〰〰〰

KIRK DOUGLAS

There was a period of time when I saw a lot of Doris—we entertained in each other's homes and went out quite often as a foursome —but I haven't a clue as to who Doris Day really is. That face that she shows the world—smiling, only talking good, happy, tuned into God—as far as I'm concerned, that's just a mask. I haven't a clue as to what's underneath. Doris is just about the remotest person I know.*

〰〰〰〰〰〰〰〰〰〰〰〰〰〰〰〰〰〰〰〰〰〰〰

Terry had also discovered that Marty had paid the accounting firm of Price-Waterhouse the sum of $25,000 to investigate Rosenthal's investments and accounting practices as they related to me. Their report was entirely negative and advised immediate termination of Rosenthal's position with me. Marty paid the $25,000 fee but completely ignored the report. Why?

By far the worst Rosenthal-related incident involved the beautiful actress Dorothy Dandridge, who killed herself a few years ago, shortly after her agent had called to tell her that he had checked on certain investments which her lawyer, Jerome Rosenthal, had made for her, and had discovered that she was penniless. Of course, she

---

* The picture I made with Kirk, *Young Man with a Horn*, was one of the few utterly joyless experiences I had in films. I was made to feel like an outsider, an intruder. Kirk and Betty Bacall had once gone together, and this picture brought them back together again, so I guess that had something to do with it. Kirk was civil to me and that's about all. But then Kirk never makes much of an effort toward anyone else. He's pretty much wrapped up in himself.

273

had no money to sue Rosenthal; not very long afterward she had committed suicide.

So the start of that trial, as you can see, had great psychological meaning for me. It was an opportunity to exorcise something that had been gnawing at me for many years. I looked to God for the prevailment of justice, hoping that it had been preordained in the order of things for me to triumph over this man who had brought such evil into my life and the lives of so many others.

For five years I had been put through the legal wringer: long days of being examined by deposition; months and months devoted to defending vexatious lawsuits Rosenthal had brought against me in such places as New Mexico, Oklahoma, and Texas (where the oil wells and hotels were located); endless hours of conferences with my lawyers to aid them in their preparation of all the paper work that so much litigation required. I cannot deny that I approached that trial feeling outrage toward Rosenthal. But I had been warned that the judicial process is very strict in its demands for proof, and that many a slippery lawyer, knowing the ins and outs of that process, has escaped through its loopholes. That worried me— for certainly Rosenthal had proved himself to be a consummate escape artist.

The case was tried before Judge Lester E. Olson, without a jury. Judge Olson, it seemed to me, was strict, fair, amiable, and very knowledgeable. During the trial seventy boxes of files, containing tens of thousands of papers, almost 2,500 exhibits in all, were introduced into evidence, but Judge Olson seemed to handle it all pretty effortlessly, and to stay abreast of what was in the boxes. He also remained unflappable in the face of some weird maneuvering on the part of Rosenthal and his lawyers. For example, they refused to give my attorney a list in advance of the witnesses they were going to use (as they are required to do), offering as an excuse the fact that the witnesses were scared to death of Terry Melcher because five years previously he had associated with the Manson family, a band of killers. In particular they cited Harry Melcher, Marty's brother, who was coming from the East to testify for them, as being in abject fear of what killer Terry might do to him! Judge Olson calmly rejected their contention and ordered them to hand over the list of witnesses. Terry managed to control his killer instincts and not rub out any of them during the course of the trial.

I particularly enjoyed the moment during the trial when Rosenthal had finished testifying about a meeting which he said he had had with me in his office on May 11, 1956. Rosenthal spent two and a half hours on the witness stand, telling the court how he had informed me on that day of everything he was doing with my money—thereby proving that he was open and aboveboard with me. Bob Winslow's cross-examination consisted of showing Rosenthal his own office diary for that day, which showed that I had been in his office for twenty-five minutes. "Mr. Rosenthal," Judge Olson said, "it took you two and a half hours to tell us what you allegedly told Doris Day. How did you manage to cram all that into twenty-five minutes?"

The best description of what happened at the trial and its result is contained in what Judge Olson said in open court on the day he gave his decision. We were all summoned to his courtroom and I must confess that as I sat there, waiting to hear his decision, I was filled with a tenseness and an anxiety such as I had never before experienced. All those years of effort, money, and emotion—talk about a moment of truth!

Judge Olson took his place on the bench and explained that he was going to give an oral decision in the case, and not issue a formal, written opinion. "For this court to write a formal opinion," he said, "would be an exercise in futility or an ego trip." He began to talk, and the impact of his words will stay with me as long as I live.

> The tragic drama in this case started to unfold back in the late Forties or early Fifties when Jerome B. Rosenthal began to represent Doris Day and Martin Melcher. It involves not a case of crude theft or misuse of a client's money by an attorney to whom it was entrusted. Rather, it involves an attorney so intent on doing business with his clients' money that he lost sight of ethical and legal principles. It involves a pattern by the attorney of placing his clients in business deals in which he was likewise involved—not just Doris Day and Martin Melcher but scores of clients to be mentioned later.
>
> The case from beginning to end oozes with attorney-client conflicts of interest, clouding and shading every transaction and depriving Doris Day and Martin Melcher of the independent legal advice to which they were entitled. It involved kickbacks and favored treatment of one client over others; it involves attempts to deal in the hotel and oil business so amateurish that they would be humorous but for the tragic consequences. It involves the extraction of fees from Doris Day and from other clients or entities for the same work performed. It involves an undertaking to provide financial and investment advice, and a complete and utter failure to provide it. It involves a tortured effort by Rosenthal to maintain for years in the future the indentured posi-

275

tion in which he had held Doris Day since 1956, even after she had ceased to permit him to act as her attorney. It involves a "percentage retainer" agreement that in the context of the facts of this case is void and against public policy because of the violation of the rules of professional conduct. It involves a carving up of the efforts of a talented entertainer by her attorney and her husband-manager, so that the attorney got 10 percent off the top, the husband-manager got 25 percent off the top—then the attorney got 10 percent of the 25 percent; after which the attorney received thousands of additional dollars in fees from other entities for work for which he had already been paid.

The evidence so reeks of negligence, a violation of the Rules of Professional Conduct and all that is basic in the traditional relationship of attorney and client as to require that the court, as best it can, undo the transaction that occurred so as to attempt to put Doris Day back to a position as if she had not become enmeshed in the machinations of Rosenthal's twisted sense of professional responsibility.

Rosenthal's conduct is doubly gross and outrageous because he recognized his ethical and professional responsibilities and yet did not follow them.

It is hard to understand some of the insane financial machinations that occurred over these twenty years unless one assumes Martin Melcher suffered under delusions of grandeur, that he had an aggravated impulse to play "Monopoly," and a blind awe of Rosenthal— and that Rosenthal was impelled to take advantage of this situation.

The lawyer, when he receives his license to practice, is armed with the ability to do great and good things, but he also can commit great harm and mischief. It is therefore right and proper that an attorney, when he acts as an attorney, be held to standards higher than the market place. To do otherwise would be to ignore the awesome power gained by an attorney by reason of his position of faith and confidence placed in him by his client.

The seriousness of Rosenthal's conduct, and the great damage flowing from it, are heightened by the fact that his great genius for the creation of paper work created an aura of propriety. To the unskilled, to the even sophisticated client, it would have appeared to be a very proper law office operation. The "Dear Folks" letters, the maze and swirl of memos, meetings, and other P. R. efforts were designed to impress—and impress they did. The evidence shows an impressive roster of former clients—investors in oil and other business deals, such as Kirk Douglas, The Chip Monks, Frank DeVol, Billy Eckstine, Irene Dunne, Zsa Zsa Gabor, Gogi Grant, Norman Granz, George Hamilton, Stanley Kubrick, Ross Hunter, Harold Mirisch, Art Laboe, Gordon MacRae, Van Johnson, Dorothy Dandridge, and others. Show-biz clients were obviously impressed by all the patina of files, papers, accounting machines, and other trappings.

The fact that Rosenthal chose to have both Martin Melcher and Doris Day as separate clients, and the evidence is absolutely uncontrovertible on this point, magnifies the problem. He had a continuing duty to both—independent of the other—and failed as to each. The gravity of the problem is also increased by the length of the attorney-client relationship, some twenty years.

Having made these general comments, some specific issues require comment: It is clear from the evidence that the Melchers relied upon Rosenthal when he decided to put them into the Federal Land Bank Bond scheme in 1953 along with other clients. Back in 1953, Rosenthal advised Melcher to provide three million dollars in United States Land Bank bonds in a sham transaction. Rosenthal himself bought $1,950,000 worth of land-bank bonds and other securities, and Rosenthal's partner, Norton, some $1,700,000 worth. Rosenthal advised another client, Gordon MacRae, to purchase $1,000,000 of land-bank bonds. In all of this they were sham transactions.

Rosenthal's advice was clouded with an incredible conflict of interest in that he obtained for his own investment terms from Cantor, Fitzgerald and Company—the promoters of the scheme—terms much better than those allowed his clients, and his purported disclosure of this personal advantage to his clients was not sufficient to eliminate the taint.

Rosenthal received what amounted to a kickback on commission from Cantor, Fitzgerald and Company for supplying them with these millions in bond transactions in the form of over $50,000 disguised as attorney fees. Exhibit 1425 shows the money received by Rosenthal from Cantor, Fitzgerald. Exhibit 691, Rosenthal's own time books, shows no services performed by Rosenthal, although it does show services performed by Rosenthal for other retainer clients at the same time. The conclusion is inescapable that over $50,000 in fees was an undisclosed and disguised kickback.

After the original bond transactions, Rosenthal failed, in the years '54 and following, to supervise the complicated transaction, nor did he learn it was being performed in a way that was certain to create adverse tax results to the clients; he was negligent in failing to terminate the transaction, back it off and attempt to trim the adverse tax exposure.

When the adverse Internal Revenue Service tax assessments were levied in about 1958, his negligence continued. His conduct of the tax litigation with the government was negligent and fraught with additional conflicts of interest. This is so because of his own personal tax liability, together with the continued need to induce Martin Melcher to pour money into ill-advised oil and gas ventures rather than consider settlement with the government and payment of the tax.

The oil and gas ventures in which Rosenthal placed his clients stand out as an incredible saga of attorney negligence. They resulted in a private "community chest" for drunken and dishonest operators, a loss to the government with respect to unpaid taxes, and worst of all, vast losses to the clients. They were amateurishly conducted and

277

ill-conceived. It would take the court several hours to present even a brief synopsis of the oil and gas ventures, ranging through Texas, Oklahoma, New Mexico and Kentucky, and nothing would be gained thereby. Through the diligent efforts of counsel for Doris Day, the evidence is in the record.

The conduct of Rosenthal with respect to the oil and gas ventures represents a breach of his fiduciary duty of full disclosure arising out of his personal participation in the oil and gas deals and the participation by other clients of the Rosenthal firm. The Rosenthal firm also failed to furnish accurate financial statements to the Day-Melcher parties, and failed to provide adequate legal advice to them concerning the oil and gas ventures.

The Midland Equipment fiasco represents one high-water mark in the unfortunate oil and gas ventures. "Cattleman" Fred Luke hires Bailey; then Bailey, using his wife as a subterfuge, cheats the Rosenthal clients. The Rosenthal office "discovers" the dishonesty their negligence had permitted and works out a settlement, unwittingly financed by Doris Day, and then Rosenthal hits the clients with $70,000 in fees and costs to resolve the mess his own negligence had created.

The check switch ceremony in December, 1966, in Lexington, Kentucky, stinks to high heaven and the attempts to explain it are saddening. Tom Atkins' testimony concerning it was a lie. Approximately $140,000 of clients' money was sent to Kentucky and checks issued to drillers as if to pay their bills, but upon phony invoices. Then approximately $31,000 of this money was channeled back to California and put into the Rosenthal firm as fees. The present defense efforts to rationalize and explain the 1966 skulduggery, although Herculean, are of no effect. One can only wonder what other items of similar nature are yet uncovered in the mass of papers created by Rosenthal. This also exposed his clients to tax fraud charges.

Other examples of negligence or worse: The use of outdated oil engineering reports, such as the 1964 reports in crucial 1966 financial statements; duplicative or dummy lists of equipment on oil leases indicated in the testimony of Mr. Sampson—and the list could go on.

In short, the oil and gas ventures represent a sad story of ill-advised and illegal transactions; of efforts to avoid paying income taxes at the risk of improvident investments; of an attorney bent on personal gain at the expense of his clients; of Martin Melcher apparently imbued with a false sense of his own intelligence and overly awed by his attorney, and of Doris Day too busy making movies to really pay attention to her own affairs, but each client still being entitled to competent legal advice and complete fidelity free from a conflict of interest—neither of which they got.

If the oil and gas ventures were bad, the hotels were worse. Again, incredible conflicts of interest existed both at the inception

278

and over the years; such as the relationship of Rosenthal with Heinz and Sarno, the promotors.

There were amateurish efforts to build and operate two large and expensive hotels, an incredibly complicated and risky business. The conduct involved costly, inefficient computer programs, management inefficiency, disorganized accounting practices, poor personnel policies, inappropriate draining of needed cash to Cabana Management to benefit Rosenthal, adverse to the Melchers. Were it not so sad, the memos put in by the defense about the price of chicken Kiev, about which manager slept with which waitress, and related garbage, would be humorous.

The lack of proper capitalization of these hotel operations boggles the mind and created from the start an aura of financial crisis. This permitted Rosenthal to exercise greater influence on Melcher because of "scare" tactics, thus permitting Rosenthal to drain Doris Day of cash as fast as the money rolled in at the box office. Again, Rosenthal failed to give adequate legal advice, failed to provide accurate financial data, and breached his duty to the clients because of adverse interests.

The highest-water mark of all was the assertion by Rosenthal, after Martin Melcher's death, that he, Rosenthal, had an oral agreement with Martin Melcher by which he, Rosenthal, owned 50 percent of the Day-Melcher empire—presented by a man who ordinarily created paper work for everything he did, yet lacked a shred of credible documentary evidence to prove this alleged oral agreement, which if true, would have involved millions of dollars.

Rule 9 of the Rules of Professional Conduct provides that an attorney shall not commingle the money of a client with his own and that he shall promptly report to the client the receipt by him of all money belonging to such client. Rosenthal failed miserably to comply with this requirement. The trustee account, at first blush, has the appearance of accuracy by reason of the Burroughs accounting machine system. In actual practice, the system was negligently maintained. Rosenthal has failed to account to his clients for trust funds.

Exhibit 1681, the journal sheets, and exhibit 1681-B, the ledger cards, have been examined carefully and the manner with which millions of dollars was handled through this trust account rises to the grossest of negligence. The failure to keep proper records amongst the various ventures and the transactions between them boggles the mind. By Rosenthal's own accountant's version, some $2,965,358 of Doris Day and Melcher's money was paid by them into the Rosenthal trust account and an additional $5,751,737 of other clients' money has been paid into that trust account, close to $10,000,000.

Since there has been a total failure to accurately account, the court finds that Jerome B. Rosenthal is personally liable to Doris Day for this amount. The Union Bank, Beverly Hills Regional office, is to be ordered to pay over the trust funds presently on deposit in the sum of $30,684.69 forthwith. Rosenthal's outrageous conduct concerning the trust account is best exemplified by the failure, over the five years this litigation has been pending, to make available the trust ledger cards and journal sheets until they were finally brought into the court on demand by this court.

The conduct of Rosenthal in the Dallas bankruptcy proceedings concerning the hotels was sad and disgraceful. The record shows Rosenthal was contemptuous and contumacious and that he could not be controlled by his own attorneys. He abused the legal process in the bankruptcy court, the United States District Court, the United States Court of Appeals, and the United States Supreme Court. He filed false claims in the bankruptcy proceedings; his petition to stay proceedings in that court was a sham; he misused the deposition process to prolong proceedings and gain an advantage in unrelated cases, and he prosecuted bad faith appeals.

In all of this, he acted with malice; the so-called advice he received from counsel is no defense because he failed to disclose to his own attorneys important facts to them, crucial to the weight to be given their advice; it is clear from the record that Rosenthal used the various attorneys of record in Texas in the various proceedings to shield him and give his vexatious conduct a patina of propriety. The court finds that the Day-Melchers have been aggrieved by this conduct and have standing in this court to urge the wrongs inflicted upon them, contrary to the defense position in this regard.

Martin Melcher died in April of 1968. 1967 had been a year of financial crisis, heightening in early '68. One can only speculate as to the effect this had on Martin Melcher's health.

His son Terrence was appointed special administrator of the estate in April 26, 1968. He elected to employ other attorneys as attorneys for the estate.

The affairs of Martin Melcher at the time of his death were a maze of complex business interests; financial records were not current; Rosenthal made insatiable demands for cash to fund current operations. He had induced Terrence to advance over $100,000 for his own benefit. Estate counsel made legitimate requests to Rosenthal to supply information and records. Rosenthal retaliated with a sham petition to seek removal of Terrence as special administrator and again refused to turn over Doris Day's files.

Some records were gradually turned over, but in view of the full extent of records now known to this court, Rosenthal's conduct with respect to the records he did turn over was deceptive, calculated to mislead and delay, and was worse than if none had been turned over. Rosenthal's demands to be compensated for his time in connection with record turnover was tantamount to extortion.

The financial crisis facing Doris Day, vis-à-vis the impending television show, the crisis with the hotels, the crisis with the oil and gas ventures, the equipment leases—to name just a few problems—

all of these made the question of records and files of imperative importance.

What did Rosenthal do when he lost the receivership battle? He refused to comply. At virtual gunpoint, aided by armed sheriff's deputies, the receiver had to pick the locks of Rosenthal's office to gain access to the records and files the court had ordered Rosenthal to turn over. Rosenthal aggravated his wrongful retention of files by utilizing confidential information contained therein to commence various lawsuits against Doris Day before she had access to her own records.

In summary, nearly twenty lawsuits and petitions were commenced by Rosenthal using confidential information he had obtained from his former client, all the while refusing to supply Doris Day with the same information.

It is true that Doris Day granted to her husband, Martin Melcher, a general power of attorney and that he used the power of attorney over a long period of time to sign documents on her behalf. It is also true that she had knowledge of this fact.

The defense has urged that this fact precludes Doris Day from now complaining as to the documents signed by Martin Melcher but the court does not agree. In fact, the extensive use of this power of attorney and Rosenthal's knowledge of the relationship between Doris Day and her husband heightened rather than lessened the need for independent legal advice to be given to her. This she did not receive.

Rosenthal took advantage of the confidential relationship which existed between himself and Martin Melcher.

He grossly failed to meet his obligations as an attorney for Doris Day and Martin Melcher.

He misled them with false, misleading, and inaccurate financial statements.

When Martin Melcher died he misused his position of trust and engaged in loan transactions involving over $100,000 with Terrence Melcher to his own benefit without disclosing all of the facts.

When discharged as attorney for the Melchers he failed to meet his obligation of trust and fidelity in turning over his clients' records.

He misused the confidential information previously imparted to him by his clients for his own gain, in filing unfounded claims, vexatious lawsuits and other legal proceedings in California, New Mexico, Oklahoma, and Texas. He skillfully and with malice abused the process of the courts to harass his former clients.

The evidence shows a pattern of conduct by Rosenthal with respect to litigiousness, taking adverse claims against former clients, and the retention of their papers—all showing a constant course of conduct adverse to his clients and contrary to the public faith and trust to be upheld by an attorney.

The evidence shows a pattern of kickbacks and rebates disguised as attorney fees, and the implication of his clients thereby in tax fraud.

For all of this, Rosenthal's conduct as an attorney was out-rageous; it was fraudulent and malicious, and exemplary damages should and will be imposed.

Based on the evidence and the law, and for the reasons previously stated, the court hereby awards damages in favor of Doris Day, and against Rosenthal and others, as follows:

For damages in connection with the oil and gas ventures, the sum of $5,589,000, together with interest in the sum of $1,956,150.

For damages in connection with the hotel ventures, the sum of $3,437,000 together with interest in the sum of $1,202,950.

For damages in connection with the investments in Guided Space Transmissions and Global Industries, the sum of $137,500 together with interest in the sum of $48,125.

For damages in connection with the tax malpractice concerning the land-bank bonds, $534,675 plus interest in the sum of $186,900.

For damages for tax malpractice in the home purchase transaction, the sum of $15,763, plus interest in the sum of $5,517.

For damages to recoup the fees previously paid the Rosenthal firms, $2,268,538, together with interest thereon of $793,800.

For damages to recoup the fees and costs paid by Arwin Productions to the Rosenthal firms, $252,600 together with interest in the sum of $88,410.

For damages to recoup the loans of money to Rosenthal by Martin Melcher as reflected by exhibit 1426, column 3, in the sum of $219,375, together with interest in the sum of $76,781.

For damages for the costs of the receivership and other damages relating to Rosenthal's wrongful retention of records, $169,329 without interest.

For damages for attorneys' fees in these actions, $850,000 without interest.

For punitive damages, the sum of $1,000,000.

For damages in fraud for unaccounted trust funds, the sum of $2,965,358 plus interest thereon in the sum of $1,037,875, subject to certain credits heretofore indicated to prevent duplication.

Total damages awarded are $22,835,646.

These proceedings are adjourned.

The courtroom exploded around me—but I just sat there, too overwhelmed to move. I had been trying very hard not to cry, but now the tears came. Tears of relief. Of gladness that this ugly business was finished. Bob Winslow came over to me, a picture of joy, having received a verdict far beyond his wildest anticipation. He was a bit puzzled by my tears.

"Doris," he said, "Doris, it's the largest amount ever awarded in a civil suit in California. Twenty-two million! Ah, Doris . . ."

I got up and put my arms around Bob and hugged him. He

deserved a laurel wreath and a bolt of godly approval from Olympus.

It was over. All over. God in his heaven had smiled upon Clara Bixby, and the forces of evil had been put to rout.

TERRY MELCHER

My relationship with my mother switches around from child-parent to parent-child. Depends on who has the problem and who's in the ascendency. Ninety percent of the time I have the parent role.

She wants to think that anyone involved with her in business is a father figure—someone she can lean on and rely upon without questioning. That's what happened with Marty. It's a dangerous attitude that I'm trying to correct. Also, she likes to think that she is poverty-stricken. She denies herself luxuries and pleasures—there's something almost religious about her self-denial. I don't know how much cash she has to have not to feel poor, but she has a lot more than enough. You would never know it if you listened to her talk.

She has her heart set on getting married again but she really doesn't have any idea how to react to a man's attention. She is the last one to know when a man is interested in her. Sad to say, I don't think my mother's had much of a sex life. But who knows? Maybe there's a lot in store for her.

Twenty-Two

I HAD a dream recently that I was at Frank Sinatra's wedding. I can't recall what his bride looked like, but in my dream Frank looked different than he does now. Now he has a very full, heavy look to his face that he didn't have when I first knew him back on the "Hit Parade." But in the dream he didn't look like he did then, either. Somewhere in between. The marriage ceremony was just ending, and I was desolate. I had a terrible crush on Frank, I was so in love with him, and I kept saying to myself, Why is he getting married? Oh, he's so darling, why is he getting married? Why is he doing this to me?

There were a lot of people at the wedding, and they were all congratulating Frank and his bride as they came up the aisle, crowding around them; I turned my back on them—it was just too painful to look at them. When Frank passed by me he tapped me on the back and I turned and he gave me a very loving look. I looked at him and I was crying and thinking, Oh, Frank, why are you marrying someone else?

I couldn't understand dreaming about Frank like that. I hadn't seen Frank since we made *Young at Heart* in 1955. I had received an invitation to attend his first opening in Vegas, but I hadn't gone. (I did go to his second Vegas show but had only seen him onstage.) It's possible I could have heard him on the radio the night before the dream. But how could I dream about him with such feeling when in fact I have never had any such feelings about Frank?

Of course, dreaming about marriage is quite understandable. I do think about marrying again, and Terry talks to me about it quite often. Terry is so cute with me. We're not at all like mother-son; we're more like contemporaries who are really good friends. He calls me up and says, "What are you doing? Come on up—I've got a great fire going, we'll open a bottle of wine and talk."

One of his favorite subjects to talk about is why I don't go out more. He'd love to see me happily coupled, if not married. But I tell him that if somebody calls, and I don't feel that seeing the fellow has a prayer of going anywhere (I can always tell that much about a man), then I don't go out simply for the sake of going out. I'd rather read. I love being in my house. I'll know when it's the right man, and when it is, I will respond to it for all it's worth. But I really don't feel that I have to run around to a lot of cocktail parties on a looking mission. I'm not looking. I'm really not. It isn't as if I don't enjoy my life as it is.

"Now, listen, Mom," Terry said, the last time we had one of these talks, "let's face it—you are really a terrific-looking woman. You're very healthy and desirable with a terrific body. You're *young,* you really are. All my friends think that."

"Well, that's adorable of you to lay those compliments on me," I said, "but I'm just very funny about whom I go out with. My time is precious to me and I don't want to waste it. I'm just very selective, that's all. Not that I think I'm such hot stuff, but everybody has the right to be selective."

"Sure. Right. But you can't really know a guy unless you see him a few times—"

"I'll know him the *minute* I see him. He'll show up. I'm sure of that. So why should I go out looking for him? I'm in no hurry. But that doesn't mean that I wouldn't love to be married."

There's no doubt that life has more meaning when you have someone to share things with. I don't think God made us to walk around by ourselves. Male-female is a twos concept. Whether you're dying to fall in love, or you just want to *think* about falling in love, it's marvelous to have those feelings. I'm so lucky to have loved and been loved in my life, so I know what I'm looking forward to. I think about the men and women in this world who have never experienced real love. Both married and unmarried. And I pity them for what they've missed out on. As for those who have loved but not been loved in return—well, as the song says, unrequited love's a bore.

"So, who is this guy?" Terry asks. "This dude who will walk in and cause you to faint?"

"Well, he is someone who will turn me on sexually, but he's also someone who is as turned on by listening to Joel Goldsmith tapes and

285

reading his books as I am. Someone who does not want to gossip about who did what to whom, or what the grosses of anything were, or any of that. He's someone who wants to learn as much about life as I do. Maybe he'll be a surgeon, gray at the temples, who would like to settle down on a big old New England farm. Oh, how I'd love that. No neighbors for miles around. Lots of room for eleven dogs to run and play. Where I could rake leaves and shovel snow and pluck rock-hard apples out of the barrel on the back porch. I'd sell everything and be out of Beverly Hills in a week's time."

"Well, Mom," Terry said, "I'd hate to lose you to the East, but bon voyage!"

What bothers me about falling in love is how impermanent it can be. In the beginning of all three of my marriages, I thought I was deeply and forever in love—but look what happened. A few years ago I was walking along Beverly Drive when a man stopped me to say hello. He was a stranger whom I took to be an *aficionado* of my movies or television shows so I returned his hello.

"Don't you remember me?"

"No," I said, "should I?"

"Well, you didn't have *that* many husbands."

I was stunned. "George? My God, you're George!"

The most embarrassing part of it was that his appearance hadn't changed very much. Can you imagine? Here was a man I was once deeply in love with . . . and married to!

I can only hope that I have learned a lot about loving, and about myself, since my young, impetuous band days. If I had known way back then what I know now, I would have said to myself, Now, wait a minute, this Al Jorden, okay, he's good-looking, he makes my heart flutter, and I like him in bed—everything about us in bed is super—but how can I love him when I don't really like him as a person? I don't like the way he thinks. I don't like his character. It's all right to go to bed with him, but that's as far as it should go. Enjoy yourself, Clara, but marriage is for people you like. What's that song? "Not only do I love you but I like you, too."

If Al Jorden had not left the band, I'm sure I would never have married him. But as I've said before, it was predestined that it work out that way. It was preordained for me to have that terrible experience, for it put some things in me that were destined to hold me together through a lot of tough times that followed. I think the Al Jorden period gave me tremendous strength and a depth of emotions from which I later drew in my acting and singing.

Looking back, I'd say the train accident was designed to turn me away from dancing and to start me toward a singing career. The one really positive value in my marriage to Al Jorden was the birth of my son. George Weidler was part of the plan in that his desertion gave me a sense of self-sufficiency, of a new inner strength.

And Marty's death—well, to be honest about it, had he lived I would have been totally wiped out. He and Rosenthal would have dissipated my five years of television earnings just as they dissipated everything else. I would have lost my house—everything. In the scheme of things, Marty had to die in order for me to survive.

I know that I am often thought of as a Pollyanna, but I'm far from it. I'm much too realistic to qualify as a Pollyanna. However, I have overcome a lot, and I have developed an inner strength on which I can rely. It has nothing to do with me. It's simply built into me and nobody can ever take it from me. I don't care about "success" in the conventional sense of my ratings or earnings. I couldn't care less about that. The success I care about is in knowing how to deal with situations, in not allowing anything in my life to get out of hand. I know that I can handle almost anything they throw at me, and to me that is real success. Otherwise, some of the things that have happened in my life, especially in the last six years, would have turned me into an alcoholic or worse. I would be doing something to excess to hide from reality, but the fact is I'm not doing anything to excess except enjoying life.

I know how I want to live. I know what's good for me. I know what brings me joy. I know what has value and what doesn't. That doesn't mean that there aren't some nights when life seems bleak and I cry myself to sleep. Okay, all right, I'll say to myself, I'll give them tonight, but tomorrow is mine. Life has to be up and down—if it isn't down once in a while, how would I know what up is? So I don't pretend. When I'm miserable, I'm miserable, and I tell everybody I come in contact with. I never try to put on a happy face. I deal with it. I try to understand why. I fight my way out of it. And when I'm happy everybody knows about that too. So many people stop themselves from feeling good—that's so hard for me to understand. They can't even accept a compliment. God, when I feel good I do pirouettes! If you squelch an emotion inside yourself, how does it get out? What happens to it? Where does it go? I'll tell you where—it shrivels up and dies inside you, but I don't think the human body is equipped for burials.

No, I let it all hang out and I suppose that outgoing quality accounts for some of the reactions I get from people who have seen me perform. I really love how most people are with me. God knows I'm not one of the awesome beauties, like Elizabeth Taylor, who epitomize the words "movie star." What I am is the truck driver's delight. People on the street always call me Doris. That's just the way I want it. We are family, my audience and I, and that's why I especially liked performing in a series that brought me into the living room every week. I think that's where I belong, as one of the family.

In one of the episodes on my television series I had a scene in which I wore a bridal gown. I received a letter from a young lady who said, "When you wore that little wedding gown on your television show, it absolutely made me cry. I'm going to be married in five months and I want a gown like that so badly—can you please tell me what store the gown came from so I can buy one like it? I want to look like you looked."

My costumer and my fitter went to work on the gown to make it even more attractive. Then they got yards of tulle and they made a beautiful headpiece decorated with lilies of the valley and little orange blossoms. It was a darling wedding dress. We sent it off to the girl who had written, with all my good wishes for her marriage. Months later, the dress long forgotten, I received a lovely letter from the girl, together with a picture of herself at her wedding in my make-believe wedding dress. So pretty. So radiant with happiness. So much the bride. It was very touching, and I shed a few tears of happiness for that sweet, anonymous girl. I thought to myself, That's what it's all about, isn't it? That's really what it's all about.

There was another wedding in my life a short time later—my son's. He married a lovely girl named Melissa, at the Spanish-style home of some friends of his in Rancho Santa Fe. It was an informal, festive event, and while we were all waiting for Melissa, who was upstairs being nervous, I began to ruminate about Terry, standing there with his best man, looking so handsome, waiting for his nervous bride. I thought about what a splendid young man he had turned into, and how much I liked him. I hoped that this adventure into marriage would be a happy one.

Melissa made her entrance, beautiful, nervous, looking lovingly at Terry, and as they took their places in front of the little improvised altar, a thought darted across my mind—we should have had a double ceremony! If only I had found someone. That would have been fun. It would really have been a kick.

Epilogue

~~~~~~

DORIS had gone to Las Vegas for Tom Jones's pants and Frank Sinatra's pajamas. I was on my way to Kennedy Airport to meet with her in Beverly Hills when word reached me to go to Vegas instead. Doris had intended to go to Palm Springs for a few days of desert sun, but the lure of Jones's pants and Sinatra's pajamas was too great.

I checked into the MGM Grand Hotel, where Doris said she'd be staying with her friend, Raquel Rael. The MGM Grand is a new hotel, twenty-six stories high, that should have been called the Taj Mahal of kitsch. The front of the hotel looks like a Castro Convertible carport, and the mammoth lobby is a conglomeration of all the gingerbread, gold-dripping lobbies of the ornate movie palaces of the Thirties. I signed the register and the desk clerk told me that a bellhop would meet me at my room. "Twenty-first floor," he said, "and turn right at Katharine Hepburn."

There were MGM lions everywhere—holding ash trays on their heads, embossed on the elevator doors, woven into the fabric of the carpets and draperies. On the twenty-first floor the corridor was lined with full-length portraits of former MGM stars, and a sharp right at Katharine Hepburn did indeed bring me face-to-face with my bellhop. I didn't bother to phone Doris's room. I just went down to the delicatessen off the lobby and there she was in a booth with Raquel Rael, surrounded by the lox-and-bagel remains of a hearty meal.

Doris explained that this trip to Vegas was a mission on behalf of the annual Actors and Others for Animals bazaar, whose main feature (and money-getter) was a day-long auction of celebrity-tainted items. "We went to see Tom Jones in his dressing room after his act last night," Doris said, "and he took off his pants and gave them to us."

"He split them in the seat during his windup number," Raquel said. "That ought to fetch a pretty penny."

"I've got to tell you about this doctor friend of Tom's who came in the dressing room while we were there," Raquel said, and she started to laugh. "A very handsome, distinguished-looking, man who really took to Doris . . ."

"That doctor?" Doris said. "Why, I didn't know he was interested."

Raquel shook her head and continued to laugh. "It's no wonder you don't have a man—you don't even know when you've got one. Well, anyway, the doctor is obviously gaga over Doris and he offers her his Lear jet to fly her back to L.A. when she's ready to go—and you know what she says? She says, 'Is it a nonscheduled flight? I never travel on nonscheduled flights.' It broke up everybody in the room, the doctor included. End of romance."

Doris had already received several items to auction from Liberace and she felt bad that she couldn't go to his opening at the Desert Inn that evening. Her friends, Jack Cassidy and Shirley Jones, were also opening at the Grand and she had promised to be there. But Doris's big quest was Sinatra's pajamas. He was opening at Caesar's Palace the following night, after a long retirement, an event, by Vegas standards, of prodigious importance, and Doris planned to stalk him after the performance and carry off the pajamas which had been promised to her.

We went to see a Grand Hotel vice-president, Bernie Rothkopf, to get a courtesy car because Raquel wanted to shop for a dress to wear to the Sinatra opening. Bernie Rothkopf was very pleased that Doris was going to use one of the Grand's cars, and while he had her in the office he seized the opportunity to try to overcome her long-standing resistance to Vegas offers.

"Look, Doris," he said, "just three weeks, even *two* weeks—you open New Year's Eve, and I tell you, you can write your own ticket. Do you know what you can make? And you do the show any way you like. Do you *know* what kind of audiences you'll get? Why, they'll love the pants off you! What do you say, Doris? Two weeks—you sing a few songs, what's the big deal?"

Doris laughed at his earnestness. "Okay, Bernie, I'll do it—"

"You will!"

"If I can do one show in the afternoon at four-thirty."

"Well," Rothkopf said sadly, "if you ever change your

mind . . ." He turned to me. "How can anyone pass up money like that?" he asked.

Doris had arranged for us to have a booth by ourselves at the Sinatra opening but when we appeared in the Circus Maximus, Doris was immediately set upon by a large, lumpish man with orange-tinted shades, wall-eyes, and insufficient hair teased across his scalp. He was Sinatra's major factotum, Jilly Rizzo, who emphatically informed Doris, "Frank wants you and your party at his poisonal table."

Frank's table was a long, narrow runner that extended out from the stage, everyone jammed tightly together on both sides. There were maybe sixty poisonal friends at Frank's table, people like Leo Durocher, Howard Cosell, Sonny Bono, Joey Heatherton. Doris had no sooner taken her seat than a crush of autograph seekers descended upon her from the upper reaches of the room. These people blocked the surrounding aisles, making it difficult for the waiters. Several Caesar's Palace men tried to clear the aisles but they didn't have much luck with the determined autograph seekers. Finally, the mob scene caught one of Jilly's eyes and he stomped over. "All right, all of youse," he said, in a voice that meant business, "you are to cease and desist from crowding in on Miss Doris Day. Get on back to your tables." The crowd wavered but did not back off. This time Jilly waded right into them. "I said MOVE!"

The crowd got the hell out of there.

The program opened with Count Basie and his orchestra, the Count at the piano playing in his clean, restrained manner. Then there was Miss Ella Fitzgerald, singing with as fluid and mellow a voice as you'd ever want to hear. "There'll Never Be Another You" for openers, "Mister Paganini" to warm up the house, and then a virtuoso duet with her bass man, Keter, on "The Man I Love." I watched Doris watching Ella, and her expression was one of pure adoration. Up there on the stage was her earliest heroine, the singer who had meant so much to her back in Cincinnati when she first got interested in singing. Now here she was, at some outrageously advanced age, sounding just as good, just as much the Ella that she was thirty-odd years ago, coming out of Doris's Atwater Kent radio. And I had no doubt that if Doris did decide to do a turn on a Vegas stage, her voice would be just as effective, just as much the Doris Day voice as it was back in the Fifties, when she was cutting all those albums that put her at the top of the international charts. That's what these two ladies had in common—longevity, plus a great way with lyrics, and an ability to come at you from somewhere inside the music.

Ella was followed by Pat Henry, a pal of Sinatra's, who was billed as a comedian. "Boy, Frank's really big here, ain't he? Look at the names he brings in—what names! Fungi Terenazi. Gaetano di Lupidicci. Bananas Scarnalo. There ain't a goddamn fruit stand open in New York this whole week."

While Pat Henry was delivering his hilarious material a man across from Doris leaned forward and identified himself as the owner of the Tropicana Hotel. "Listen, Doris," he said, as sotto voce as his voce would permit, "I got a great proposition for you. You come on for three weeks at the Tropicana and I spring fifty thousand dollars for that there Actors and Others for Animals, plus what you pull down. You wanna help those doggies—fifty G's buys a hell of a lot of dog food. What d'ya say? New Year's Eve for three weeks and you can fatten up every hound in L.A."

"All right," Doris said.

"You mean it? Shake!" The owner thrust his pudgy hand across the table.

"But only one performance . . ."

"One performance . . . ?" The Tropicana owner took his hand back.

". . . on closed circuit."

Up on the stage Pat Henry had a drink in his hand which he had filched from Leo Durocher. He fished out an ice cube. "Hey, looka there! An ice cube wit' a hole in it. I was married to one for eight years."

Sinatra appeared at the mike without introduction. His voice was raspy and crinkled at the edges. It didn't matter. His style was the style of a man who knew how to make love to his audience. Whatever his offstage failings, onstage he could do no wrong. Doris was listening but I could tell that she was thinking about those pajamas. Doggedness was one of her strong points—she had come for Frank's pajamas and she was not going to go away empty-handed.

We went backstage after the performance and Doris was greeted warmly by Count Basie, an old friend who had recently performed for Doris at an Actors and Others benefit dance. Doris went looking for Ella and they embraced and asked each other how they were. Frank, though, was not around. Doris was told that he had gone up to his room but he expected her at a party he was giving in a roped-off section of the Lounge.

There were a lot of people at the party, but not Frank. At the table across from us was Joe Louis, in a golf cap and blazer, talking to Johnny Weissmuller, in a blazer without golf cap; these two heroes of my boyhood with their puffed faces and shrunken eyes. Doris made several inquiries about Frank, finally was told by Pat Henry that Frank had had a couple of stiff drinks and gone to bed for the night. Someone ran up to see if he had left pajamas for Doris—the word came back, no, Frank's valet knew nothing about any pajamas. Doris was upset, but she didn't show it. Pat Henry brought Jilly over.

"Pat says Frank promised you somethin'—pajamas or somethin'—'at right?" Jilly asked.

"Yes, for the bazaar auction."

"Okay, pajamas—you got 'em. When you need 'em?"

"Next week."

"No problem. I'll poison'ly get the pajamas put on Frank's plane and fly 'em to ya."

"I hate to trouble you, but we really need—"

Up went Jilly's right hand in a stop signal. "Puh-lese, Doris! No trouble. Frank promises pajamas—you get pajamas."

The day of the bazaar came and went but Sinatra's pajamas never arrived. The bazaar itself was a phenomenal event, in that thousands of people came all the way to Warners' vast Burbank lot in the Valley and paid three dollars a head primarily for the purpose of seeing Doris in person. Pilgrims to the Burbank Lourdes. There were a few other celebrities present—Bea Arthur, Lassie, Earl Holliman, Jonathan Winters, and McLean Stevenson—but from the moment she appeared, it was evident that Doris was the prime reason they had come. Several girls with sashes were assigned to stay with Doris for the day, to collect ten cents for each autograph she gave, and twenty-five cents every time she posed for a picture. They did a booming business. Everyone called her Doris, and everywhere she went they pressed and swirled around her so tightly she could hardly manage to write her name. But from ten in the morning, when she arrived, until eight that evening, Doris was of unceasing good cheer —for these people were contributing to "the animals," and Doris's gratitude to them was boundless.

There were auctioneers but Doris handled a good part of the auction herself. She had contributed scores of personal objects that she exhorted the people to bid for. There were also many movie items—a life preserver from the S.S. *Poseidon,* Robert Redford's cap from *The Sting,* expensive gowns that had been contributed by Eydie Gorme, Debbie Reynolds, Kaye Ballard, and others, Paul Newman's pajamas from *The Sting,** Doris Day movie posters—hundreds of such items vigorously bid on by the crowds.

Toward the end of the afternoon, Doris went to the photo area, where for a dollar a person could pose for a photo with Doris. Immediately, a line formed that stretched halfway across the lot. It was terribly hot and Doris had not eaten all day, but she remained in the photo area until the last person in the line had been taken care of. "They've been waiting here for a long time," Doris explained, "and it would be wrong of me to disappoint them."

At eight o'clock, when the last photo had been taken, Doris and I went back to her trailer. She was wilted and exhausted but happy, for obviously a lot of money had been raised for the animals, and in the process a lot of people had enjoyed themselves.

"All those people today," I said, "I've been watching them, watching their faces when they looked at you and talked to you— I've never seen so much love."

She kicked off her shoes and leaned back in her chair. "If so many people love me," she asked, "how come I'm alone?"

On the eve of my departure from Hollywood, I took Doris to a little party at Gus Schirmer's house. Doris's friend, Kaye Ballard, was there, as was Paul Lynde and Jim Bailey, the impressionist. It was a lively evening of good food and show-business worry. Lynde was worried about the welfare of his dog, Harry Dinwiddie, while Lynde was gone East to do a play. Gus was worried about his weight. Bailey was worried about his voice (he does imitations of Judy Garland and other lady singers). Kaye was worried about (a) the impending musical version of *Come Back, Little Sheba,* in which she was to star in Chicago, and (b) the fact that Johnny Carson had suddenly stopped asking her to appear on the *Tonight* show.

Doris had very good, positive things to say to all of them, and by the time the evening was over the pall of show-business worry that had hung over the living room seemed to have lifted somewhat.

As we were all leaving, Doris and Paul having a last laugh as

---

* When I told Paul that his pajamas had been bid in for sixty dollars, he said, "That's nice—but I didn't wear pajamas in *The Sting.* I slept in my underwear."

they preceded me down the steps, Kaye Ballard came up beside me and smiled down on them.

"Oh, that Clara Bixby," she said. "You know something—I think God did a little dance around her when she was born."

Appendix

〰〰〰〰〰〰〰〰〰〰〰〰〰〰〰〰〰〰〰〰〰〰〰〰〰〰〰〰〰〰〰〰〰〰〰

The Care and Decoration of the Body:
Diet, Clothes, and Makeup

Exercise

If it isn't practical for you to ride a bicycle, then get one of those stationary bikes that you can ride in the house. I have one in my bedroom, and there is no better instant tonic than to jump on it and pedal away for ten minutes.

Swimming is another of my favorite exercises and relaxers. I usually swim backstroke or sidestroke because I find that the crawl and breaststroke put too much strain on my lower back. I'm a sway-back and like all swaybacks I have problems in my lower back, so I avoid the crawl and breaststroke. My doctor put me on to that. Also, the backstroke and sidestroke keep my hair pretty dry.

On days that I don't care about getting my hair wet, I do the dead man's float for as long as I have time, usually for forty or forty-five minutes. Just hang in the water, face down, arms outstretched, feet floating, everything just inertly hanging on the surface of the water. Greatest tonic for anxiety and nerves that I know. The ultimate relaxer.

But before I do the dead man's float, I will have backstroked twenty laps or more. Some people get in a pool, swim two or three laps, and call that exercise. I don't. For people who swim regularly, twenty laps is a moderate workout. Swimming is the most complete exercise I know, and not owning a pool, these days, is no excuse for not swimming. There are pools everywhere, and one can join a health club for a modest amount and swim all year round.

As important to me as biking and swimming is my slant board, which, in case you've never seen one, is simply a wooden board that you lie on that elevates your feet twelve inches higher than your head. You can buy them at sports stores and department stores. I consider my slant board vital to my sense of well-being. I'm on it fifteen minutes in the morning and fifteen minutes at night; and sometimes when I'm working I lie on it every chance I get. I usually put on some soft music —Bach strings, for example—close my eyes, and meditate. All of my body runs counter to the gravity pull that has been at it all day long. Lying slanted does wonders for the skin and for the scalp, and is much better than standing on your head, which achieves the same result but is very hard on your neck and not nearly as restful.

I also do some limbering-up exercises which are designed to keep me loose. I danced on my last television special, and afterward I got a lot of inquiries as to how, at fifty years of age, I could be so supple. Well, there's no trick to it if you just keep yourself free and easy. I usually hold onto the back of a chair and do a lot of kicks and squats and toe-and-heel things that hark back to my old dancing-school days. You can do it just as well. Just move your legs around, trying to make them as limber as possible. You've seen dancers on the *barre,* holding on with one hand while bending and kicking. It doesn't matter what you do as long as you've got your legs, knees, and waist in motion.

Then I drop to the floor on all fours, let my back sag, completely relaxing, then arch my back up like a cat as far as I can; then I drop everything down again, up and down, up and down, really stretching up my back as far as I can each time.

Next I sit on the floor with both legs stretched in front of me. I grasp one of my feet and pull it all the way toward me, as close to my crotch as I can, then slowly I bend forward, trying to touch my forehead to the floor. Afterward I try the same thing with the other leg. This exercise does wonders for the hamstrings; if the hamstring tendons are pliant and supple, then you can be loose in almost all your moves. Another good exercise is to lie on your side, with your lower arm off at an angle, and scissor your legs. Wonderful for the hips. Turn over and repeat scissors for the other hip. I don't do too many of these exercises. That's boring. Just enough to *feel* them do their work.

An exercise that I do that is designed to keep the buttocks firm and well-conditioned consists of getting down on all fours, bringing one knee up to my chin, then thrusting my leg quickly out to its full length. I do this about five times with each leg.

Another one that is good for the neck and the waist is to stand in the middle of the room, bend my trunk forward, and do the crawl stroke just as if I were swimming in the pool. I usually finish off with the old standby—with my legs eighteen inches apart and knees straight, I reach way out to the side, touch the floor, straighten, and repeat on the other side, each time bending my torso as far as I can. Marvelous waist exercise.

I also have a few exercises I do after I get in bed. One is isometric and consists simply of tightening my entire body, head to foot, relaxing, tightening. Also, just before I put out the light I close my eyes, completely relax my head, and roll it from side to side like a dead weight. Wonderful relaxer that helps induce sleep.

One exercise I do in the morning before I get out of bed consists of rolling my shoulders forward and then back, as high as I can, slowly lifting them until I feel as if they're touching my ears, pushing with all my might but letting my head hang and drop, all concentration being on my shoulders. Then slowly I bring my shoulders back and drop them on the sheet. I repeat this several times, and it's amazing how stimulating but relaxing it is. Certainly gets the day off on the right foot.

As far as face-lifting, breast-lifting, and other surgical cosmetic aids are concerned, I'm all for them as long as you can afford a good surgeon and you can bear the pain and discomfort that are involved. A lot of women say, "Well, I know my face has gone to pot but my husband loves me the way I am. He wouldn't have me look different for all the world." If they're overweight, those same women say, "Oh, my husband loves every extra pound." Don't kid yourself. Not about yourself or your husband. No one wants to look unattractive or be overweight. And that old husband excuse is just a cop-out. Those husbands who allegedly adore the excess wrinkles and jiggly fat of their wives are perfect candidates for affairs with their secretaries.

I weigh the very same today as I weighed in 1948, when I made my first movie. I don't think exercising is what keeps my weight constant so much as the fact that I don't overeat. People who are too fat eat for reasons other than hunger, to compensate for frustrations of one kind or another; and they *over*eat. The bigger their problems, the more they overeat.

Of course, *what* you eat is also relevant. I eat some foods that I don't particularly like but which I know are good for me. Yogurt is one of them. I'm not very fond of yogurt and I could happily live without it, but I make it a point to eat yogurt every single day. Cottage cheese is another food I could do without, but I eat it regularly. My favorite way of eating it is on toasted rye, with salt and pepper and a large slice of onion. The fact is, I eat simple foods but I often start the day with a big breakfast that includes bacon and eggs, and I eat a well-balanced dinner. I also accommodate some candy and ice cream somewhere along the course of most days. I have never in my life been on a calorie-counting diet. Or any other kind of diet.

Makeup

Outdoorsy type that I am, I don't like a lot of makeup. My pet dislike is the heavy pancake foundation that is applied with a sponge. It really wipes out any individuality your face may have. Now, though, there are liquid foundations that are very, very thin, hardly noticeable; so that if you do have a blotchy skin or one with uneven pigmentation, this kind of foundation evens the look of the skin but is almost invisible. A touch of rouge and your face has a very natural but even look. Most times I don't use any foundation, not even the new thin liquids. But if I want to be dressy in the evening, I use a touch of translucent foundation around my eyes, and then I use a little tawny-colored gel which comes in a stick.

But makeup is very personal, and no two faces can really be treated in the same way. I have a friend who has very sallow skin with a yellow tinge to it. She tried going without foundation makeup, as I do, but it was wrong for her. I worked with her on it one afternoon, and we came up with a rose-colored liquid foundation that absolutely transformed her. That touch of pink on her rather yellow skin gave her a beautiful color. Changed her whole look. She has brown eyes, which we shadowed with a pale-lavender tone, and we used brown and rosy beige on the lids and a touch of pink liquid rouge on her cheeks. She was a vision!

Of course, if you have a good suntan, you just have to do your eyes and that's it—but I am very careful about the sun. I love the feel of the sun on my body but I don't like what it does to my skin. At first I'll allow myself ten minutes in the direct sun, not a minute more, and slowly, over many, many days, I'll work up to twenty minutes— but never, under no circumstances, more than that. It's important not to bake the skin, for that dries it out and creates all kinds of havoc. One trick, if you really like the sun, is to wear a big hat that completely protects your face, and tan only your body. Then use a foundation to darken your face to match the color of your body tan. I'm also very careful about my lips. I cover them with zinc oxide before I go out in the sun and never let them get exposed to direct sunlight.

The only time I have to use heavy pancake makeup on my body is when I'm making films. Even if I have a suntan. With the amount of light that's thrown on me, if I weren't evenly pancaked I would look like I'd been in a flour barrel. But not on my face. I make myself up for television (except for the pasting on of my false eyelashes, which I never get straight) and I have found how to keep my natural, unpancaked look and still not burn whitely under the lights.

The fact of the matter is that I don't spend much time on makeup. Outdoorsy types shouldn't. What I do is done quickly. I don't want to look contrived. I can't look slinky or *femme fatale*-ish, no matter what I do, so it's silly to try. And besides, I simply don't have the time for it. Good, careful, intricate makeup takes at least an hour to apply. Ten minutes is my maximum.

Of course, most time and attention is given to eye makeup. Some women I know spend almost an hour every day on their eyes alone. I do spend quite some time on my eyes when I'm going before the camera because there is no way to do good eye makeup quickly. But, in general, an outdoorsy type who overloads her eyes just looks silly. I have a friend, Raquel Rael, an interior decorator, who is an indoorsy type if ever there was one. She has shocking black hair and dark skin, and she concentrates her makeup almost entirely on her eyes. No lipstick, very light foundation, and those dramatic eyes coming out of that black-haired frame. Very effective. But I'm not dramatic-looking and no amount of eye makeup is going to change my look.

So many women make the mistake of wearing bright-red lipstick for dramatic effect, when in fact if they wore no lipstick and concentrated on their eyes they'd be much better off. I'm very much against bright-colored lips. Very muted colors are so much more effective. And, in general, I'd say that outdoorsy blondes like myself should forget eye makeup. If I go out in the daytime with eye makeup on I feel like I'm in some kind of carnival. And at night I feel like I'm pretending to be somebody else. All I do for my eyes is to curl my eyelashes and use a soft-brown mascara to darken the tips, because the tips are very blond. Once in a while I'll put on a faint touch of gray eye shadow. Most people think my eyes are blue (they do photograph quite blue) but I think they are more gray than blue, so I add that slight touch of gray shadow. I never use an eye liner except for the camera.

But I don't mean to suggest that all blondes should follow my lead. There's a young lady who works for my dentist who is very blond and has the palest skin you ever saw. Without a makeup base, she says, she looks ghastly. She wears a liquid base with a glowing pink tone to it, and she delicately rouges her cheeks. She also does her eyes to a fare-thee-well. But everything about her, especially her long, silky blond hair, suggests indoorsy. Her eyes are predominantly shadowed with gray-silver ash and then touched up with a little yellow and gold. But it's all put on so well, and so delicately, that her eyes don't jump out at you—they seem to blend with her face and hair. So what it comes down to is that each woman must be honest with herself as to what type she is, and then pay careful attention to how she can enhance her own individual personality.

The same goes for perfume. It's wrong to choose a perfume because Catherine Deneuve looks beautiful in an ad, or because you like it on someone else, or because it's a status scent like Arpège or Joy or Shalimar. Years ago, the status perfume was White Shoulders. I was dancing with a man who said, "I know what perfume you're wearing—White Shoulders." I was surprised that he could identify the scent so easily. "Nothing to it," he said, "that's what practically every woman in this room has on." I got the message. I gave away my bottle of White Shoulders and went to find a scent that was right for me. Since then I've never told anyone what I use. But I stopped using perfume long ago. I much prefer cologne, and I've used the same one for many years.

In general, I'd say that outdoorsy types should avoid heavy, seductive perfumes. A light, clean fragrance suits them much better. Actually, I don't like a heavy perfume on anyone. There is a tendency to put on more than one should and the smell is usually overpowering. I should think it would turn men off rather than on.

I remove makeup with cleansing cream. I wash my face with soap only once a week, if that. After the cleansing cream, I apply freshener with cotton. I like to use a body lotion after my shower, and I use one that has a very light scent that quickly disappears. I splash on my cologne, run my hands through my hair, pat my face, and that's about it. Studio Girl, which I am now affiliated with, has a cucumber skin freshener that I really like, and I use it whenever I shower.

I use eye-makeup remover to remove mascara. It's different from the regular mascara remover but I like the way it works. I just rub it across my eyelashes, let it set for a moment, then wipe off the mascara. Its advantage is that it doesn't break my eyelashes.

Once a week I use a beauty mask. It's good for circulation and it makes my skin tingle and glow. It has the consistency of toothpaste and is easy to apply. I cover my entire face and neck with it and leave it on for about twenty minutes, then rinse it off with tepid water. I'm using a Studio Girl facial mask now that peels off after use.

I like to do my fingernails and toenails when I'm in a good hot tub. I use a good cuticle remover to get off dead skin, and I use a terry facecloth to push back the cuticles. I never cut the cuticle on my nails or toes, because the more you cut it, the more you have to.

I do my own fingernails. I put cuticle oil on them at night and just push the cuticle back after it has soaked in the oil. When I use polish, which is not too often, I use a clear one. I use an emery board and a buffer and keep my nails at medium length. I don't like brightly colored nails or very long nails, because they give a woman's hands an unnatural look. Of course, some women unfortunately have rather yellowish nails and have to wear a colored polish. My guess is that men don't like brightly colored nails, no matter what women say. I subscribe to the old saw that women dress for women and for themselves, not for men.

I wash my hair every other day and use a blow comb to shape it while it dries. I rarely go to a beauty parlor. I use three rollers on the top with a little hair-setting lotion. When it has to be cut, Barbara comes to my house and does it. (I realize that a lot of women have very fine hair that won't hold a curl so they go to beauty parlors, where they have it rolled and set with a lot of hair-setting lotion and tons of spray that keep it in place for the rest of the week. I would never do that. If I had hair like that, I would either have my hair cut short and shaped by a really good hairdresser, so I could just run my hand through it and it would fall in place, or I would grow it very long and wear it as I once did, piled on top, or pull it back with a barrette and tie it with a velvet ribbon or some such.) Every four months I have my hair streaked. Its natural color is very light so all I need is highlights.

One night a week I make it a practice to cover my entire body, forehead to toes, with Vaseline. I buy Vaseline in huge jars for this purpose. I rub it in thoroughly and apply it thickly. I then put on a flannel nightgown and lightweight socks to cover my feet and go to sleep like that. Of course, if you're sleeping with a man, husband or otherwise, you are not a very appetizing number in this condition and it's best to be in a separate bed on this occasion. Vaseline has a rather pungent odor, which is not exactly offensive but neither is it very pleasant. But the Vaseline, sticky and gooey as it is, does wonders for the body, especially the feet. I like to walk barefoot, which tends to roughen up the bottoms of my feet and the back of my heels. Well, after a Vaseline soak and a little work with a pumice stone, feet, elbows, knees—those vital places that have a tendency to rough up— are good as new. The only danger connected with the overnight Vaseline soak is that you can slide out of bed—which I have.

Clothes

One of the lessons I learned during my Warner Brothers years was how not to dress. Name any picture I made for Warners, and I will show you Doris Day in a ludicrous costume. Off-the-shoulder dresses with heart-shaped necklines, satin stoles that slid off my neck at the wrong time, flounces and frills and Barbie Doll crinolines. I would look at myself on the screen and go home and cry all night. How many women I see on the streets today who are still dressed in the mode of early Warner Brothers!

The only rule I know is: don't dress for the sake of fashion, or because you see something in a window that's pretty. Put on your body only that which looks good on *your* body. The number of plump women I see who dress in big print dresses that flounce out and make them seem even stouter! Dressing up is often achieved by dressing down. Imagination is so much better than imitation. When I was working on my television show and they brought dresses to me, sometimes I'd try one on and say, "I like it but I think I'll put it on backwards." My costumer and dear friend, Connie Edney, almost flipped, but I'd put it on backward and it would be great.

There are such prejudices about clothes, almost none of them valid. Like the prejudice against gray—that it's an old-lady color— but it isn't, it's beautiful. Two of my favorite combinations are gray-and-white and gray-and-camel. I have grays in dresses, pants, coats, jackets, and pants suits. I just love going against most prejudices.

As far as jewelry is concerned, my taste runs toward old pieces. I have some antique bracelets that I like and some nice Indian jewels although I don't wear them very often. I have a lovely turquoise ring that is a favorite, and some pretty pearls that I like to wear. Pearls seem to be in again, after a long banishment, but isn't that dumb? I never stopped wearing my pearls. With me, what looks good on me and what I like is in.

I don't wear big beads or other pieces that are heavy-looking and seem to carry me rather than the opposite. I feel the same way about the clothes I wear. I don't want my clothes to wear me. So often I see women who are wearing overpowering clothes. You can't find the woman, you can hardly see her, so lost is she in the big hats and furs she is wearing. And speaking of furs—I don't think any woman is ever justified in wearing any fur that comes from an animal. Fake furs are fun and should be the only furs we ever put on our backs.

One last word about cosmetics, about what really does the most wonders for a person's face and body. I think the greatest face-lift is a thinking-lift. Our faces reflect what we're thinking, and when we have clouded, negative, bitter thoughts, thoughts with fear and hate in them, our faces and our eyes show these things no matter what we do with foundations and eye shadows. When thoughts are positive and loving, a person's entire face relaxes. Down lines go up. Worry lines ease out. The body lifts in spirit; the soul is uplifted. It's the greatest cosmetic of all, and it doesn't cost a cent.

Filmography

~~~~~~

U.S.A. RELEASE	STUDIO	FILM TITLE	PRODUCER(s)	DIRECTOR(s)	COSTARS
7/1948	WB	*Romance on the High Seas* (Technicolor)	Alex Gottlieb	Michael Curtiz	Jack Carson, Janis Paige, Oscar Levant, S. Z. Sakall
4/1949	WB	*My Dream Is Yours* (Technicolor)	Michael Curtiz	Michael Curtiz	Jack Carson, Adolphe Menjou, Eve Arden, S. Z. Sakall
8/1949	WB	*It's a Great Feeling* (Technicolor)	Alex Gottlieb	David Butler	Dennis Morgan, Jack Carson, Bill Goodwin
3/1950	WB	*Young Man with a Horn* (Black & White)	Jerry Wald	Michael Curtiz	Kirk Douglas, Lauren Bacall, Hoagy Carmichael
9/1950	WB	*Tea for Two* (Technicolor)	William Jacobs	David Butler	Gordon MacRae, Billy De Wolfe, Patrice Wymore, Gene Nelson, Eve Arden, S. Z. Sakall
11/1950	WB	*The West Point Story* (Black & White)	Louis F. Edelman	Roy Del Ruth	James Cagney, Virginia Mayo, Gordon MacRae, Gene Nelson, Alan Hale, Jr.
2/1951	WB	*Storm Warning* (Black & White)	Jerry Wald	Stuart Heisler	Ginger Rogers, Ronald Reagan, Steve Cochran
3/1951	WB	*Lullaby of Broadway* (Technicolor)	William Jacobs	David Butler	Gene Nelson, S. Z. Sakall, Billy De Wolfe, Gladys George

Date	Studio	Title	Producer	Director	Cast
7/1951	WB	*On Moonlight Bay* (Technicolor)	William Jacobs	Roy Del Ruth	Gordon MacRae, Jack Smith, Rosemary De Camp, Mary Wickes, Leon Ames
12/1951	WB	*Starlift* (Black & White)	Robert Arthur	Roy Del Ruth	Gordon MacRae, Virginia Mayo, Gene Nelson, Ruth Roman, Jane Wyman, James Cagney
1/1952	WB	*I'll See You in My Dreams* (Black & White)	Louis F. Edelman	Michael Curtiz	Danny Thomas, Frank Lovejoy, Patrice Wymore, James Gleason, Mary Wickes
6/1952	WB	*The Winning Team* (Black & White)	Bryan Foy	Louis Seiler	Ronald Reagan, Frank Lovejoy, Eve Miller, James Millican, Rusty Tamblyn
1/1953	WB	*April in Paris* (Technicolor)	William Jacobs	David Butler	Ray Bolger, Claude Dauphin, Eve Miller
5/1953	WB	*By the Light of the Silvery Moon* (Technicolor)	William Jacobs	David Butler	Gordon MacRae, Leon Ames, Rosemary De Camp, Mary Wickes, Billy Gray
11/1953	WB	*Calamity Jane* (Technicolor)	William Jacobs	David Butler	Howard Keel, Allyn McLerie, Philip Carey, Dick Wesson

(Music: Sammy Fain/ Paul Francis Webster . . . "Secret Love" Academy Award-winning song)

U.S.A. RELEASE	STUDIO	FILM TITLE	PRODUCER(s)	DIRECTOR(s)	COSTARS
4/1954	WB	*Lucky Me* (WarnerColor-CinemaScope)	Henry Blanke	Jack Donohue	Robert Cummings, Phil Silvers, Eddie Foy, Jr., Nancy Walker, Martha Hyer
1/1955	WB	*Young at Heart* (Arwin Prod.) (WarnerColor, Print by Technicolor)	Henry Blanke	Gordon Douglas	Frank Sinatra, Gig Young, Ethel Barrymore, Dorothy Malone, Robert Keith, Elisabeth Fraser, Alan Hale, Jr.
6/1955	MGM	*Love Me or Leave Me* (Eastmancolor-CinemaScope, with Perspecta Stereophonic Sound)	Joe Pasternak	Charles Vidor	James Cagney, Cameron Mitchell, Robert Keith, Tom Tully, Harry Bellaver
6/1956	PARA-MOUNT	*The Man Who Knew Too Much* (Technicolor-VistaVision)	Alfred Hitchcock	Alfred Hitchcock	James Stewart, Brenda De Banzie, Bernard Miles, Daniel Gellin, Christopher Olsen
		(*Music: Jay Livingston/Ray Evans . . . "QUE SERA, SERA" Academy Award-winning song*)			
11/1956	MGM	*Julie* (Arwin Prod.) (Black & White)	Martin Melcher	Andrew L. Stone	Louis Jourdan, Barry Sullivan, Jack Kelly, Frank Lovejoy
8/1957	WB	*The Pajama Game* (WarnerColor)	George Abbott/ Stanley Donen	George Abbott/ Stanley Donen	John Raitt, Carol Haney, Eddie Foy, Jr., Reta Shaw, Barbara Nichols, Thelma Pelish, Jack Straw

Date	Studio / Title	Producer	Director	Cast
4/1958	PARA-MOUNT *Teacher's Pet* (Black & White-VistaVision)	William Perlberg	George Seaton	Clark Gable, Gig Young, Mamie Van Doren, Nick Adams
11/1958	MGM *Tunnel of Love* (Black & White-CinemaScope)	Joseph Fields/Martin Melcher	Gene Kelly	Richard Widmark, Gig Young, Elisabeth Fraser, Gia Scala, Elizabeth Wilson
6/1959	COLUMBIA *It Happened to Jane* (Arwin Prod.) (Technicolor-CinemaScope)	Richard Quine	Richard Quine	Jack Lemmon, Ernie Kovacs, Steve Forrest, Teddy Rooney, Gina Gillespie
10/1959	UNIVERSAL *Pillow Talk (Arwin/Universal Prod.) (Eastmancolor-CinemaScope)	Ross Hunter/Martin Melcher	Michael Gordon	Rock Hudson, Tony Randall, Thelma Ritter, Nick Adams

Miss Day's performance nominated for Academy Award

Date	Studio / Title	Producer	Director	Cast
4/1960	MGM *Please Don't Eat the Daisies* (MetroColor-CinemaScope)	Joe Pasternak (Asst. Prod. M. Melcher)	Charles Walters	David Niven, Spring Byington, Janis Paige, Richard Haydn, Patsy Kelly, Jack Weston
11/1960	UNIVERSAL *Midnight Lace* (Eastmancolor)	Ross Hunter/Martin Melcher	David Miller	Rex Harrison, Myrna Loy, John Gavin, Herbert Marshall, Roddy McDowall, Hermione Baddeley
3/1962	UNIVERSAL *Lover Come Back* (Eastmancolor)	Stanley Shapiro/Martin Melcher	Delbert Mann	Rock Hudson, Tony Randall, Edie Adams, Jack Oakie, Jack Kruschen

U.S.A. RELEASE	STUDIO	FILM TITLE	PRODUCER(s)	DIRECTOR(s)	COSTARS
7/1962	UNIVERSAL	That Touch of Mink (Eastmancolor-PanaVision)	Stanley Shapiro/ Martin Melcher	Delbert Mann	Cary Grant, Gig Young, Audrey Meadows, Dick Sargent, Allan Hewitt
12/1962	MGM	Billy Rose's JUMBO (MetroColor-PanaVision) (MGM/Euterpe/Arwin Production)	Joe Pasternak/ Martin Melcher	Charles Walters	Jimmy Durante, Stephen Boyd, Martha Raye, Dean Jagger
8/1963	UNIVERSAL	The Thrill of It All (Eastmancolor, Print by Technicolor (Ross Hunter/Arwin Production)	Ross Hunter/ Martin Melcher	Norman Jewison	James Garner, Arlene Francis, Edward Andrews, Zasu Pitts
12/1963	20th C/FOX	Move Over, Darling (De-Luxe Color-CinemaScope) (Arcola/Arwin Production)	Aaron Rosenberg/ Martin Melcher	Michael Gordon	James Garner, Polly Bergen, Chuck Connors, Thelma Ritter, Fred Clark
11/1964	UNIVERSAL	Send Me No Flowers (Technicolor) (Martin Melcher Production)	Harry Keller (Exec. Prod. M. Melcher)	Norman Jewison	Rock Hudson, Tony Randall, Edward Andrews, Paul Lynde, Hal March, Clint Walker
12/1965	20th C/FOX	Do Not Disturb (De-Luxe Color-CinemaScope)	Aaron Rosenberg/ Martin Melcher	Ralph Levy	Rod Taylor, Hermione Baddeley, Sergio Fantoni

Date	Studio	Title	Director	Producer	Cast
7/1966	MGM	Glass Bottom Boat (MetroColor-PanaVision) (Arwin/Reame Production)	Frank Tashlin	Martin Melcher/Everett Freeman	Rod Taylor, Arthur Godfrey, John McGiver, Edward Andrews, Paul Lynde, Eric Fleming, Dick Martin
6/1967	20th-C/FOX	Caprice (De-Luxe Color-CinemaScope)	Frank Tashlin	Aaron Rosenberg/Martin Melcher	Richard Harris, Ray Walston, Jack Kruschen, Michael J. Pollard, Edward Mulhare, Lilia Skala
11/1967	UNIVERSAL	Ballad of Josie (Technicolor-TechniScope)	Andrew V. McLaglen	Norman Macdonnell (Exec. Prod. M. Melcher)	Peter Graves, Audrey Christie, George Kennedy, Elisabeth Fraser, Andy Devine
5/1968	MGM	Where Were You When the Lights Went Out? (MetroColor-PanaVision)	Hy Averback	Everett Freeman/Martin Melcher	Robert Morse, Terry-Thomas, Patrick O'Neal, Lola Albright, Steve Allen, Jim Backus
8/1968	WARNER-PATHE	With Six You Get Egg Roll (Technicolor-PanaVision) (Arwin & Cinema-Center Film Production)	Howard Morris	Martin Melcher	Brian Keith, Pat Caroll, Barbara Hershey, John Findlater, George Carlin, Alice Ghostley

SUMMARY: THIRTY-NINE MOTION PICTURES OVER 20 YEARS . . . WB = 18 . . . U.I. = 7 . . . MGM = 7 . . . 20th C/FOX = 3 . . . PARAMOUNT = 2 . . . COLUMBIA = 1 . . . WARNER-PATHE (Cinema-Center) = 1